eye-music:
kandinsky, klee
and all that jazz

frances guy

simon shaw-miller

michael tucker

Published on the occasion of the exhibition
Eye-Music: Kandinsky, Klee and all that Jazz

Pallant House Gallery, Chichester
30 June–16 September 2007
Sainsbury Centre for Visual Arts, Norwich
2 October–9 December 2007

Curator: Frances Guy, Pallant House Gallery

First published in 2007 by
Pallant House Gallery
9 North Pallant
Chichester
PO19 1TJ
United Kingdom
www.pallant.org.uk

Paperback
ISBN-10   1-869827-03-1
ISBN-13   978-1-869827-03-8

Designer: David Wynn
Production Editor: Andrew Churchill
Editorial Support: Harriet Wailling
Picture Research: Daniella Norton

Set in Foundry Sterling and Architype Bayer
Printed in the United Kingdom by Selsey Press Ltd

Eye-Music Funded by

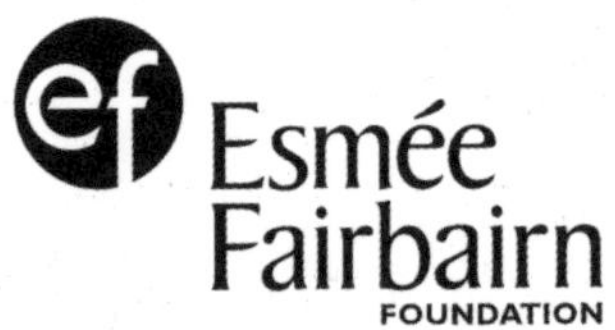

This exhibition has been funded by Esmée Fairbairn
Foundation's Regional Museums Initiative (RMI),
one of ten exhibitions taking place at twenty venues
across the UK between 2004 and 2007. RMI aims
to encourage museums to develop important
and engaging exhibition programmes, to support
organisations to play an enhanced role in the
cultural life of the country and to help attract a
constant and enthusiastic public. It is particularly
interested in collaborations between museums,
and exhibitions that tour.

Eye-Music Supported by

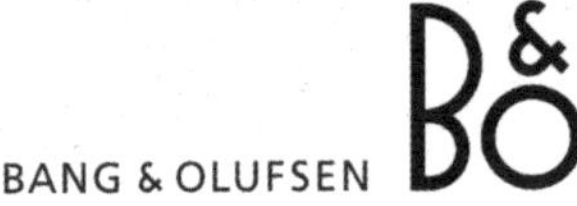

Supporter of the Collection 2007

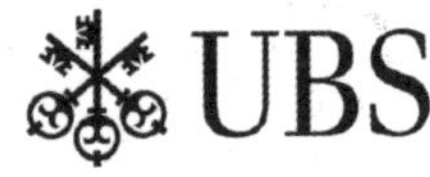

Supporter of the Gallery 2007

contents

director's foreword

A cathedral city in England is always a centre of music. The enduring tradition of church music and cathedral choirs is unique in the world and in Chichester we are fortunate to enjoy the outstanding quality of that tradition. In the twentieth century, the Dean of Chichester Cathedral, Walter Hussey (1955–1977), combined a passion for both the visual arts and music. We enjoy the fruits of his collecting of fine art here in the Gallery on a daily basis but, of course, he was equally instrumental in commissioning Leonard Bernstein, Benjamin Britten and William Walton among others. In the same century, artists have explored opportunities to express music into a visual language: we think of Der Blaue Reiter, Bauhaus, the members of De Stijl, and many others. Our collection is also strongly linked with the birth of popular culture in Britain as Pop Art and pop music go hand-in-hand in work by artists such as Peter Blake and Richard Hamilton.

Eye-Music: Kandinsky, Klee and all that Jazz, our first international loan exhibition, explores this theme, and the curator, Frances Guy, has combined her passion for the visual arts and music in this exciting interdisciplinary project. The exhibition encompasses a wide range of artists from the early until the late twentieth century who translated their passion for music - be it Bach, Debussy or Schönberg, ragtime, jazz or boogie-woogie - into a visual language. Frances has succeeded in presenting a challenging theme beautifully, and the result is a real feast for the eyes. I am most grateful for the generosity of British and international lenders, whose loans made it all possible. As well as Frances, who has worked tirelessly on this exhibition catalogue, I would also like to acknowledge Dr. Simon Shaw-Miller and Professor Michael Tucker for their contributions.

This exhibition is part of the Esmée Fairbairn Foundation's Regional Museums Initiative which enabled 10 exhibitions to be shared by 20 venues across England. This initiative has been hugely successful and we are most grateful for the foundation's support. As part of that programme, this exhibition will travel to the Sainsbury Centre for Visual Arts, Norwich in October 2007.

I would finally also like to thank Bang & Olufsen of Chichester as Supporter of the Exhibition, as well as Bonhams in their role as Supporter of the Collections, and UBS as Supporter of the Gallery for 2007, all of whom are, I hope, proud to be associated with the Museum of the Year, winner of the Gulbenkian Prize for museums and galleries 2007.

Stefan van Raay

curator's acknowledgements

My heartfelt thanks go to Dr. Simon Shaw-Miller and Professor Michael Tucker for their insightful essays and invaluable advice and expertise, which was so willingly given throughout. The catalogue was published by our superb in-house team under the direction of Andrew Churchill with David Wynn (design) and Harriet Wailling (editorial support). In addition to the Director's thanks, there are many others without whom Eye-Music would have been impossible to realise. I would particularly like to acknowledge Professor Peter Vergo for his encouragement from the outset. Others who have offered their time, knowledge and support are:

Peter Batten, Dr. Michael Baumgartner, Jo Beggs, Richard Bernas, Finella Boyle, Christine Butler, Paul Carr, Juliet Ceresole, Catherine Clement, Sara Cooper, Peter Copley, Harvey Daniels, Alan Davie, Jonathan Dodd, Steve Dummer, Colin Dunn, Sophie Duplaix, Patrick Elliott, Roger Emery, Mark Forkgen, Dr. Rainer Fuchs, Amanda Geitner, Shreela Ghosh, Sally Goldsmith, Mel and Rhiannon Gooding, Vivienne Hamilton, Keith Hartley, Michael Head, Neil Hennessy, Robert Hepburne-Scott, Daniel Herrmann, Simon Hucker, Bob Jaroc, Nichola Johnson, Stuart King, Tessa Lewin, Barry Littlechild, Professor Norbert Lynton, Chris McHugh, Thor McIntyre-Burnie, Dr. Christian Meyer, Ian O'Riordan, Tilman Osterwold, Alfred Pacquement, Tom Phillips, Sandra Prusa, Sean Rainbird, Ben Rivers, Nicholas Roberts, Simon Robinson-Elms, Pascal Rousseau, Mark Rowan-Hull, Matthew Rowe, Christian Rumelin, Dr. Dieter Scholz, Amanda Sharp, Peter Shepperd Skaerved, Jack Smith, Robin Spencer, Chris Stephens, Mary-Anne Stevens, Alistair Stewart, Alan Thurlow, Rebecca Wallace, Giles Waterfield, Ernst Vegelin, Prof. Brian Whitton, Dr. Pete Wilson, Christian Wolsdorff, Judith K. Zilczer.

Finally, my thanks to the Gallery team: Stefan van Raay, Director and Bob Bentley, Elaine Bentley, Tom Brodie, Ann Broomfield, Sarah Deere, Nick Higbee, Greg Liffen, Stewart Maclean, Simon Martin, Ian Milford, David Miles, Valerie Möller, Linda Neve, Antonio Rodriquez-Rivera, Helen Ward, Russell Webb and Matthew Weekes. In particular I would like to thank Daniella Norton for her invaluable administrative support and Marc Steene for his unwavering encouragement and enthusiasm.

I would like to dedicate this exhibition to my mother and father who filled my life with art and music.

Frances Guy

making overtures:
an introduction
to eye-music

frances guy

I have to confess that this is a personal dream for me, the opportunity to curate an exhibition on a subject of my own choosing, a rare occurrence. And whilst I apologise for this, I also hope that the enthusiasm and fascination I have for the subject will present itself in this small selection of works that show the relationship between abstract art and music at the beginning of the twentieth century, and that those who see it or read this catalogue will be inspired to find out more.

As a musician myself, I know what it is to be in the centre of a symphony orchestra and to be physically and mentally consumed by a performance. As a lover of music, I am always overwhelmed by the visual spectacle of a favourite piece being performed by a group of musicians playing as one and the memories and associations that are stimulated by the sounds that fill the concert hall. In my professional career as an art historian, abstract art has always held a peculiar fascination. The circumstances surrounding the imaginative leap into a new world when the imitation of the real world had previously been so highly regarded, is a compelling story. What propelled artists towards this unknown territory and how did they develop their highly individual visual languages? When I understood that for many artists music became a model for their experiments in abstraction, I wanted to discover why. Now, in my role as curator of this exhibition, I hope to present some of the ideas and developments that lay behind this fascinating journey and the resulting revolution in the visual arts.

There were many reasons why avant-garde artists were turning their backs on figuration at the turn of the century. The Impressionists had already liberated painting by introducing new techniques to capture atmospheric effects and new subjects that spurned the artistic canon of history painting

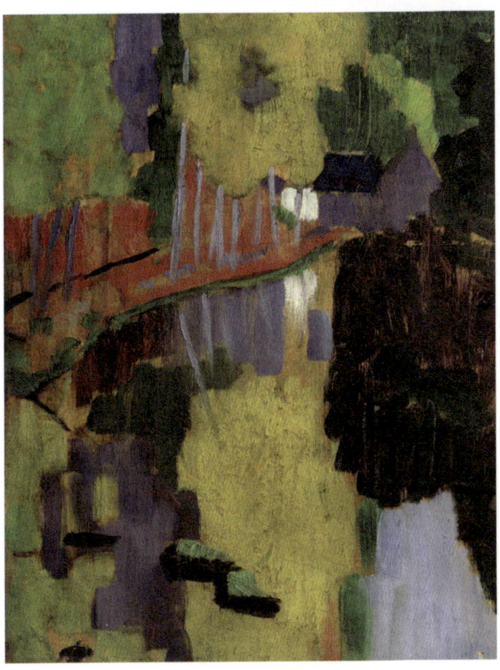

and mythological subjects. The Post-Impressionists took this further in their work where colour and form were given independence of subject matter and became the real focus of their paintings. Take Paul Sérusier's *The Talisman* (fig 1.), so named because of the significance it held for the group of artists, the Nabis, whom Sérusier was painting with when he created it 1888 under the tutelage of Paul Gauguin. Gauguin had instructed his contemporaries to 'think too of the musical role, which colour will now begin to play in modern painting. Colour, which is just as much oscillating waves as in music, is capable of expressing the most universal and this the most vague thing there is in Nature: its intrinsic force.'[1]

In England, James Abbott McNeill Whistler had linked musical terms with colours in the titles of his paintings since the 1860s to exemplify his theory that art should essentially be concerned with the beautiful arrangement of colours, not with the accurate portrayal of the natural world: 'As music is the poetry of sound, so is painting the poetry of sight, and the subject-matter has nothing to do with the harmony of sound or of colour... Art...

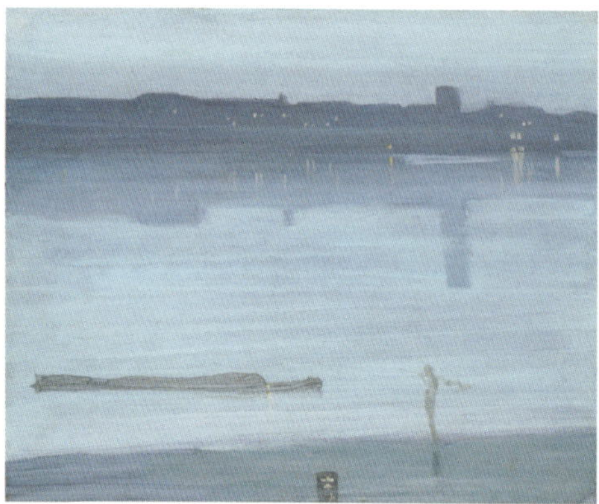

Fig. 2
James Abbott
McNeill Whistler
(1834–1903)
Nocturne: Blue and Silver – Chelsea
1871
oil on wood
Tate, London

should stand alone, and appeal to the artistic sense of eye or ear, without confounding this with emotions entirely foreign to it... that is why I insist on calling my works "arrangements" and "harmonies".' [2] To further the analogy, the composer Claude Debussy wrote *Nocturnes* (1897–99) as musical equivalents of Whistler's colour compositions of the same name (fig. 2), and the Czech artist František Kupka - an artist who will crop up time and again in this exhibition - painted *Nocturne* in 1911, a purely abstract work of vibrating units of blue light, possibly also in response to Whistler.

Kupka had studied in Vienna where he became involved in the intellectual and artistic circle of the Viennese Secession with whom he exhibited throughout the early 1900s, despite his move to Paris in 1896. The ultimate expression of this artistic movement was the Secession building in Vienna that, in 1902, was decorated with Gustav Klimt's remarkable frescoes and Max Klinger's statue in an exhibition in homage to Ludwig van Beethoven. The exhibition was intended as an envisioned ideal of the combined efforts of art, music and poetry and Klimt's decorative scheme included a symbolic choir of angels hymning Schiller's 'Ode to Joy', the final chorus of Beethoven's *Symphony no. 9* (fig. 3). However it was the geometric designs in the Secession building created by the architect Josef Hoffmann that particularly inspired Kupka to paint his series composed of clusters of rectangles, which he later exhibited in Paris in the Salon des Indépendants of 1912. Whilst visiting the exhibition, Roger Fry, Duncan Grant and

   Making Overtures: An Introduction to Eye-Music

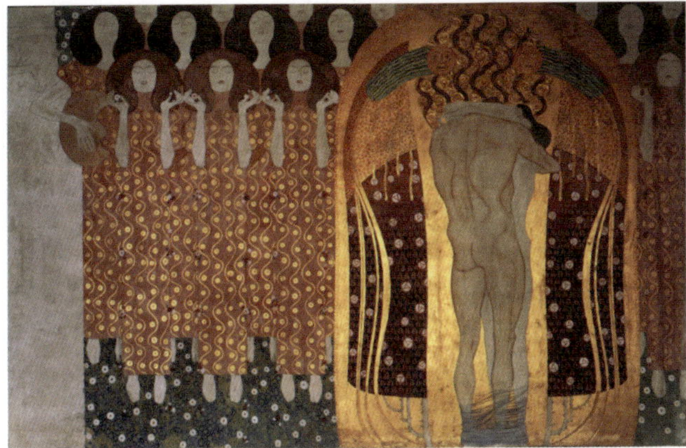

Vanessa Bell, as well as Piet Mondrian, were perhaps inspired by Kupka's revolutionary compositions to make their own abstract experimentations based on simple horizontal and vertical forms.

Music had a symbolic role for many artists, including Georges Braque, Juan Gris and Pablo Picasso, each of whom frequently included musical instruments as a motif in their work, particularly in the period 1911–12. This coincided with a crucial phase in the development of Cubism with the gradual disintegration of the picture plane. In particular, Braque frequently referenced J.S. Bach in his paintings (fig. 4), perhaps as a pun on his own name, and sometimes including the titles of musical works or examples of musical notation. By fragmenting the objects in their paintings and introducing layering into the spatial structure, they each introduced an element of motion and temporality into their paintings, which contemporary commentators likened to the polyphony of Baroque music. One art gallery director was prompted to say 'One experiences this transcendental dynamism in a way no different from the metaphysical counterpoint of Bach's fugues.' [3]

The nineteenth century had witnessed a growing interest amongst artists, composers, poets and theorists in the potential for the arts to draw on each other to develop a new language that would communicate its message by stimulating a range of sensory reactions. The idea that colour and

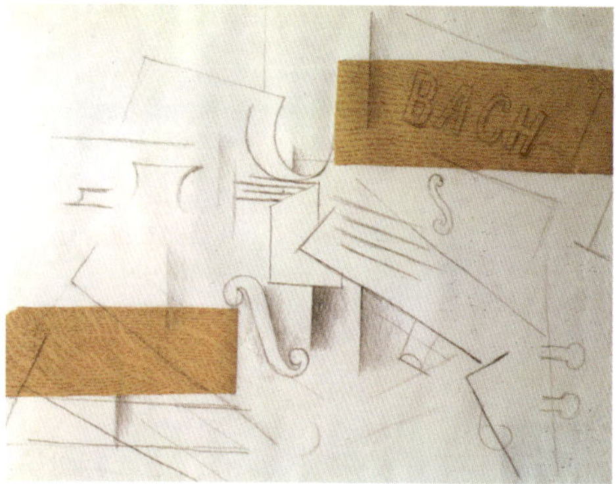

Fig. 4
Georges Braque
(1882–1963)
Still life Bach
1912
collage & pencil on paper
Musée National d'Art Moderne,
Centre Pompidou, Paris, France

musical notes were intrinsically related had been in existence in Western theoretical understanding since Isaac Newton split the optical spectrum into seven colours and linked them to the seven notes of the musical scale. Goethe and his contemporaries, whose writings were to become key to the development of abstract art, proposed that colour had the ability to stimulate a range of sensory reactions, and this was long before synaesthesia – the neurological phenomenon where two or more senses are combined – was identified in the 1880s.

Synaesthesia is a problematic issue for this exhibition, since many artists believed they possessed it but perhaps not to the extent that scientists would now equate with a true manifestation of the condition. However most people do have a degree of synaesthetic experience. It is embedded in our language since we call colours 'warm' or 'cold', and we tend to associate high and low sounds with bright and dark colours respectively. This intermingling of sensory perception was exploited in the work of Symbolist writers and poets, such as Charles Baudelaire in his poem and theory of *Correspondances* (1852–56) and Joris-Karl Huysmans. In *À Rebours (Against Nature)* (1884), Huysmans describes the sensory indulgence of his hero Des Esseintes who corresponds the flavour of liqueurs with particular sounds of orchestral instruments: 'dry curaçao matched the clarinet whose note is penetrating and velvety; kummel, the oboe with its sonorous, nasal resonance; crème de menthe and anisette, the flute, at once honeyed and pungent, whining and sweet'.

Such sensory decadence fuelled some of the most extravagant and outrageous innovations in art. Before his untimely death from blood-poisoning in 1915, the Russian composer Alexander Scriabin was planning a grandiose multi-media work entitled *Mysterium* based on his theosophical beliefs, to be performed in the Himalayas, involving music, scent, dance and light. Had it been realised, it would have been an incredible development of the concept of the *Gesamtkunstwerk*, a 'total work of art' fusing many art forms into one glorious whole that had been established earlier in the nineteenth century in the operas of Richard Wagner.

Scriabin's earlier groundbreaking symphonic work *Prometheus (The Poem of Fire)* (1910) included a part written for the 'luce' or colour organ, another nineteenth century obsession. From Louis-Bertrand Castel's colour organ of 1734, a stringed instrument that correlated the seven colours to the seven notes of music using moving transparent coloured tapes, to Alexander Wallace Rimington's patented version of 1893 which was demonstrated to an audience at St. James' Hall in London in 1895, many scientists, artists and composers proposed their own version of a machine that could project coloured light to music. Castel's aim was 'to paint sounds, I say, really paint them; not merely paint them, but paint them using the appropriate colours – in a word, to render sounds perceptible to the eye, just as they are to the ear, in such a way that a deaf person would be capable of enjoying and of judging the beauty of a piece of music.' [4] Scriabin's work premiered without the projection, and a planned performance in England using Rimington's machine was cancelled because of the outbreak of World War I, but the work was finally realised in its entirety in New York in 1915.

However, for the artists included in this exhibition, it was the ability of music to transcend the material world that became such an important motive in their drive towards abstraction. Music had been associated with the cosmos and a more spiritual world since Ancient Greece, when Pythagoras had analysed its arithmetic and developed a system of musical ratios, the basis of Western music today, which he equated with the divine order of the universe or 'the music of the spheres'. Its freedom from representation or narrative content, and its ability to communicate directly with the soul and evoke an emotional response, was an inspiration for artists who wished to do the same in their own work.

The exhibition and the catalogue have been divided into sections, each
with a separate introduction, that illustrate some of the different ways in
which artists used music as a model in this common aim: from Kupka and
Klee's admiration of Bach and polyphonic composition [5] to the correlation
between modern music and modern art in the significant relationship
between Schönberg and Kandinsky; from the ground-breaking artistic
synthesis of *Der Blaue Reiter Almanac* to the studies of colour, form and
line in the teachings at the Bauhaus; and the lasting impact that the vitality
of dance-music and jazz was to have from the 1920s into the second half of
the twentieth century.

One of the principles behind the exhibition was to discern between those
artists who referred to music in writings about their own art rather than
those whose art was critiqued in musical terms, an easy resort for writers
commenting on abstraction for the first time. Despite the subject being
a very Continental phenomenon, particularly in the first decades of the
twentieth century, I wanted to include some British artists and to make
the subject more relevant to the Gallery's collections of Modern British
art. Many artists and artistic movements have not been included, simply
because to do justice to such a vast subject is beyond the scope of this
Gallery, whereas the Centre Pompidou in Paris has the resources to do an
in-depth survey, as it did so magnificently just a few years ago with
'Sons et Lumières'. [6]

As well as the essays by Simon Shaw-Miller and Michael Tucker included
in this catalogue, the programme that accompanies the exhibition is a vital
tool in aiding further understanding of the subject, including screenings
of early abstract films curated by Ben Rivers of Brighton Cinematheque.
The programme contains some of the pioneers in this field for whom
the medium was the ultimate means of bringing movement, rhythm and
musicality to their artistic vision. Also the accompanying exhibition of
musical notation 'Sighting Music', curated by Simon Shaw-Miller, illustrates

how music itself is an inherently visual art and how composers and artists have exploited its graphic language to innovative ends. Most of all, concerts of works from Bach to Schönberg, and John Taverner to Jim Aitchison will enliven the Gallery with music performed amongst the paintings. So, in Kandinsky's own words:

'Lend your ears to music, open your eyes to painting, and… stop thinking! Just ask yourself whether the work has enabled you to 'walk about' into a hitherto unknown world. If the answer is yes, what more do you want?' [7]

Endnotes

[1] Gauguin in a letter to critic André Fontainas in 1899

[2] Whistler in a letter to 'The World', 22 May 1878

[3] Erich Kuppers, *Der Kubismus, Ein künstlerisches Formproblem unserer Zeit, Leipzig,* 1920, quoted in Maur, Karin von, *The Sound of Painting. Music in Modern Art,* Munich/London/New York: Prestel, 1997

[4] Castel in an article published in *Mercure de France,* 1725

[5] For a brief explanation of musical terms used in the book see p. 186

[6] *Sons et Lumières. Une histoire du son dans l'art du XXe siècle (Sound and Light: A history of sound in 20th century art),* Paris: Centre Pompidou, 2004. For a select bibliography see p. 190

[7] Kandinsky quoted in Cytowic, Richard E., *The Man Who Tasted Shapes,* London: Abacus, 1996, p. 56

kandinsky and schönberg: musicality and abstraction

simon shaw-miller

The links between the visual arts and music are manifold and multifarious and no single essay can hope to do much but scratch the surface of this fascinating topic.[1] My aim here, therefore, is to provide a case study around the relationship between one of the twentieth century's greatest painters and one of its greatest composers: Wassily Kandinsky and Arnold Schönberg respectively (fig. 1 and 2).

Kandinsky's aim, in his quest for abstraction, was to produce a 'pure' art; one that moved beyond a direct figuration of the observed world to an exploration of the subject through the materials of painting itself. In the first two decades of the twentieth-century, Kandinsky based his paintings on historical subject-matter but dissolved the figurative elements in a haze of lines and colours. Through this process the figural means became independent of the original motif (cat. 11).

In this quest, music, accepted as the most abstract of the arts, provided Kandinsky with a quintessential paradigm that was both structural and ideological. Kandinsky found sustenance in two crucial, related areas: art theory (especially his own copious writings on art) and music. Similarly, his friend, the Austrian composer Arnold Schönberg, was driven fundamentally to re-evaluate his own artistic means of expression. Like Kandinsky, he did this in two main ways: one was through music theory, particularly his own profuse writing on the subject, and the other was in looking in the opposite direction to Kandinsky, beyond music to visual art.

One way of considering their relationship would be to explore their parallel development of stage works (*Die glückliche Hand* and *Der gelbe Klang*, both c.1910–13). But this is a large topic, and in relation to this exhibition it seems

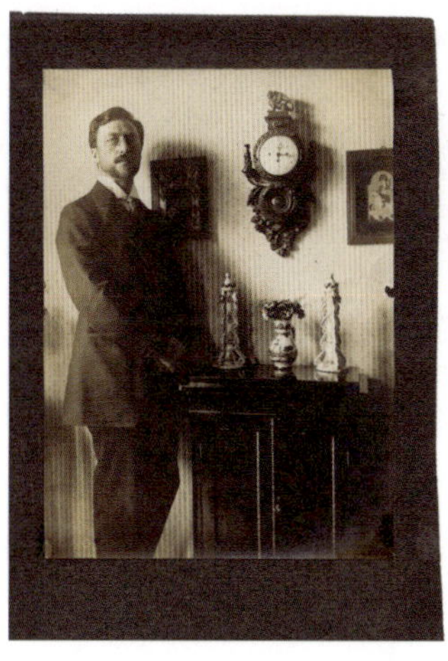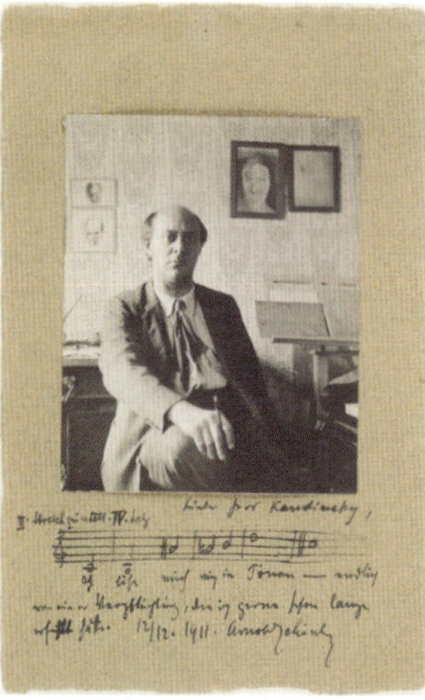

to me more appropriate to focus instead on the relationship of their ideas more generically, through the concepts of abstraction and musicality. Unlike many other artists who turned to music in the early decades of the twentieth century, Kandinsky was drawn, not to conventional music and theory, but rather to the most radical developments on the fringes of the avant-garde: to the music and writings of the composer Arnold Schönberg.

Like Kandinsky, Schönberg stands astride the aesthetic assumptions of the classical tradition and modernism. While there are elements of their aesthetic theories that are relatively conventional (for example, their employment of conventional formal structures including Kandinsky's use of historical subjects and Schoenberg's employment of traditional phrase structures) there are also more radical developments. I shall focus on these in order to draw the musician and artist into alignment.

Schönberg enunciated a new and relativistic conception of dissonance. 'The question of whether dissonances or consonances should be used is not a question of beauty' he said. For him, the difference between consonance and dissonance is 'in a gradated manner'; they are not in opposition, dissonances are merely more remote consonances (in terms of the harmonic overtone series).

Writing at the same time and in a passage that quotes Schönberg, Kandinsky also announces a new relativity. New art is simply a part of a single beauty, and it is art historians who will one day look back and see a new harmony, a new beauty [2]. Indeed, perhaps Kandinsky's most radical relative conception is in uniting all the arts at the level of 'inner sound' whilst also maintaining that 'the different arts have set forth on the path of saying what they are best able to say, through means that are peculiar to each. And in spite of, or thanks to this differentiation, the arts as such have never in recent times been closer to one another than in this latest period of spiritual transformation. In all that we have discussed above lie hidden the seeds of the struggle towards the non-naturalistic, the abstract, towards inner nature... the richest lessons are to be learned from music.' [3]

Schopenhauer, a philosopher appreciated by both Kandinsky and Schönberg, had characterized music as not of the world but of the will. In Kandinsky's terms, music was the least material art and hence already a spiritual one. While the different arts can be distinguished from each other (they have different means), they correspond insofar as they embody the same ultimate truth or 'sound'. Further, and this is an idea he takes from the realm of music and from Richard Wagner specifically, it is possible for this same impulse to be expressed through synthesis (as a sort of *Gesamtkunstwerk*), hence his *Der gelbe Klang*: 'finally one will arrive at a combination of the particular forces belonging to the different arts. Out of this combination will arise in time a new art... a truly monumental art.'

However, the dissolution of naturalistic artistic means was not easy. The main obstacle to negotiate was the issue of the relationship between content and meaning. In the attempt to dissolve identifiable representational motifs to promote inner sound and emotional empathy in the viewer, Kandinsky was concerned not to allow painting to become merely ornamental. He wrote in 1913, 'A terrifying abyss of all kinds of questions, a wealth of responsibilities stretched before me. And most important of all: What is to replace the missing object? The danger of ornament revealed itself clearly to me.' [4] Most of his early abstract paintings, therefore, maintain a dual iconography as subject pictures (fig. 3). [5] Like Schönberg's compositions of the same

     Kandinsky and Schönberg: Musicality and Abstraction

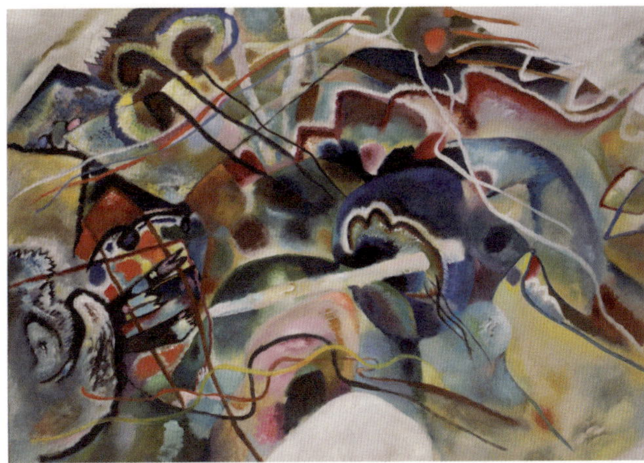

period, what these works express above all else, is the struggle for artistic expression itself - the content and subject is the struggle, an attempt at resolution between different pictorial or artistic codes.

Like Kandinsky, Schönberg also saw a tension at the heart of creativity between inner and outer expression. In music, this was not expressed as a conflict between naturalism and abstraction, but rather a tension between the laws of sound ('the demands of the object or material'), and the laws of cognition ('the demands of the subject'). Whilst he held that there were some sonoric universals, these should not be equated with aesthetic universals. In other words, nature provides material which composers make subservient to music. He clarifies this in a neat analogy:

There is no reason in physics or aesthetics that could force a musician to use tonality in order to represent his idea. The only question is whether one can attain formal unity and self-sufficiency without using tonality. The appeal to its origin in nature can be refuted if one recalls that just as tones pull towards triads, and triads towards tonality, gravity pulls us down towards the earth; yet an airplane carries us up away from it. A product can be apparently artificial without being unnatural, for it is based on the laws of nature to just the same degree as are those that seem primary.[6]

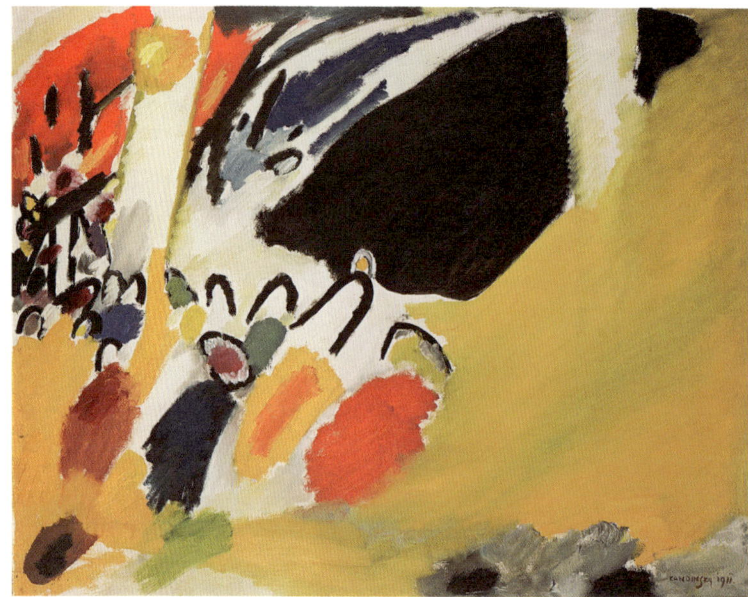

Art enables resistance to universals for aesthetic purposes: this attitude
unites Schönberg and Kandinsky, although aesthetic relativism was not
unique to these two. 'Abstract art', wrote Piet Mondrian, 'is opposed to
a natural representation of things, but is not opposed to nature as is
generally thought.'[7]

What music offered Kandinsky was justification for the move away from
the object (fig. 4). The idea of musical composition offered an artistic
structure for the abstract configurations of lines, colours and forms that
were self-sustaining and expressive. But I say the 'idea' of music advisedly.
In practice, things were less straightforward.

Western art music is distinguished by its harmonic sophistication. Increasing
harmonic complexity had brought music to a crisis point in the early
years of the twentieth century. The gravity of tonality had been greatly
weakened by intense reliance on chromaticism, to a point where in Wagner,
for example, the fact of tonal resolution was endlessly postponed.

The movement from consonance to dissonance and back was an ever more difficult journey. As tonality (the ultimate resolution of dissonance into a consonant framework) was made increasingly unstable, the possibility for transcending it was raised. It is this problem that Schönberg confronts in his 'emancipation of dissonance'. As we have seen, his resolution of this problem was a form of relativism, where the oppositions of consonance and dissonance are replaced by a sliding scale of relative dissonance or consonance. This was supplemented by an increased concern with tone colour (*Klangfarbe*). He writes in the final chapter of his *Theory of Harmony*, 'In a musical sound three characteristics are recognized: its pitch, colour and volume. Up to now it has been measured on only one of the three dimensions in which it operates, the one we call pitch.' [8] Schönberg outlines his notion of a *timbre*-structure, in which successions of changing tone-colours might create independent formal shapes, and which might be organised analogously to pitch structure. It is arguable that Schönberg's pupil Webern put this more effectively into practice. In his *Five Pieces* for orchestra (1910–11), for example, there are frequent changes of timbre within a single melodic phrase which sets up an independent set of relationships across and between the melodic groupings.[9] It is also possible that Schönberg would have looked with envy on the relatively sophisticated discussions of colour that were evident in art theory, and which occupy Kandinsky significantly in *Concerning the Spiritual in Art*.

1908 was a very difficult year for Schönberg, a time of personal and musical crisis. His wife had temporarily left him for the painter Richard Gerstl (fig. 5) and, in the same year, he started but then temporally abandoned work on his music drama *Die glückliche Hand* (cat. 14 and 15). It was also during this year that he definitively abandoned tonality. With his friend and supporter Gustav Mahler absent from Vienna, Schönberg only had a single concert of his music that year. It was around this time that he was most active as a painter.

This is a time for Schönberg when formal issues are at their most critical. The conventional structures of music are closely dependant on tonality, for example, sonata form, a structure that continues to occupy composers

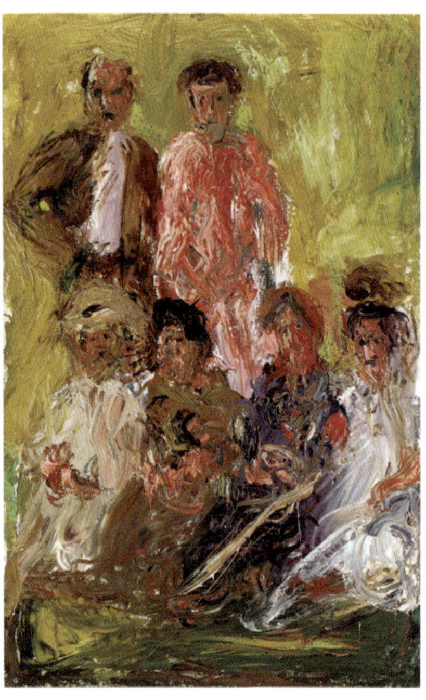

Fig. 5
Richard Gerstl
(1883–1908)
The Schönberg Family
n.d.
oil on canvas
Österreichische Galerie Belvedere, Vienna

to this day, is here a theme that is not merely stated and repeated, but transformed. The music begins in one key and moves to another, usually from the tonic to the dominant, and then works its way back to the tonic. This can be a simple or elaborate and protracted journey but, in either case, orientation is provided by a sense of departure from a home key and a return, via interesting (chromatic) byways. Once tonality is abandoned overall structure disappears as does any sense of orientation. There is no fixed home, just a beginning, and all distances from it are now equal so a sense of narrative journeying is lost. As a consequence, many of his pieces from around this time are relatively short. For longer pieces, such as the Second String Quartet, *op. 10*, the *George Songs op. 15*, *Erwartung op. 17*, *Die glückliche Hand op. 18* and *Pierrot Lunaire op. 21*, texts become very important for Schönberg. By texts I mean both theoretical texts (Schönberg wrote his *Theory of Harmony* at approximately the same time as Kandinsky was writing *Concerning the Spiritual in Art*) and texts that give the music a shape and provide a narrative for the journey. Schönberg explained it thus:

A little later I discovered how to construct larger forms by following the text or poem. The differences in size and shape of its parts and the change in character and mood were mirrored in the shape and size of the composition, in its dynamics and tempo, figuration and accentuation, instrumentation and orchestration. Thus the parts were differentiated as clearly as they had formerly been by the tonal and structural functions of harmony.[10]

Schönberg's repair to painting was, I would suggest, also an important element in this process: it was part of his re-evaluation of his identity as an artist. Painting allowed Schönberg to be provisional and experimental without the pressure to be successful; his sense of identity was not central to his activities as a painter. What painting gave him was permission to equate the self with a radical reduction in the language of art. This reduction took the form of isolated physiognomic elements against a spaceless background, such as paintings of eyes or hands (cat. 12 and 13). We might also think of them as paintings of actions, the act of looking, a reduction to the crux of visual art.

The influence of the Austrian Expressionist painter Richard Gerstl on Schönberg's style is undeniable. Gerstl helped Schönberg achieve a reduced technique best suited to his dilettante efforts, but given his personal circumstances it is also clear why Schönberg should want continually to deny Gerstl any role in the formation of his aesthetic. That said, Schönberg did distil pictorial elements to a much greater extent than Gerstl; an isolated face in a void, bare statements on the act of seeing. These paintings struggle to communicate with an unknown viewer. Their subject is the desperate hope for communication at a time when Schönberg was estranged from both his wife and a sympathetic audience for his music. These works are a poignant appeal for communion.

Both Kandinsky and Schönberg shifted the issue of meaning from being solely invested in the object to the site of its reception. Schönberg believed in the cultivation of perceptive power. He emphasised a participatory conception of listening, believing certain effects to have 'an effect on more

experienced and trained listeners'. This is also a symptom of the way in
which listening changes through history with knowledge and familiarity.
Kandinsky's image of a great triangle of spiritual life slowly moving
forward and upward, likewise implies perceptual change through time.[11]
If, with Impressionism, materiality had been presented through the filter
of subjective vision, with the advent of a pure abstract art the time had
come, Kandinsky hoped, for a more spiritual art to sound.

I want to conclude by pulling together the strands that feed the issue of
abstraction in art and music. For Kandinsky, the issue of abstraction was
propelled by the desire (or need) to explore the qualities of form, line,
colour and facture as independent formal entities, rather than as pictorial
elements for the depiction of subjects from life. What he sought was
emancipation from imitation, representation and figuration; from a realistic
or naturalistic depiction of the world. Instead, he wished to promote an
inner spiritual or emotional reality, one more directly accessed through
abstract pictorial means. Such a perspective was not new for music.
The Viennese musicologist Edward Hanslick's view, that music was the pure
and paradigmatical non-representational art form, was a dominant one
by the early twentieth century. Schönberg saw this as the reason why the
study of musical composition had been conventionally more theory-laden
than the equivalent study of composition in painting. He lamented the fact
that 'Music does not simply have instructions in its craft and techniques,
as does painting, music has, rather, Instruction in Theory'. Unlike figurative
art, musical language needs no empirical anchor outside its own terms
of reference. He continues to modify his analogy thus: 'Musical composition
is more theoretical than carpentry... The carpenter could never understand
his craft in a merely theoretical way.'[12] What is new and unique to the idea
of musical abstraction in the twentieth century is therefore not its non-
representational nature, for music has never been representational in the
way the visual arts have, but rather its ever increasing dependence on
theoretical models, accompanied by a weakened link between acoustic and
perceptual laws and organisational theoretical concepts. This is especially
true in twelve-note music, where the organisational structure is rarely
detectable by the ear alone, and eyes and a score are needed.

The twentieth century has seen the proliferation of musical and artistic languages. Music and art become less a form of shared or communal expression and more explicit, culturally-constructed systems of originality dependent on the individual systems of artists. However, it is worth noting that if Schönberg is one of the progenitors of this in music, he maintained that music only has meaning through enactment (doing). Likewise, for Kandinsky in his 'Compositions', 'Here reason, the conscious, the deliberate, and the purposeful play a preponderant role. Except that I always decide in favour of feeling rather than calculation.' [13]

Endnotes

[1]   For more on this see my own *Visible Deeds of Music: Art and Music from Wagner to Cage*, Yale, 2002 and 2004

[2]   Kandinsky, 'Whither the "New" Art' in *Complete Writings on Art*, vol. 1, p.102. Schönberg 'New Music: My Music' (1930), in Style and Idea, p. 101

[3]   Kandinsky, 'Concerning the Spiritual in Art' in *Complete Writings on Art*, vol. 1, pp. 153–5

[4]   Kandinsky, 'Reminiscences/Three Pictures' in *Complete Writings on Art*, vol. 1, p.370

[5]   *Painting with White Border* of 1913 is, for example, based around the abstracted motif of St. George and the dragon, but veiled by an abstract, non-naturalistic, linear and colour composition.

[6]   Schönberg, 'Opinion or Insight' (1926) in *Style and Idea*, p. 262

[7]   Mondrian, 'Plastic Art and Pure Plastic Art' in *The New Art – The New Life: Collected Writings*, p. 293

[8]   Schönberg, *Theory of Harmony*, p. 421

[9]   See also Webern's orchestration of the ricercare from Bach's *Musical Offering*.

[10]   Schönberg, 'Composition with Twelve Tones' (1941), in *Style and Idea*, p. 217–18

[11]   See 'Concerning the Spiritual in Art' in *Complete Writings on Art*, vol. 1, p. 133

[12]   Schönberg, *Theory of Harmony*, p. 7

[13]   See 'Concerning the Spiritual in Art' in *Complete Writings on Art*, vol. 1 p. 218

as if mirroring a (jazz) melody

michael tucker

In June 1907 the poet Rainer Maria Rilke saw an exhibition of watercolours by Paul Cézanne at the Bernheim Jeune gallery in Paris; a few months later, he would return again and again to the Cézanne retrospective at the Salon d'Automne. Writing to his wife Clara about the Bernheim Jeune show, Rilke spoke of 'Landscapes, very light pencil outlines, and, here and there, as if just for emphasis and confirmation, there's an accidental scattering of colour, a row of spots, wonderfully arranged and with a security of touch: as if mirroring a melody - .' (fig. 1) [1]

Rilke's letters on Cézanne have long been valued as one of the prime examples of the influence of one art form upon another in early twentieth-century art: for the gradually emergent, immense constructive power of Cézanne encouraged Rilke to concentrate less on the feelings to be expressed in a poem, and more on the means by which those feelings might be shaped into an artistic utterance of what Rilke called lasting, thing-like consequence. Comparing the rendering of various fruits by that earlier master of still life, Chardin, to that which is to be found in Cézanne, Rilke remarked how, in the work of the latter painter, fruits 'cease to be edible altogether, that's how thing-like and real they become, how simply indestructible in their stubborn thereness.' [2]

A century later, while our concepts of landscape, melody and still life may have changed considerably since those operative in his time, each of the above remarks by Rilke (1875–1926) will surely continue to strike a chord with any painter (or poet) concerned with what remain the central generative mysteries of art: the relations of form and content, the sign and what is signified; what is presented and/or represented in a work of art, to and for the audience's attention. In the Western tradition, from at

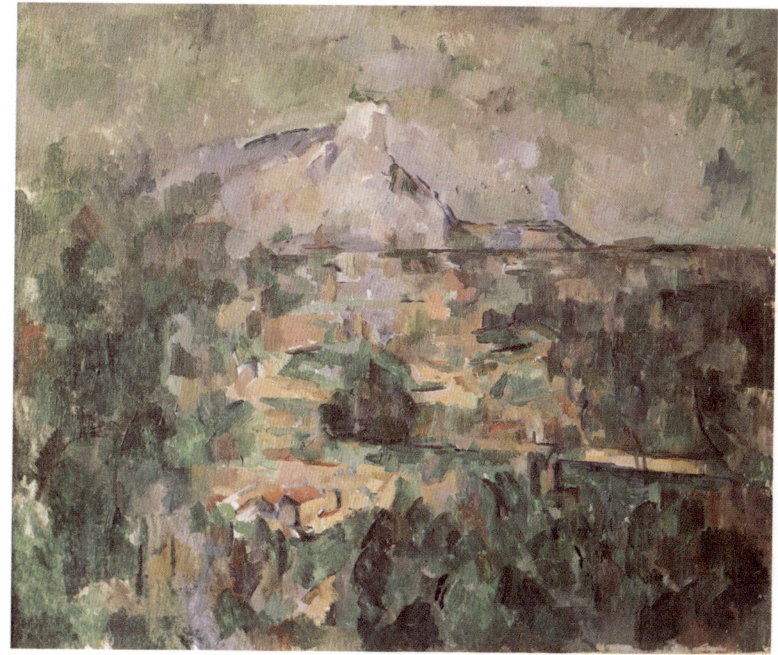

Fig.1
Paul Cézanne
1839–1906,
Montagne Sainte-
Victoire from Les
Lauves,
1904-06,
oil on canvas,
Kunstmuseum, Basel,
Switzerland

least Plato and Aristotle onwards, such mysteries have fuelled a continuing philosophical debate about the nature of poetics, or the understanding of the making of meaning in art. In the context of the present exhibition, the particularly - and particular - musical inflection that Rilke brought to this archetypal theme in his letters on Cézanne compels especial attention. So too does the paradox that it was by reference to that most intangible of mediums, music, that Rilke sought to underpin, or illuminate, his emphasis on the increasingly concrete or "thing-like" nature of Cézanne's achievement in painting.

In the musical analogy quoted above, Rilke - for whom music was an art of the utmost import - speaks equally of the accidental and the arranged, of both 'a scattering' and 'a row' of visual effects. While the analogy was precipitated by the qualities of those Cézanne watercolours which Rilke saw in Paris, anyone familiar with subsequent avant-garde developments in Western painting will most likely consider, and with justification, that Rilke's analogy could apply equally to a good many of such developments.

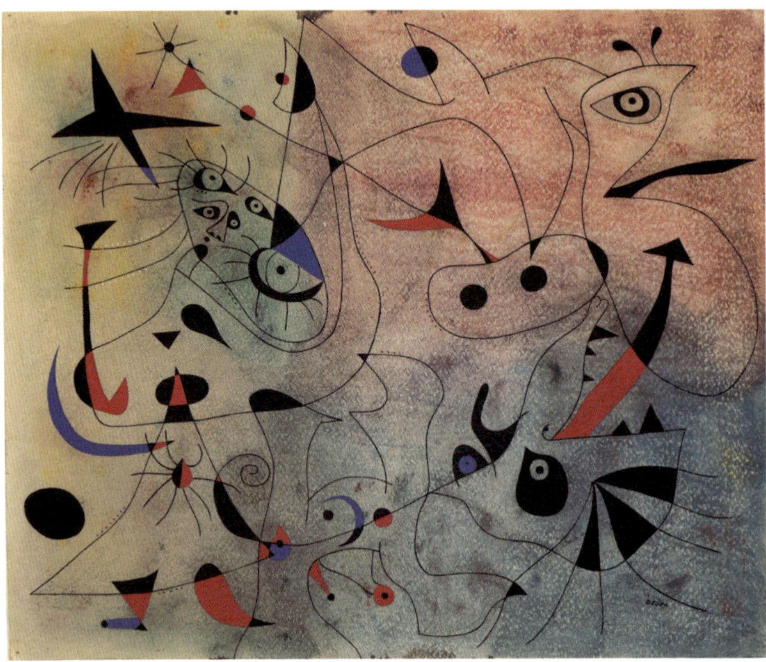

Take the work of Joan Miró, for example, and in particular, the seminal *Constellations* series of twenty-three gouaches from 1940–41, which had such an impact on Jackson Pollock and others of the emergent generation of Abstract Expressionists, when they were exhibited for the first time in New York in 1945 (fig. 2).

References to the interplay of music, poetry and painting abound in Miró's *Catalan Notebooks* of 1940–41. It was here that Miró made his famous remark that, above all, he wanted his work to be like a poem set to (or made into) music by a painter. Like so many visionary artists of the twentieth-century avant garde, Miró's blending of the factors of accident and arrangement in his work was deeply affected by his sensitivity to music (fig. 3). He responded with equal enthusiasm to the elegance of Mozart and the anonymous singing of hymns in Palma Cathedral; to what his compatriot, the poet and dramatist Federico Garcia Lorca, called the *cante jondo* or 'deep song' of the folk forms which fired flamenco music, as well as to the more cosmopolitan innovations of such diverse figures as John Cage and Karlheinz Stockhausen - and Duke

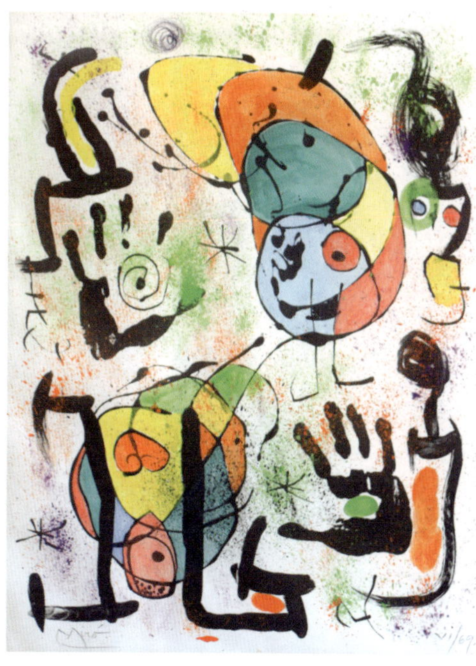

Ellington. A photograph, taken in summer 1966 in the courtyard of the recently opened Fondation Maeght in southern France, for which Miró had created an extensive sculpture labyrinth, documents Miró's relishing of the open-air piano trio jazz of Ellington, bassist John Lamb and drummer Sam Woodyard.[3]

From Léger, Mondrian and Matisse to Miró, Picasso and Pollock, and from Romare Bearden and Daniel Larue Johnson to Stuart Davis and Larry Rivers, Karel Appel and Jean Dubuffet, Alan Davie, Harvey Daniels and Jean-Michel Basquiat, artists have long been fascinated by jazz. When Jean Cocteau first heard this new American music in 1918, he felt that it was as fertilising to the artist 'as life itself'. The Dadaists celebrated the life-force in what they called 'Negro rhythms'; and the poet and critic (and good friend of Miró) Michel Leiris spent many a Paris evening in the 1920s enjoying jazz in the company of André Masson. Believing that jazz 'unfurled an orgiastic banner to the colours of the moment', Leiris considered the effect of the hot jazz he heard to be comparable to a form of possession: a practically religious experience involving music, dance and eroticism.[4]

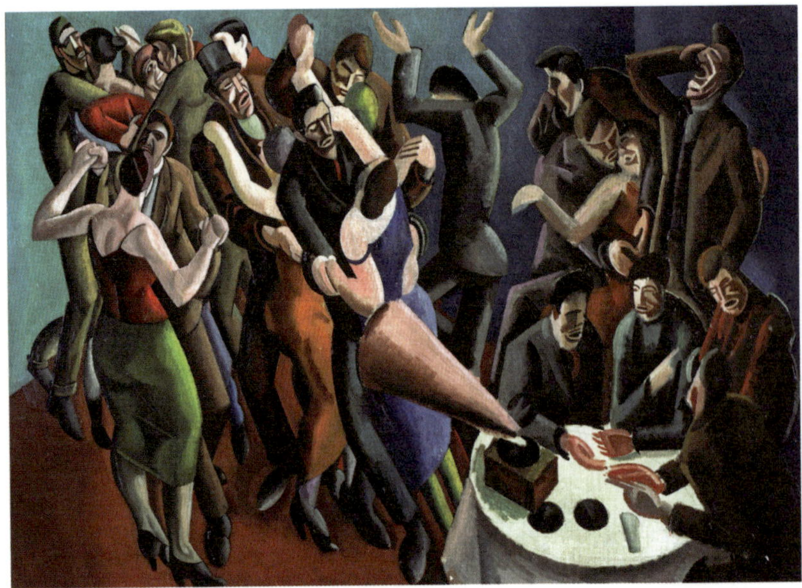

Such a perception, of a piece with such jazz-oriented paintings of the period as Otto Dix's *Homage To Beauty* (1922) and William Roberts' *The Dance Club (The Jazz Party)* of 1923 (fig. 4), contains a substantial measure of truth. Like these paintings, Leiris's words anticipate the Jungian insights of a key work of the so-called Jazz Age, Hermann Hesse's 1927 novel *Steppenwolf*. Here, the strains of a dance band alto saxophone prompt the self-loathing Harry Haller to take the first steps of a healing journey towards what Hesse called the Magic Theatre of Haller's deeper or more fully integrated sense of self. [5] However, paradigmatic as it remains, Leiris's insight risks conjuring one or another variety of potentially regressive or limiting myths about jazz. Consider, for example, Max Beckmann's *Self-Portrait* from 1930, with its phallic fantasy of a saxophone wrapping itself, serpent-like, around the painter's body (fig. 5).

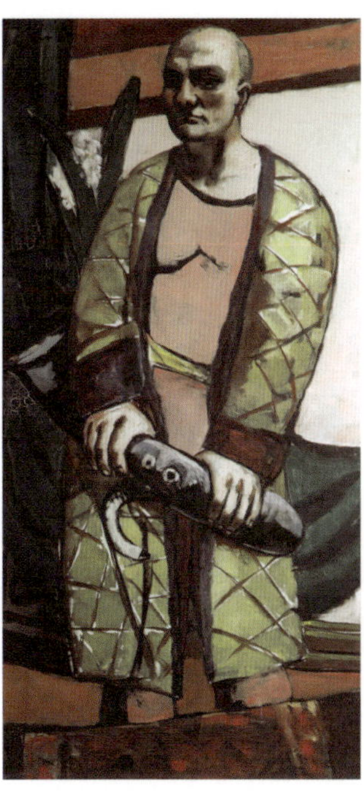

Jazz is a highly sensuous, even sensual, music. But if the motor rhythms of jazz might be said to owe much to the elemental cyclical power of the blues, we should not forget that, early on, the compositional and rhythmical complexities of ragtime also fed into the development of the music. Absorbing both the complex harmonic language of Western classical music and the modal principles of much non-Western classical and folk music, the improvisational flair which lies at the heart of jazz has developed what one might call both idiomatic and non-idiomatic aspects of instrumental colour and expressive capacity to previously unsuspected levels. And the instrumental, or soloing, side of jazz has long been matched by a congruent capacity for innovative arrangement, whether for piano trio or big band. Jazz, in fact, has long been a music of considerable intellectual consequence. It has attracted the attention of such diverse and distinguished musical minds as Milton Babbitt, Gunther Schuller and George Russell: not to speak of Duke Ellington and Jelly Roll Morton, Coleman Hawkins and Oscar Peterson, Bill and Gil Evans; John Lewis and Lalo Schifrin, Charles Mingus, Miles Davis and Oliver Nelson; John Coltrane and Don

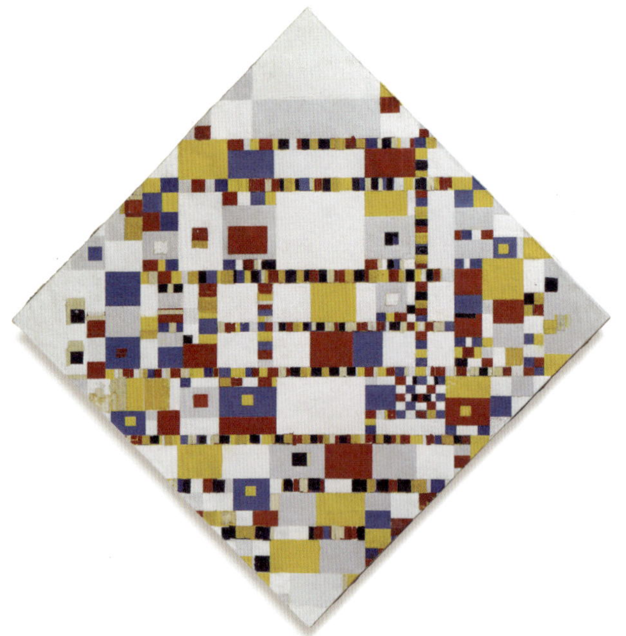

Cherry, Keith Jarrett and Jan Garbarek, and many, many more. And with a history which stretches from turn-of-the-nineteenth-and-twentieth-centuries New Orleans, through key developments in Chicago and Kansas City, New York and Los Angeles, to the world-wide art that it is today, jazz has been, and will surely continue to be, many things to many people.[6]

To the Nazis and the Communists of the 1930s and 1940s, the music was anathema. While the Nazis vilified syncopated or swing music in one crude piece of poster propaganda or another, the USSR twice tried to ban jazz officially. They might just as well have tried to drain the oceans. From its earliest roots in gospel music and the songs of travelling blues messengers, jazz has spread to clubs and concert halls the world over, speaking to people of all colours and creeds. Born from the unspeakable misery of a people who had been branded as unworthy, jazz was the means whereby that people asserted its worth, its dignity. And in giving the world jazz, African-American culture did far more than encourage a foot to tap here or a finger to snap there, in careless abandon.

For a painter like Piet Mondrian, and others of the De Stijl generation such as Theo van Doesburg, jazz was a kind of vitalised mathematics that could help feed a social, intellectual and artistic myth of progress, moving modern life from the realm of the suffering individual to the triumph of the abstract and the collective, to the creation of that dialectical harmony (born from the opposition of contraries) which marks such late works of the New York-domiciled Mondrian as *Broadway Boogie-Woogie* (1942–43) and the unfinished *Victory Boogie-Woogie* (1943–44) (fig. 6). In his monograph on the painter, the art historian Hans L. C. Jaffé speaks of 'a new tempo' in these works, underlining both social and formal aspects of their jazz-inflected modernity (and modernism): 'Whereas Mondrian's early paintings were built up out of long continuous lines and large planes, which could be compared to whole or half notes in music, there now appear much smaller forms, comparable to eighth or sixteenth notes [...] boogie-woogie music, with its unexpected syncopation of rhythm, is elaborated visually [...] Passionately devoted as he was to dancing and rhythm, Mondrian had always been attracted by the latest in ballroom music, advocating the tango and one- and two- steps over the waltz.' [7] In a definitive phrase, Jaffé observes how, in the unfinished *Victory* work, 'a syncopated movement now predominates; the beat of the measure dissolves into shifts of accent.' [8]

The beauty of jazz, such as it has been sensed by many painters, lies precisely here: in the way in which, no matter whether its emotional temper be hot (Louis Armstrong and Sidney Bechet, Dizzy Gillespie and Charlie Parker) or cool (Miles Davis and Chet Baker, Stan Getz and the Modern Jazz Quartet), jazz takes us as far as possible from the strait- (and, in jazz parlance, 'straight'-) jacket of the parade ground. As the late critic Martin Williams observed, jazz handles the paradoxes of life - all those tensions between the arranged and the accidental - in creative ways that no other music has done before. It brings individual and group, body and mind, heart and soul into as dynamic, fluid and fruitful a field of relation as structure and improvisation. [9] The blues, the backbone of jazz, and the so-called blue or flatted notes of jazz scales, handle emotional complexities and contradictions in ways which may serve to release us from the false promises of absolutes; including, it must be said, those which fuelled the essential Puritanism of much of Mondrian's art.

Around the time that Miró was working on his *Constellations*, a young Philip Larkin wrote a short and extraordinary essay on jazz, which has been published only recently. Sensitive to the faculty of intuition so crucial to the potency of the music, Larkin began his essay by suggesting that 'The decay of ritual in everything from religion to the lighting of a fire is resulting in the insulation of the unconscious which finds its daily fulfilment in such ritual [...] The predicament in which the unconscious is finding itself today is reflected in the general upheaval in all the arts, and particularly in the emergence of a new art, American Jazz music.' [10] Larkin concluded his essay with the ringing declaration that 'the unconscious is in a new state, and has a new need, and has produced a new art to satisfy that need, and it is as well that we should understand.' [11]

Within the present exhibition, the creative tensions of picture plane, spatial and linear rhythm, colour and imagery in such contrasting works as John Tunnard's *Ascension* (1945) (cat. 55), Alan Davie's *Jazz by Moonlight No.3* (1966) (cat. 57) and Jack Smith's *Musical Painting Touching no. 2* (1992) (cat. 43) speak, not of any simplistic illustration of the lasting perspicacity of Larkin's words, but rather of exactly the sort of musically inflected *embodiment* of trans-rational feelings which, following his exposure to Cézanne, Rilke had pursued in the consciously wrought figures and forms of his own work.

In the case of Alan Davie, whose (recorded) achievements in improvised, jazz-oriented music are considerable, the vivid contribution of his imagery to the sort of jazz-driven, newly refreshed myth of the unconscious of which Larkin wrote in 1940 is such as to epitomise the border-crossing, and ultimately shamanic - or visionary - impact of jazz upon painting. [12] Here, as perhaps with no other painter of the past half-century, the mirroring of a (jazz) melody can serve to fracture entirely any conventional notion of the (mirroring) picturing that was once held to be the task of painting. For here we are in the province of the painter-poet who would dance, who would sing, of worlds simultaneously ancient and new. The shape-shifting shamanic core of the music that is jazz and blues offers, thus, multi-toned revivification of the faith which Rilke proclaimed in the sonnets which he devoted to the most renowned of all the shamans of classical antiquity: 'Once and for all, if there is Song, Orpheus is there.'

        As if Mirroring a (Jazz) Melody

Endnotes

1   *Letters On Cézanne* (edited by Clara Rilke; translated from the German by Joel Agee),
    London: Jonathan Cape, 1988 p. 53

2   Ibid pp. 32–33

3   See Maeght, A. (ed.) *À proximité des poètes et des peintres: quarante ans d'édition maeght*, Paris:
    Adrian Maeght, 1986, p. 91. The jazz world has been equally enthusiastic about Miró. Three albums have
    been devoted to him: the Dave Brubeck Quartet's *Time Further Out: Miró Reflections* from 1961 (Columbia
    CK 64668); the Tommy Smith Quartet's *Azure* from 1995 (Linn AKD 059); and drummer Bobby Previte's The
    23 *Constellations of Joan Miró* from 2001 (Tzadik TZ 7072). In 1992, saxophonist Jane Ira Bloom, who appears
    on the Previte album, recorded 'Straight No Chaser/Miró' on her *Art and Aviation* (Arabesque Jazz AJ 0107);
    a decade later, bassist Miroslav Vitous recorded 'Miro Bop' (with tenor saxophonist Jan Garbarek, pianist
    Chick Corea and drummer Jack DeJohnette) on his *Universal Syncopations* (ECM 1863, released in 2003).
    I investigate the Miró/jazz connection in detail in a sleevenote to the Azure recording.

4   Hadler, Mona 'Jazz and the Visual Arts', *Arts Magazine*, June 1983, p. 96. See also Archer-Straw, *Petrine
    Negrophilia: Avant-Garde Paris and Black Culture in the* 1920s, London: Thames and Hudson, 2000;
    Richter, Hans *Dada: Art and Anti-Art*, London: Thames and Hudson, 1966 p. 20; Melzer, Annabelle *Latest
    Rage The Big Drum: Dada and Surrealist Performance*, Ann Arbor: UMI Research Press, 1980 pp.30-32, and
    the related discussion and further references in Tucker, Michael 'Music Man's Dream' in *Alan Davie*, London:
    Lund Humphries Ltd., 1992, pp. 70-92.

5   For extensive discussion of the impact of jazz upon twentieth-century visual art and literature (including
    writers as different as Ralph Ellison and Langston Hughes, Jean-Paul Sartre and Jack Kerouac) see Goldson,
    Elisabeth (ed.) *Seeing Jazz: Artists and Writers on Jazz*, Washington: The Smithsonian Institute, 1997.

6   Ibid passim.

7   Jaffé, Hans L.C. *Mondrian*, London: Thames and Hudson, 1990 (first edition 1969), p. 124.

8   Ibid p. 126. See also the discussion in Appel Jr., Alfred *Jazz Modernism: From Ellington and Armstrong to
    Matisse and Joyce*, New York: Alfred A. Knopf, 2002 pp. 77-78 and passim.

9   Williams, Martin *The Jazz Tradition*, New York: Oxford University Press, 1970, pp. 10-15. For a related,
    more socially specific text, see Belgrad, Daniel *The Culture of Spontaneity: Improvisation and the Arts in
    Postwar America*, Chicago & London: The University of Chicago Press, 1998.

10 Palmer, Richard & White, John (eds.) *Reference Back: Philip Larkin's Uncollected Jazz
    Writings 1940–84*, Hull: The University of Hull Press, 1999, p.169.

11 Ibid p. 170. Unpublished in his lifetime, Larkin's ideas offer uncanny anticipation of a fair portion of what
    Martin Williams would say in the excellent, somewhat Jungian-inflected introduction to his 1970 *The Jazz
    Tradition*. After a lengthy discussion of the many (creative) paradoxes of jazz, including the central dialectic
    of suffering and affirmation, pain and joy, Williams concludes: 'Perhaps in jazz, then, the gods, in some small
    way, prepare for their metamorphosis.'(p. 15.)

12 William Feaver provides an invigorating, strongly jazz-oriented perspective on Davie in his catalogue essay
    for the 2007 show *Alan Davie: Paintings 1955–1967*, London: Thomas Dane Gallery/The Paragon Press,
    2007. For detail on the shamanic (or healing-visionary) theme, see Tucker op. cit. passim and Tucker,
    Michael *Dreaming with Open Eyes: The Shamanic Spirit in Twentieth-Century Art and Culture*, London and
    San Francisco: Aquarian/HarperCollins, 1992, which includes discussion of the work of Miró (pp. 308-316)
    and Davie (pp. 320-326). Translated by me, the Rilke quotation which closes the present essay comes from
    Sonnets to Orpheus (Part One, no 5): for a slightly different translation, see Bly, Robert, *Selected Poems of
    Rainer Maria Rilke*, New York: Harper and Row, 1981, p. 203.

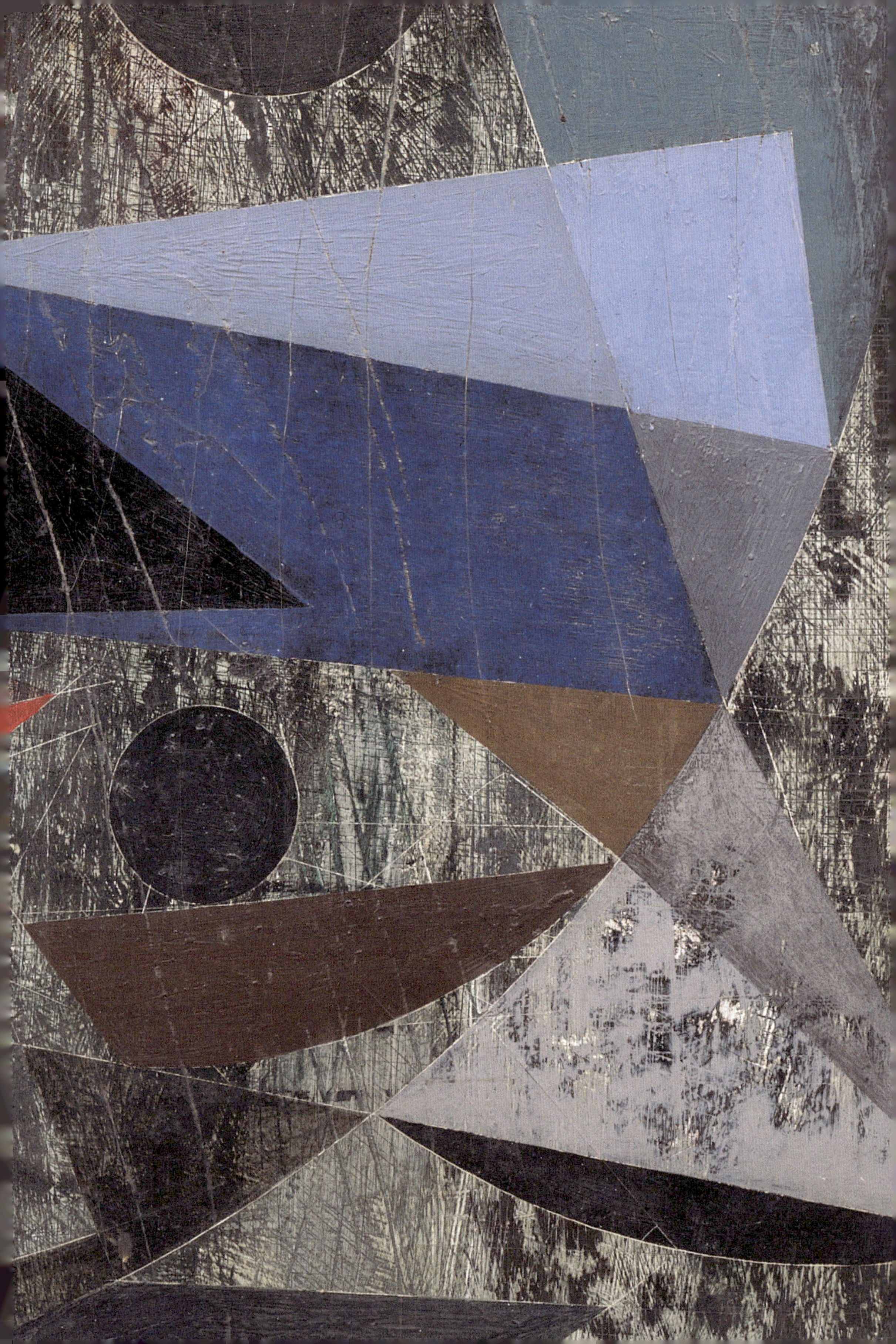

harmony

'In the eighteenth century music already perceived and resolved the paths of abstraction... Painting is only beginning this task today.'

Paul Klee, Diaries, 1898–1918

In 1829 the composer Mendelssohn staged a concert of Bach's choral masterpiece, the St. Matthew Passion. It spurred a revival of interest in Baroque music and that of Bach in particular who had long been neglected, considered too academic in style to be widely appreciated. And yet, during the Romantic period, Bach's work had been revered as the pinnacle of artistic achievement for its pure harmony and mastery of composition, interweaving musical lines to form a complex whole that was felt to reflect the harmony of the universe itself.

For many artists in the early twentieth century who wished to develop a visual language that was not grounded in mere imitation of the material world, eighteenth century music served as the ultimate model. Often prompted by scientific developments or an increasing interest in alternative belief systems, artists sought a new means of self-expression that would connect with the underlying order present in nature. Music, seen by many to be the language of the cosmos, was founded on balance and harmony for which artists tried to find visual equivalents in the form and colour of their own paintings.

John Wells, Nocturne (detail), 1946
oil on gesso, 48.5 x 42.5 cm
Private Collection

Kupka adopted the fugal structure from music to develop a method of visual composition that gave him freedom of expression and led him to comment, 'I am still groping in the dark but I believe I can find something between sight and hearing and I can produce a fugue in colours as Bach has done in music.' In his diaries of 1898–1918, Klee made continuous reference to the parallels between music and painting but he was scathing of critics who saw analogies between music and his own art based on its graphic quality alone, rather than recognising within it a structure and rhythm that was derived from eighteenth century musical forms. His preference was for the music of Mozart and Bach and was contemptuous of much contemporary music, once writing in response to a performance of Schönberg's *Pierrot Lunaire*, 'Perish, Philistine, your last hour has struck!'. Introducing music into his teachings at the Bauhaus, Klee inspired students such as Neugeboren to find answers to visual problems in Bach's compositions.

Other twentieth century artists sought to express the purity of classical harmony in abstract terms in reference to particular composers or even specific pieces of music. The Lithuanian artist Čiurlionis was both a composer and a painter who created over 300 pieces of music and 250 artworks in his short life and who influenced the circle associated with Schönberg and Der Blaue Reiter (The Blue Rider). Over half a century later, Richards found inspiration in the music of Debussy, which he felt to be particularly poetic and visual in nature. He stated 'There is certainly a deep link between music and painting – the proportions of time – the geometry of rhythms and the division of spaces. This is true also about architecture and poetry. The sensuous entity that a piece of music or painting becomes ensues from the special adjustments of these elements.'

harmony
catalogue entries

Mikalojus Konstantinas Čiurlionis

b.1875 Russia (Lithuania)–d.1911 Russia (Poland)

Sonata No.5 (Sonata of the Sea)
i. Allegro ii.Andante iii.Finale
1908
tempera on paper
approx. 73 x 63 cm each
M. K. Čiurlionis National Museum of Art

Čiurlionis studied orchestral music and composition before studying painting at the Warsaw School of Fine Arts in 1904. His interest in music theory, philosophy and cosmology found expression in tempera paintings such as the *Sonata* series, organised in 'movements' mirroring his own musical compositions. *Sonata of the Sea* was painted after Čiurlionis' three-part symphonic poem for orchestra called *The Sea*, written in 1907, followed by a piano sonata of the same name in 1908. The repeated motifs and rhythmic linearity of the paintings give them a semi-abstract quality and can be read as 'musical' elements. Čiurlionis expressed his theosophical belief in the underlying force of nature in musical terms, writing in 1901, 'I am completely immersed in counterpoint. I imagine the entire world as a great symphony and people as notes.'

In 1908 Čiurlionis joined the Union of Russian Artists led by Alexandre Benois, the set-designer of the Ballets Russes, whose son Nicolas and the artist Nina Varypaeva were both influenced by him to paint in a style directly inspired by music. One year after his death in 1911, a work by Čiurlionis was selected by Boris Anrep to be exhibited alongside other Russian artists as part of Roger Fry's 'Second Post-Impressionist Exhibition' in London.

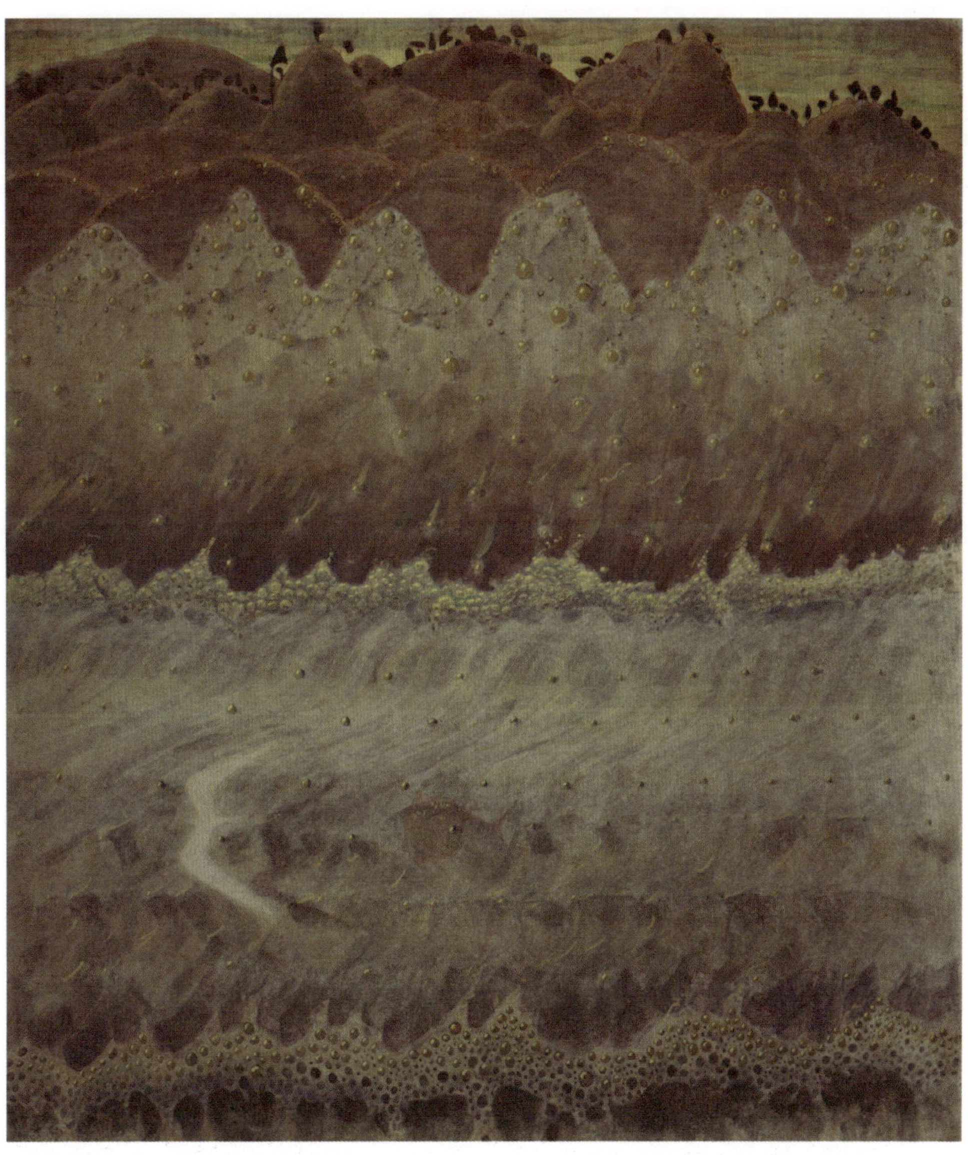

i. Allegro

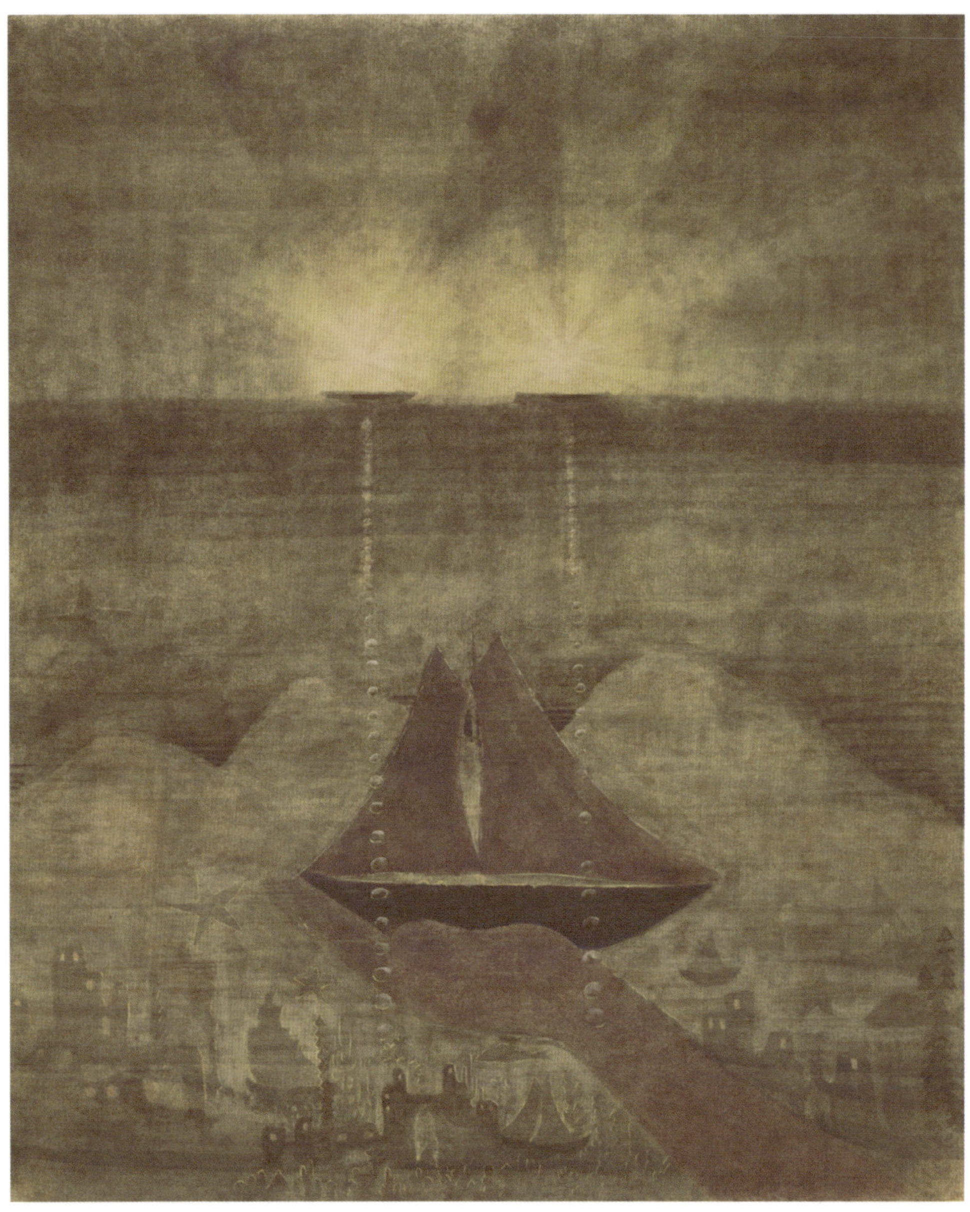

ii. Andante

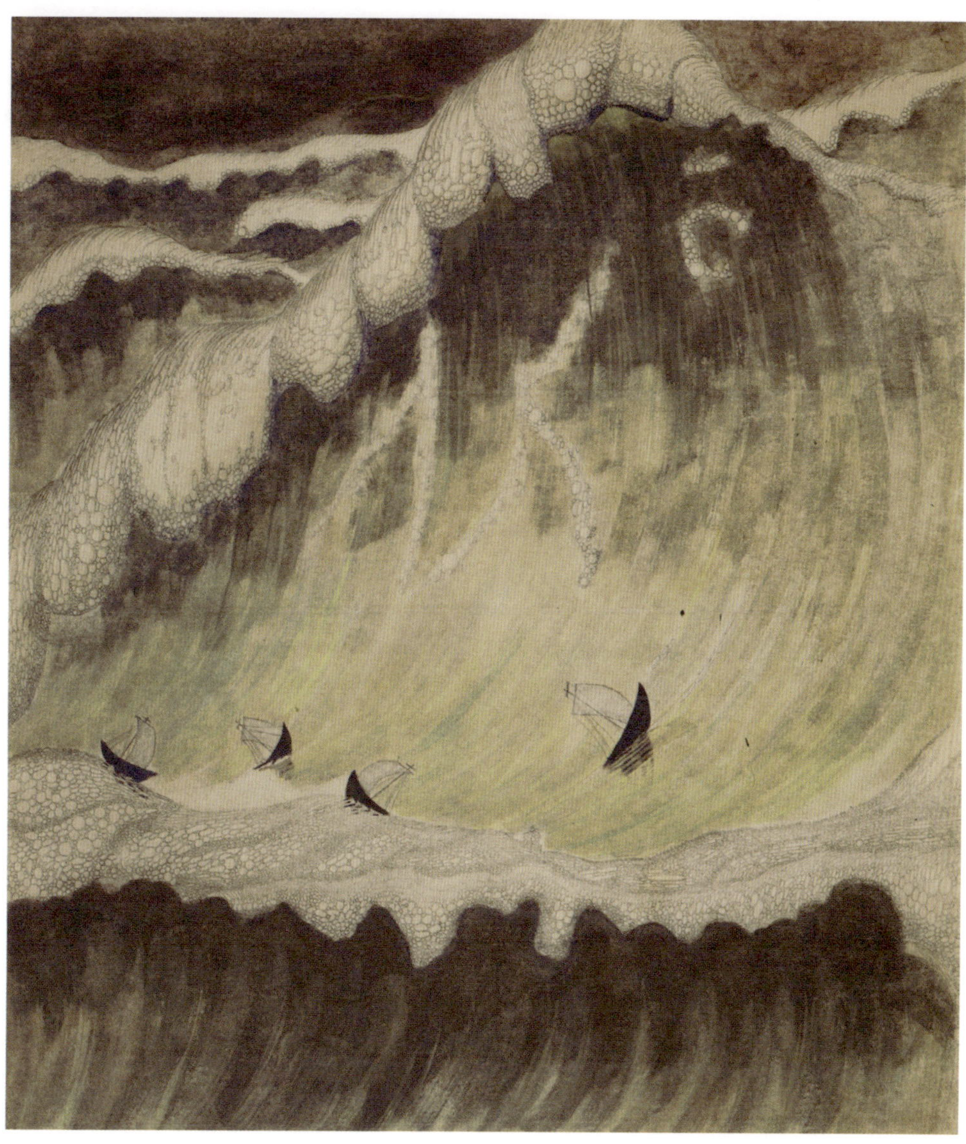

iii. Finale

František Kupka

b.1871 Czechoslovakia (Czech Republic)–d.1957 France

Study for 'Fugue'
1911–12
gouache on paper
38 x 39 cm
Museum Kampa, the Jan and
Mada Mladek Foundation

Kupka's *Amorpha, Warm Chromatics* and *Amorpha, Fugue in Two Colours*, for which this is a study, were the first purely abstract paintings to be exhibited in Paris in the Salon d'Automne of 1912. Shown alongside works by Albert Gleizes, Jean Metzinger and Henri Matisse, these paintings were deemed radical in comparison and prompted the critic Gustave Kahn to write, 'the elegant chromatic arabesques based on feminine lines by Mr. Kupka are games which are not within everyone's reach. Even with the greatest sympathy for the Cubist effort, one cannot yet admire these works.'

The *Amorpha* works (meaning 'form' in Greek) represent a synthesis of Kupka's ideas that were leading him to develop a new visual language capable of expressing the fundamental essence of nature and a cosmic vision of the universe that derived from his interest in spiritualism and theosophy, an alternative belief system promoting the concept of a universal brotherhood that enjoyed a new popularity in the nineteenth century. Through his friend Walter Morse Rummel, a pianist known for his transcription and interpretation of choral works by J. S. Bach, Kupka conceived of a style of painting that imitated the orchestration of fugues, 'where the sounds evolve like veritable physical entities, intertwine, come and go.'

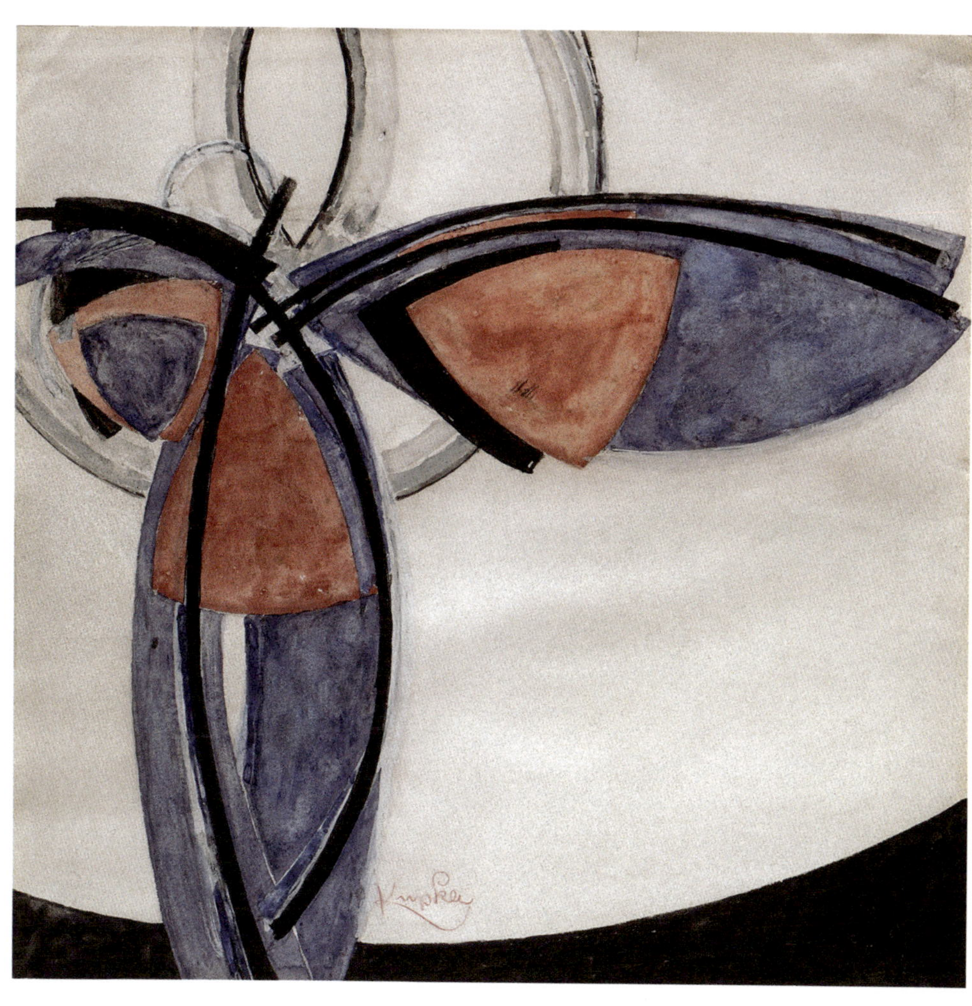

Paul Klee

b.1879 Switzerland–d.1940 Switzerland

Untitled
1917 (inscribed 1917.40 S.Kl)
watercolour, pen and ink on Ingres paper
attached to artist's mount
95 x 28 cm
Private Collection, London
On loan to Courtauld Gallery, London

Klee's father was a music teacher and his mother a trained singer, and he himself was an accomplished violinist, performing with the Berne Municipal Orchestra. In a letter of 1898, following a decision to study art in Munich, Klee wrote, 'It's terrible to marry when you are wildly in love with someone else. That's the truth. My mistress is and was music, and I embrace the goddess of the paintbrush, smelling of oil, who is also my wife.'

In his diaries written between 1898 and 1918, Klee expressed many of his ideas about art and music, testing them in watercolour studies and marking those he felt were particularly successful with a code (*Sonderklasse*). The following diary entry was written in July of 1917 whilst he was training with the German air force, the same year as the date of this watercolour: 'Polyphonic painting is superior to music in so far as the temporal element has more of a spatial quality. The sense of simultaneity emerges in an enriched form. With his choice of an over-sized horizontal format, Delaunay endeavoured to accentuate the temporal dimension of the picture in the manner of a fugue.' It is possible that Klee was experimenting with Robert Delaunay's format in this small painting to lend it the quality of a fugue that unfolds in space as well as over time.

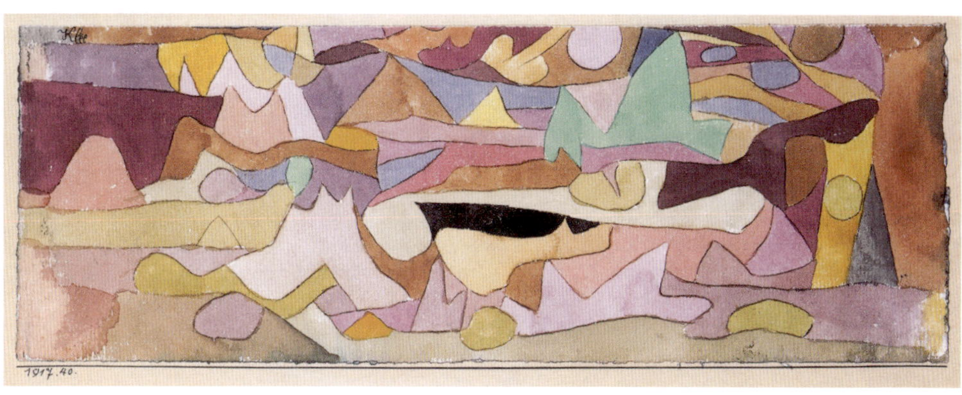

Paul Klee

b.1879 Switzerland–d.1940 Switzerland

Still Life with Little Box (Stilleben mit dem Kästchen)
1931 (inscribed 1931 L.9.)
wax and oil on vellum laid
down on artist's gouache mount
14.6 x 29.5 cm
Private Collection, London

Klee taught at the Bauhaus from 1921–31 in Weimar and then
in Dessau. He resigned in April 1931 to take up a teaching post in
Düsseldorf where this work was painted. It reflects his growing
interest in a technique similar to that of pointillism, which Klee
called 'divisionist painting' and which was to find its ultimate
expression in a later work of 1931, *Ad Parnassum*, named after
an 18th century treatise on music that taught the technique of
polyphonic harmony. In this work, the arrangement of the objects
and groups of dots in a horizontal format is also representative
of Klee's theory of polyphony, the expression of separate melodic
lines in a unified composition in painting. In this *Diaries*, he noted:

*'There is polyphony in music. In itself the attempt to
Transpose it into art would offer no special interest.
But to gather insights into music through the special
character of polyphonic works, to penetrate deep into
this cosmic sphere... and then to lurk in waiting for
these things in the picture, that is something more.
For the simultaneity of several independent themes
is something that is possible not only in music.'*

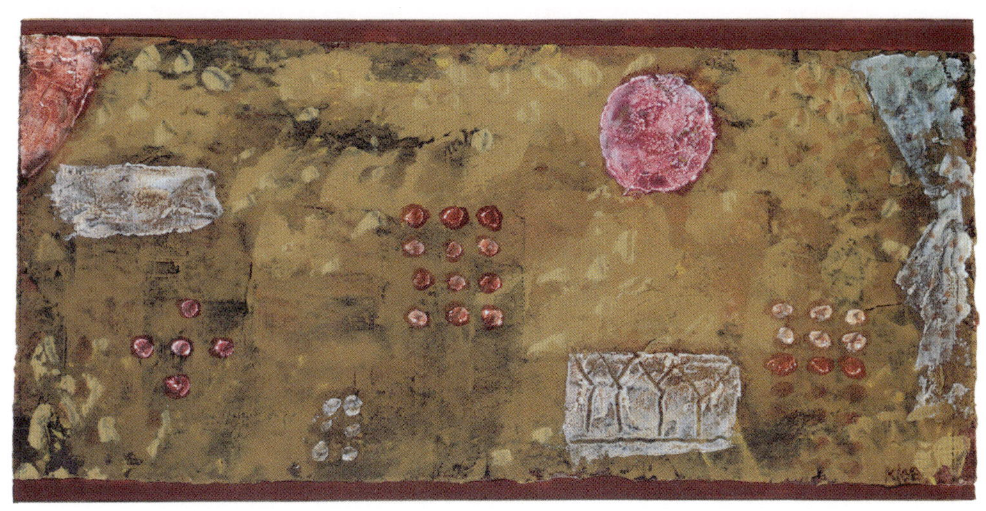

Heinrich Neugeboren (Henri Nouveau)

b.1901 Romania–d.1959 France

**Sculptural Representation of Bars 52–55 of Eb Minor Fugue
by J. S. Bach, Proposal for a Bach Monument**
1928, reconstruction 1967
stainless steel on painted black board
76 x 79.8 x 79.8 cm
Bauhaus Archive, Berlin

Neugeboren studied at the Bauhaus where he was influenced
by the teachings of Kandinsky and Klee to try out new forms of
transcription in order to translate musical structures into images
(see also Cat. 6). This sculpture is based on musical notation,
in which Neugeboren is fulfilling his 'wish not only to hear the
temporal and spatial dimensions of music, but also to see them,
and to see them more clearly than with the usual method of
musical notation.'

Music did not figure on the Bauhaus curriculum, but it was central
to the school where musical events featuring the works of both
classical and contemporary composers had their place alongside
taught classes. Tutors other than Kandinsky and Klee had affinities
with music, for example Lyonel Feininger, who was a composer
and performer as well as a painter, and Johannes Itten whose
basic courses in pictorial composition focused on musical rhythm.
Furthermore, the synthesis of the arts was encouraged through
stage workshops, which aspired to the Wagnerian concept of the
Gesamtkunstwerk or 'total work of art' where different artistic
disciplines were integrated into one production.

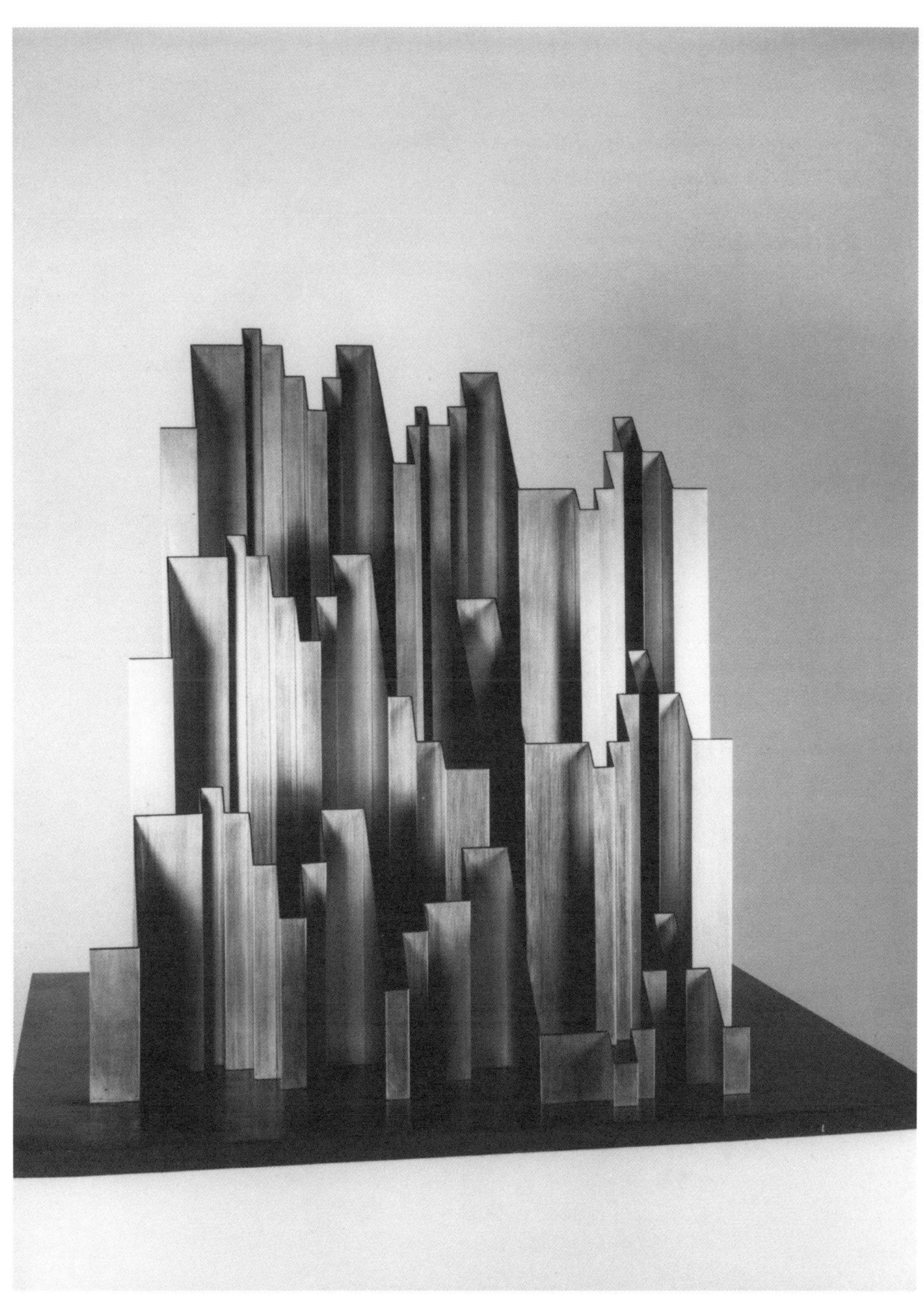

Heinrich Neugeboren (Henri Nouveau)

b.1901 Romania–d.1959 France

Graphic Depiction of Four-Part Fugue no. 1
from 'The Well-Tempered Clavier' by J. S. Bach
1928/44
black India ink (alto and bass) and
red ink (soprano and tenor) on graph paper
30 x 112 cm
Bauhaus Archive, Berlin

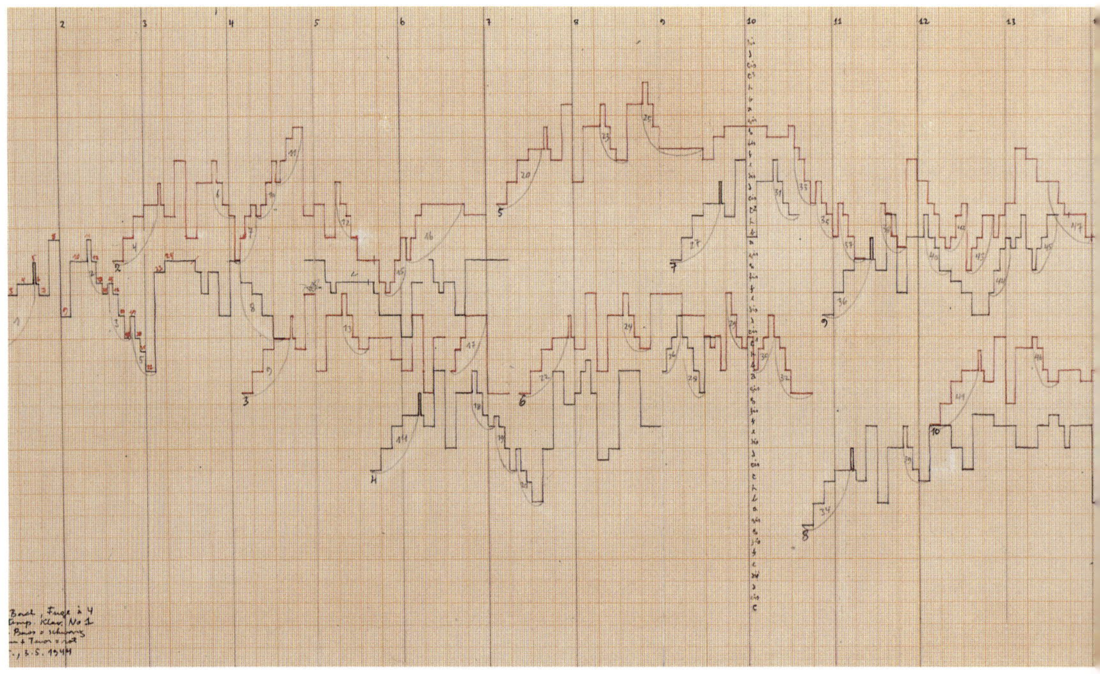

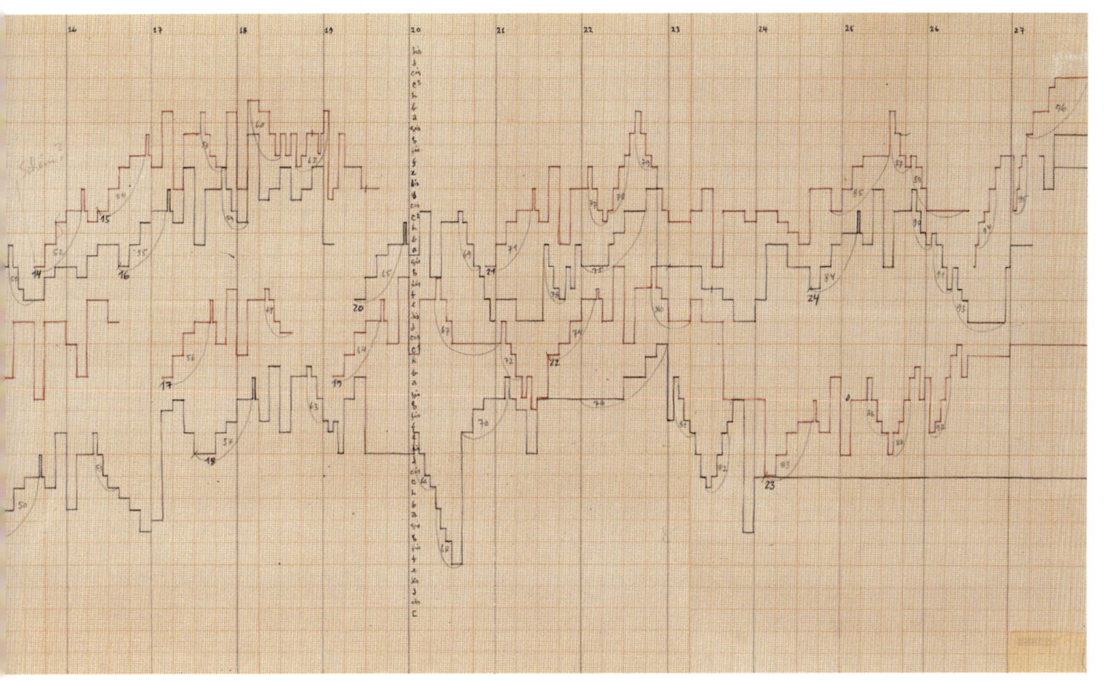

John Wells

b.1907 England–d.2007 England

Nocturne
1946
oil on gesso
48.5 x 42.5 cm
Private Collection

Whilst practising as a doctor in the Scilly Isles during World War II, Wells spent much of his spare time continuing to paint and study art, which he had done since taking evening classes at St. Martin's School of Art when studying medicine in the late 1920s. He had made regular trips to Cornwall since a child and in 1928 he met Ben and Winifred Nicholson and Christopher Wood who subsequently introduced him to Naum Gabo. Towards the end of the war, Wells returned to Cornwall to live and he became involved with the community of artists living in St. Ives. He was influenced by the Constructivist principles of Gabo and others, which sought to bring a kinetic energy to painting.

Wells was inspired by the rhythms and structures of the natural world and also music, believing that 'The analogy between great music (which is always abstract) and abstract painting seems to me of fundamental importance and not stressed nearly enough'. *Nocturne* achieves the qualities of rhythm and balance that Wells associated with Baroque music in particular. In a letter to Nicholson in 1943, he affirmed that 'The parallel between abstract music and painting intrigues me... Taking colour, form, rhythm and scale of painting or sculpture (i.e. light x space) and finding correspondences in music (i.e. sound x time) is fascinating.'

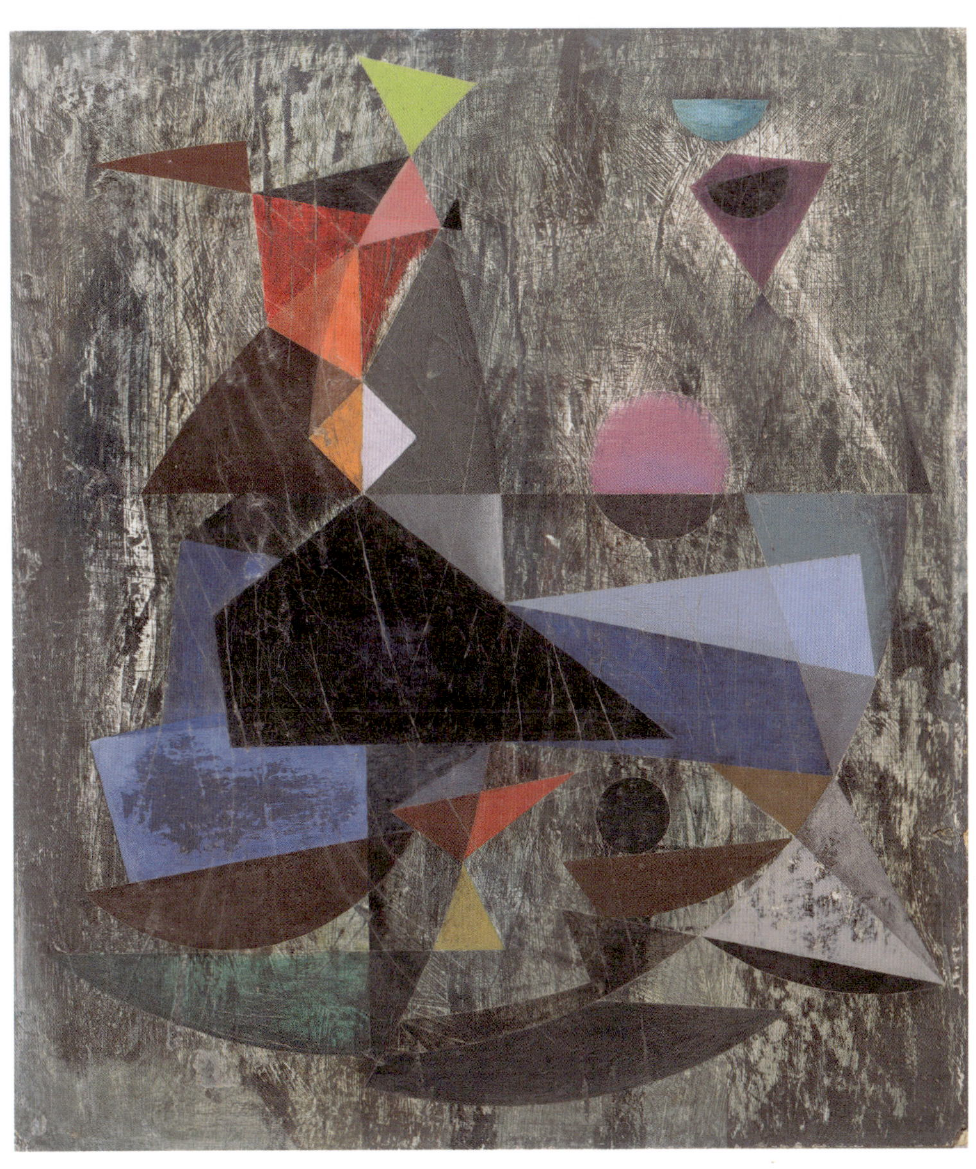

Ceri Richards

b.1903 Wales–d.1971 England

**La Cathédrale Engloutie: Blue Swirl
(The Submerged Cathedral: Blue Swirl)**
1960
relief construction: wood, metal, bells
and collage on painted wood
30 x 30 x 5 cm (framed)
Private Collection, Rhiannon Gooding

*'Music is specially significant for me and moves parallel with
my love and activity of painting – continually. One can say
that all artists – poets, musicians, painters – are creating in
their own idioms, metaphors for the nature of existence, for
the secrets of their time. We are all moved by the beauty
and revelation of their utterances – we notice the direction
and beauty of the paths they indicate for us – and move
towards them – and I have done this in most of the works
I am exhibiting here.'*

Richards wrote this introductory statement for his exhibition
'Homage to Music and Poetry' at the National Eisteddfod in Cardiff
in 1960. He had been brought up in a mining village near Swansea
where he encountered music everyday as a pianist and organist in
the local chapel. When studying at the Royal College of Art in the
late 1920s he was introduced to the work of the French avant-
garde and also Kandinsky's *Concerning the Spiritual in Art*. In an
interview with the journalist Noël Barber in 1964, Richards said,
'That Kandinsky interpreted painting in musical terms gave me
a lot of satisfaction in a vague sort of way.'

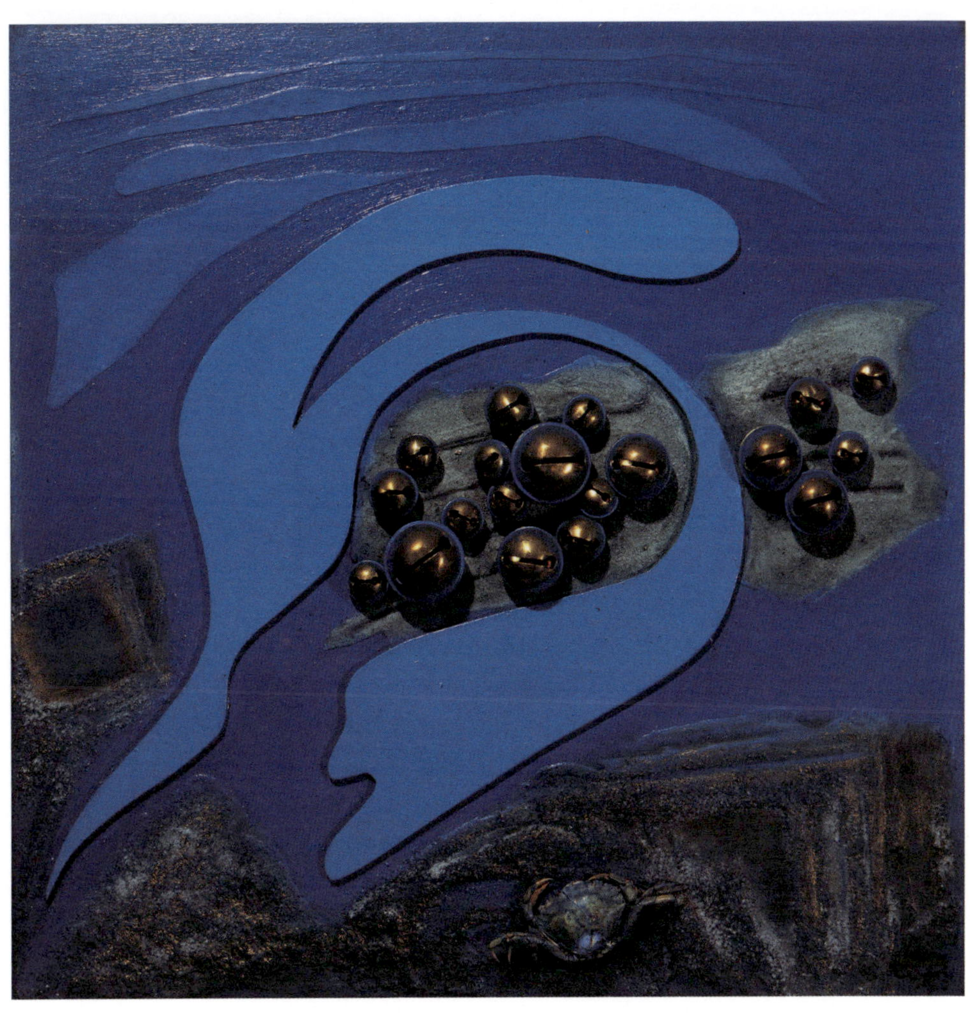

Ceri Richards

b.1903 Wales–d.1971 England

La Cathédrale Engloutie: Jeux de Vagues
(The Submerged Cathedral: Play of the Waves)
1961
oil on canvas
152 x 152 cm
Estate of Ceri Richards

From the 1950s much of Richards' work centred on musical themes, the most important being a series of paintings made between 1957 and 1962 after Claude Debussy's composition *La Cathédrale Engloutie* (1910). Debussy (1862–1918) was inspired to write this symphonic poem by the poetic legend of the submerged cathedral of Ys on the coast of Brittany, whose bells were said to ring from the depths. Richards was similarly moved by the story and also Debussy's music, which he found 'produces a visual picture immediately.'

The poet Vernon Watkins wrote of *La Cathédrale Engloutie* paintings in 1964, 'Just as a supreme composition in music has the secret of self-renewal, of endlessly beginning afresh, so these pictures hold the attention through a multiplicity of images and then return it to their imaginative source where it is confronted with them again. It is this secret that makes the effect of these works a continually changing one, like a fountain which renews its identity through exuberance, and remains sudden and fresh.'

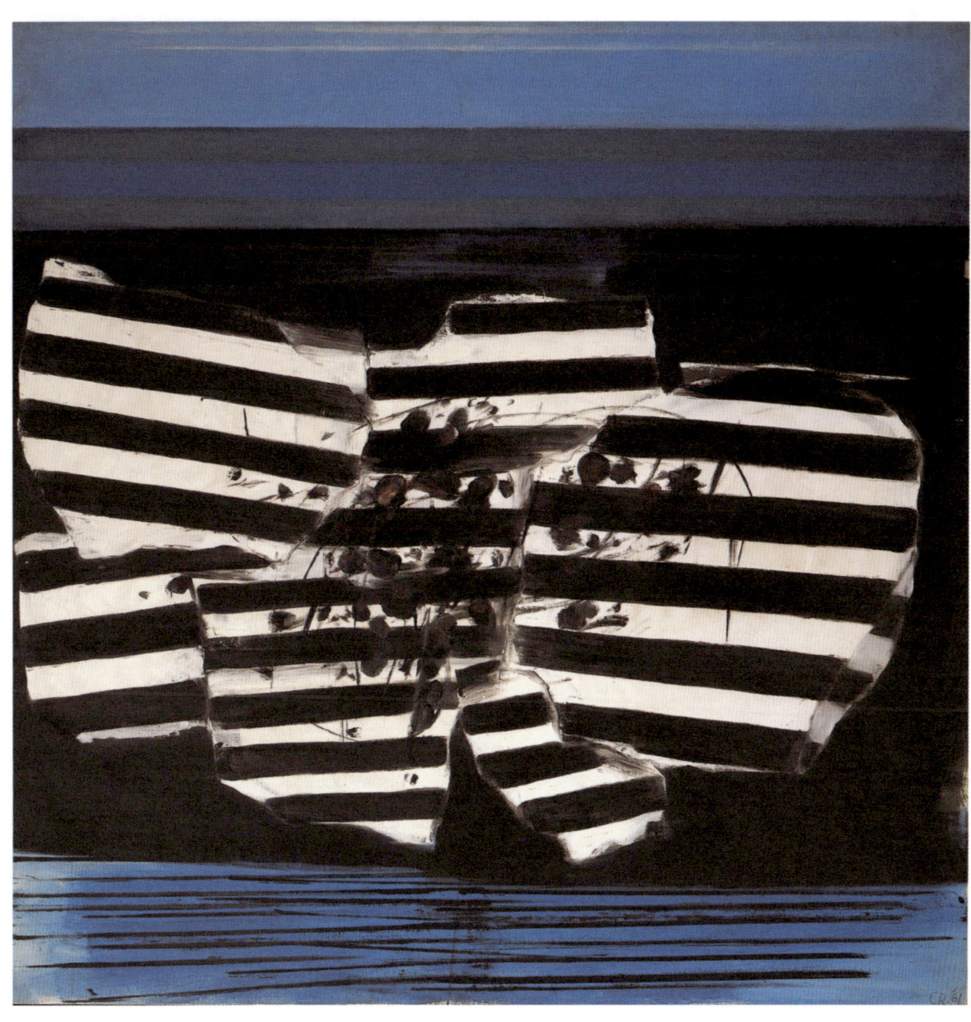

Tom Phillips

b.1937 England

Concerto Grosso
2002
oil on canvas
107.5 x 138.5 cm
Courtesy of the artist

Phillips is an artist who has been involved with music all his life, from what he calls his 'failed flirtations' whilst learning instruments at school, to producing works that form his own personal notation, either to be contemplated as paintings or to be performed as musical compositions. In his book, *Works and Text* (1992) he wrote:

> '*I am a composer in the same way as a pianist without hands could be a pianist. This is something I never stop thinking about, but which I can't really handle in its entirety because I lack a whole range of technical expertise. Nevertheless, an idea for a composition allows me to get ahead with all sorts of pieces of work. Some of these are in fact linked to the feeling I have for music and actually emerge as unplayable pieces, ones based on the almighty five lines of the stave, which dominated the life of a musician from cradle to grave.*'

Concerto Grosso was inspired by a piece of music by the Russian composer Alfred Schnittke (1934–98), known for his compositional method of combining different musical styles from the past and present.

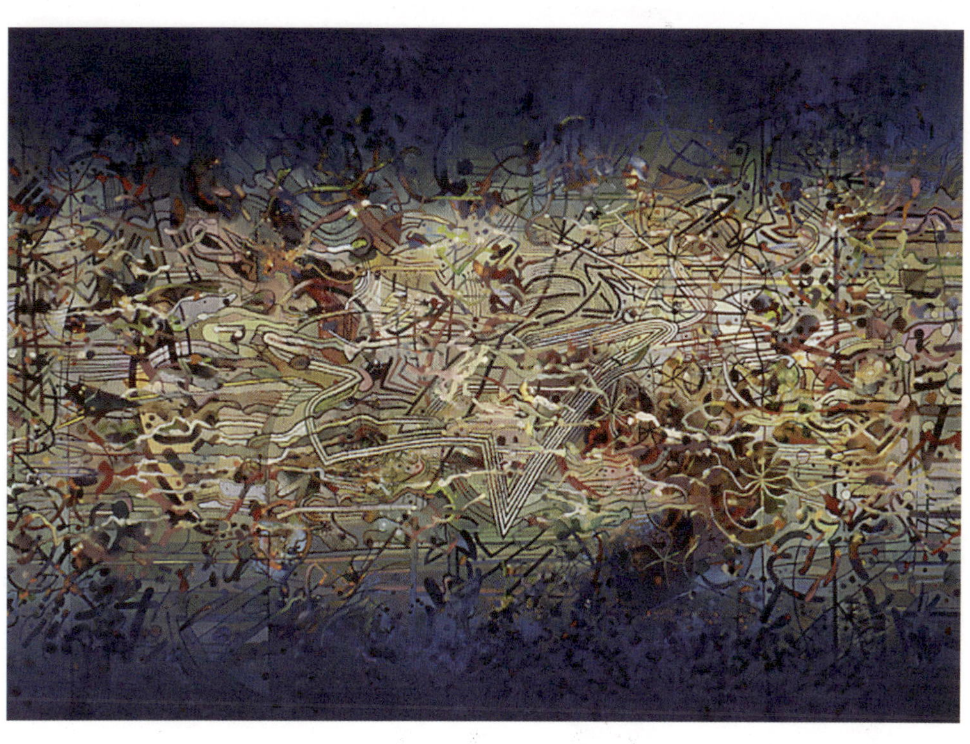

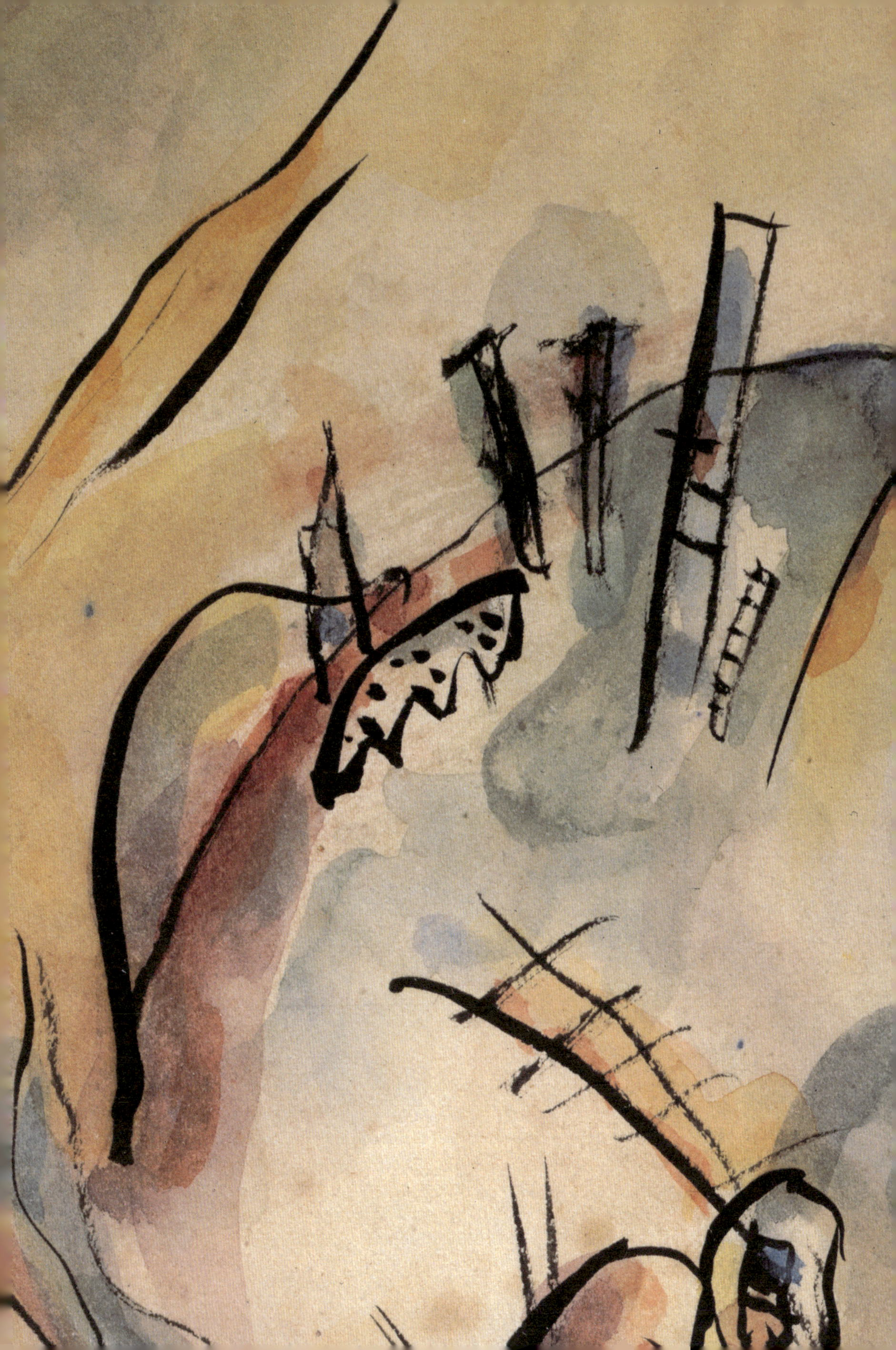

dissonance

'Kandinsky and Oskar Kokoschka paint pictures in which the external object is hardly more to them than a stimulus to improvise in colour and form and to express themselves as only the composer expressed himself previously.'

Arnold Schönberg, Der Blaue Reiter Almanac, 1912

Whilst other artists were looking to the music of the past for inspiration when experimenting with abstraction, Kandinsky and many of the artists associated with the avant-garde in Münich found a deeper resonance in the music of their contemporaries. After a concert of Schönberg's music in January 1911, where some of his ground breaking atonal works were performed, Kandinsky felt prompted to write to the composer to express his feeling that they were both striving towards the same goal in their respective disciplines, of liberating them from their formal constraints to develop a new means of expression.

Schönberg's innovation lay in compositions based on unresolved dissonance or the placing together of clashing notes commonly avoided or resolved in tonal music. He later developed this into the twelve-tone system where all twelve tones and semitones in the musical scale were given an independence from conventional harmonic arrangements. For Kandinsky, this paralleled his own use of complementary colours and his abandonment of figuration in favour of a freer, more expressive style. Their ultimate aim was to express universal truths or what Kandinsky termed the *'innerer Klang'* or 'inner sound', so that 'The artist creates not what others think is beautiful but whatever is necessary for him.'

Wassily Kandinsky, Untitled (detail), 1917
watercolour and ink on paper, 27 x 22.2 cm
Private Collection, London

Franz Marc was also at the Münich concert, and later wrote to his friend August Macke about the event: 'Can you imagine a music in which tonality (that is, adherence to any key) is completely suspended? I was constantly reminded of Kandinsky's large *Composition*, which also permits no trace of tonality... and also of Kandinsky's "jumping spots" in hearing this music, which allows each tone sounded to stand on its own (a kind of *white* canvas between the spots of colour!).'

Both Kandinsky and Schönberg published written theories in their respective disciplines within months of each other and both were working on stage compositions using light and colour as independent dramatic tools when they first met. Schönberg exhibited in the first exhibition of Der Blaue Reiter, a group founded by Kandinsky and Marc, and made important contributions to the Almanac of the same name, which became the ultimate document of ideas in twentieth century international art.

Der Blaue Reiter was short-lived, broken up by World War I and the death of Franz Marc and August Macke. It lived on, however, in the expressionist journal and gallery Der Sturm in Berlin where many of the surviving artists exhibited, and eventually reached a new epitome in the years at the Bauhaus where Kandinsky taught as a Master and renewed his friendship with Klee.

The overriding sense of optimism and excitement that was felt by artists who contributed to Der Blaue Reiter can be summarised in Marc's proposed foreword to the planned second volume of the Almanac, written in February 1914 but sadly never published: 'The world is giving birth to a new time; there is only one question: has the time now come to separate ourselves from the old world? Are we ready for the *vita nuova*? This is the terrifying question of our age.'

dissonance
catalogue entries

Wassily Kandinsky

b.1866 Russia–d.1944 France

Cossacks
1910–11
oil on canvas
94.6 x 130.2 cm
Tate, presented by Mrs Hazel McKinley, 1938

The years between 1908 and 1912 saw the transition from figuration to abstraction in Kandinsky's work and the development of his aesthetic theory which he published in his pioneering book *Concerning the Spiritual in Art (Über das Geistige in der Kunst)* at the end of 1911. At the time of completing *Cossacks*, a study for the larger work *Composition IV*, Kandinsky was still involved with the Münich New Artists' Association (Neue Künstlervereinigung München, NKVM), which he had helped establish in 1909. However, tensions grew within the group as he continued his drive towards abstraction and, in December 1911, when the selection jury refused to exhibit *Composition V* in the third exhibition of the NKVM, Kandinsky resigned his membership. His partner, the artist Gabrielle Münter and their friend Franz Marc left with him to form the counter group Der Blaue Reiter.

Cossacks contains recognisable elements but Kandinsky did not intend these to be the subject of the painting, being more concerned with the arrangement of colour and line to convey what he termed the 'inner sound'. In *Concerning the Spiritual in Art*, he wrote, 'Legitimate and illegitimate combinations of colours, contrasts of various colours, the over-painting of one colour with another, the definition of coloured surfaces by boundaries of various forms, the overstepping of these boundaries, the mingling and the sharp separation of surfaces, all these open great vistas of artistic possibility.'

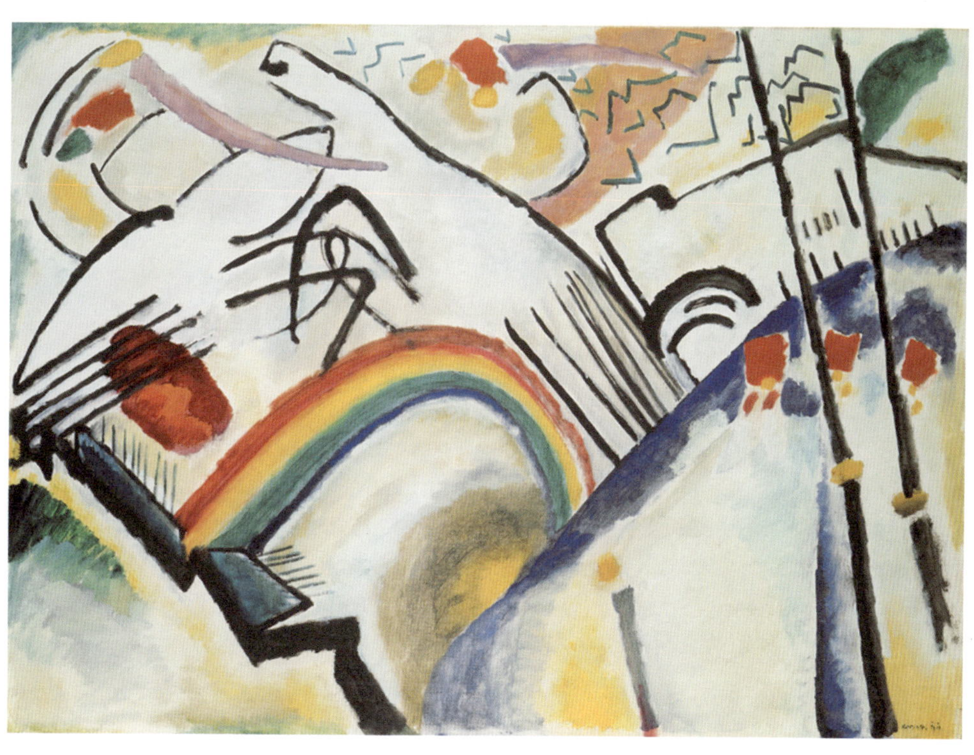

Arnold Schönberg

b.1874 Austria–d.1951 U.S.A.

Self-Portrait
1910
oil on 3-ply panel
31 x 22.7 cm
Belmont Music Publishers, Los Angeles,
lent by Arnold Schönberg Center, Vienna

On 2 January 1911, Kandinsky and other artists associated with
the NKVM - Münter, Marc, Alexej von Jawlensky and his partner,
Marianne von Werefkin - attended a concert of works by
Schönberg. This included the controversial *String Quartet no.2, op.10*
(1907–08) in which the composer had abandoned the accepted
organisation of the musical scale for the first time, and the almost
completely atonal *Three Piano Pieces, op.11* (1909). The programme
notes included excerpts from Schönberg's forthcoming treatise
Theory of Harmony, in which he wrote, 'Dissonances are only
different from consonances in degree; they are nothing more than
remoter consonances.'

For Kandinsky and the other artists, the concert was a pivotal event.
Kandinsky wrote to Schönberg, saying, 'In your works, you have
realised what I, albeit in uncertain form, have so greatly longed for
in music. The independent progress through their own destinies,
the independent life of the individual voices in your compositions,
is exactly what I am trying to find in my paintings.' The resulting
correspondence between the two, bears witness to a unique
meeting of minds and their attempts to revolutionise the
aesthetics of their respective disciplines.

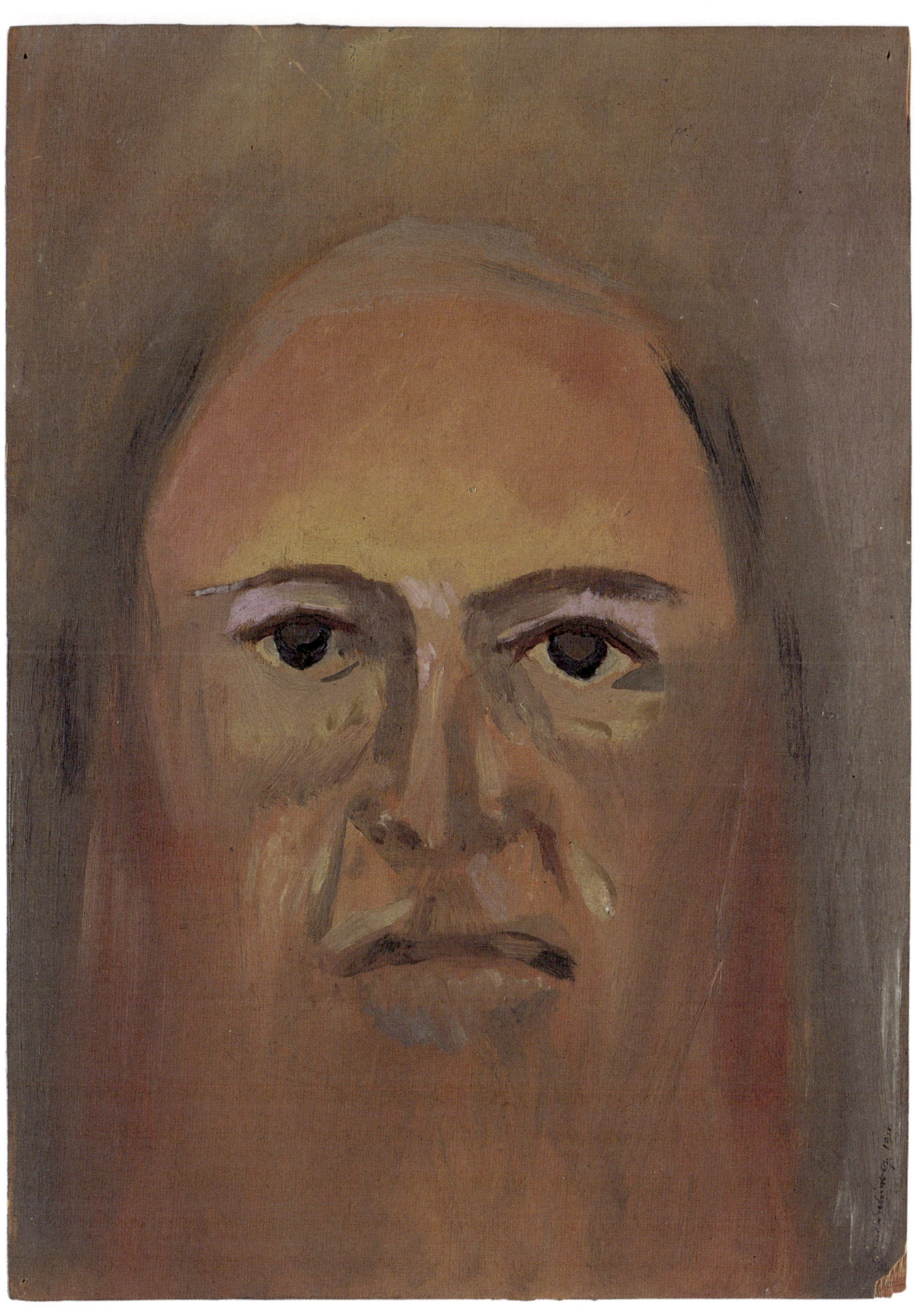

Arnold Schönberg

b.1874 Austria–d.1951 U.S.A.

Gaze
March 1910
oil on cardboard
28 x 20 cm
Belmont Music Publishers, Los Angeles,
lent by Arnold Schönberg Center, Vienna

Schönberg studied painting with the young Austrian artist Richard Gerstl, whom he met in 1905. Their friendship brought about an unfortunate chain of events: Schönberg's wife Mathilde left her husband for Gerstl in 1908, eventually being persuaded by Schönberg's pupil Anton Webern to return to her family which resulted in Gerstl's suicide. This personal crisis was to have an impact on Schönberg's creative output, both as artist and composer. It coincided with the completion of one of his most revolutionary compositions, *String Quartet no.2, op.10* and, as he developed his new musical language, painting frequently became an outlet to 'give expression to emotions that find no musical form'.

His paintings attracted considerable interest when first exhibited in Vienna in 1910. One critic wrote, 'Schönberg paints these portraits and fantasies with brutal simplicity, in the style of Kokoschka. One large blot of colour stands wild and mutinous next to another… And yet one cannot deny, that as dreadful, as audacious, as childish as his manner of painting appears to be, there is always a flash of something elemental and peculiar to the person or mood portrayed.' Schönberg sent photographs of his work to Kandinsky after receiving the artist's first letter and was subsequently invited to take part in the first exhibition of Der Blaue Reiter in Munich in December 1911.

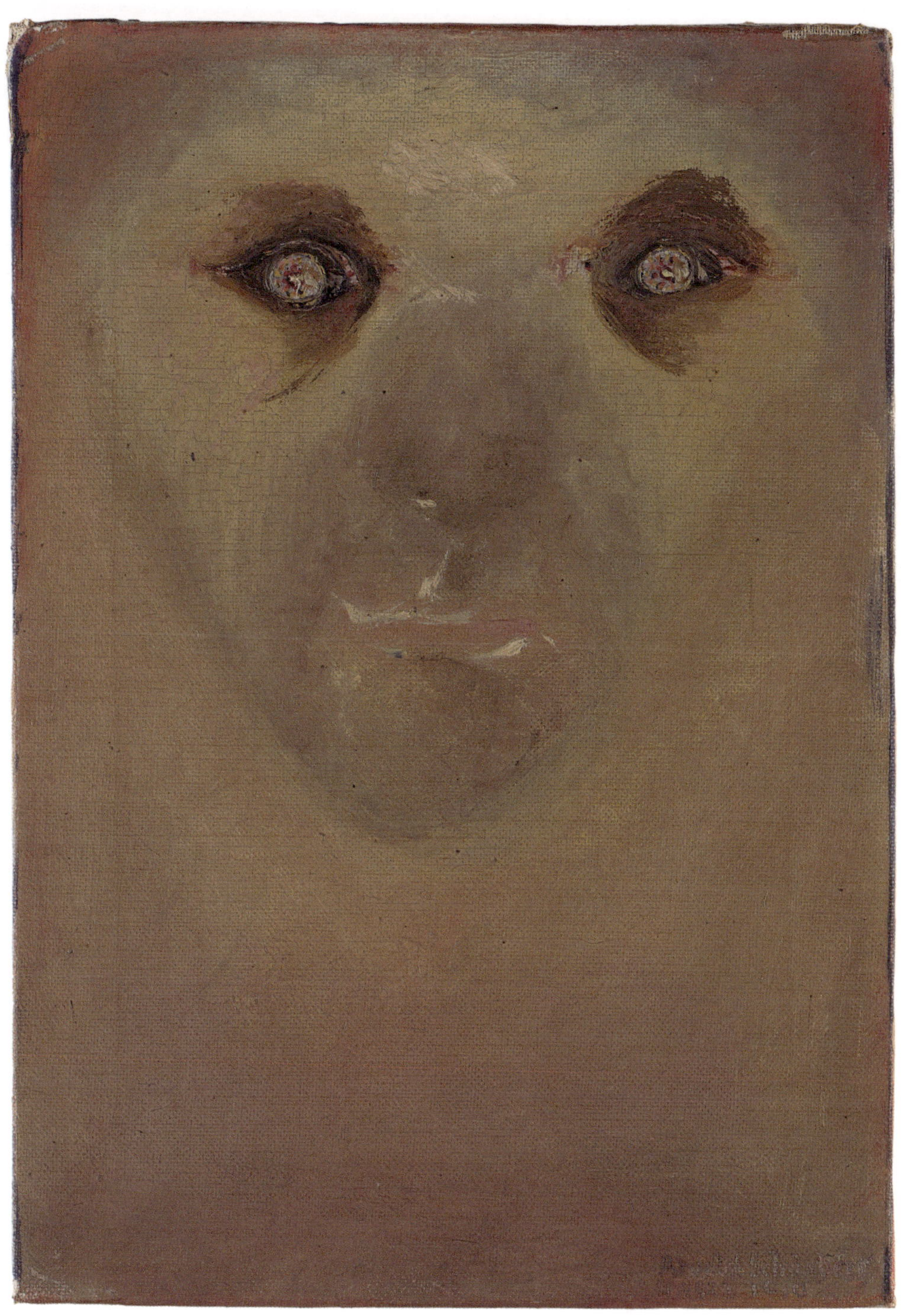

Arnold Schönberg

b.1874 Austria–d.1951 U.S.A.

The Lucky Hand, Scene 1
(Die glückliche Hand)
1910
oil on cardboard
21.8 x 30.2 cm
Belmont Music Publishers, Los Angeles,
lent by Arnold Schönberg Center, Vienna

Schönberg wrote his opera *The Lucky Hand* in 1910, a year after Kandinsky had written his own music-drama *The Yellow Sound (Der gelbe Klang)*. Both artists had independently sought to create works where colour was an integral part of the performance, perceived on the same level as sound and action, and both works represented their respective interpretations of the Wagnerian *Gesamtkunstwerk*.

As part of the direction, Schönberg sketched a 'colour crescendo' in which lighting effects were coordinated with a succession of specific musical gestures, very much in the same vein as Kandinsky's own synaesthetic experiments in *The Yellow Sound*. Both artists were aware of the Russian composer Alexander Scriabin (1872–1915) and his masterwork *Prometheus: The Poem of Fire* (1910), in which the top line of the music score is written for the 'luce', a colour organ played like a piano but which projected coloured light onto a screen in the concert hall. This piece was beset with technical difficulties and was not fully realised until its performance at Carnegie Hall, New York in March 1915. For both Kandinsky and Schönberg, their works were similarly restricted in that they pre-empted the advent of modern lighting.

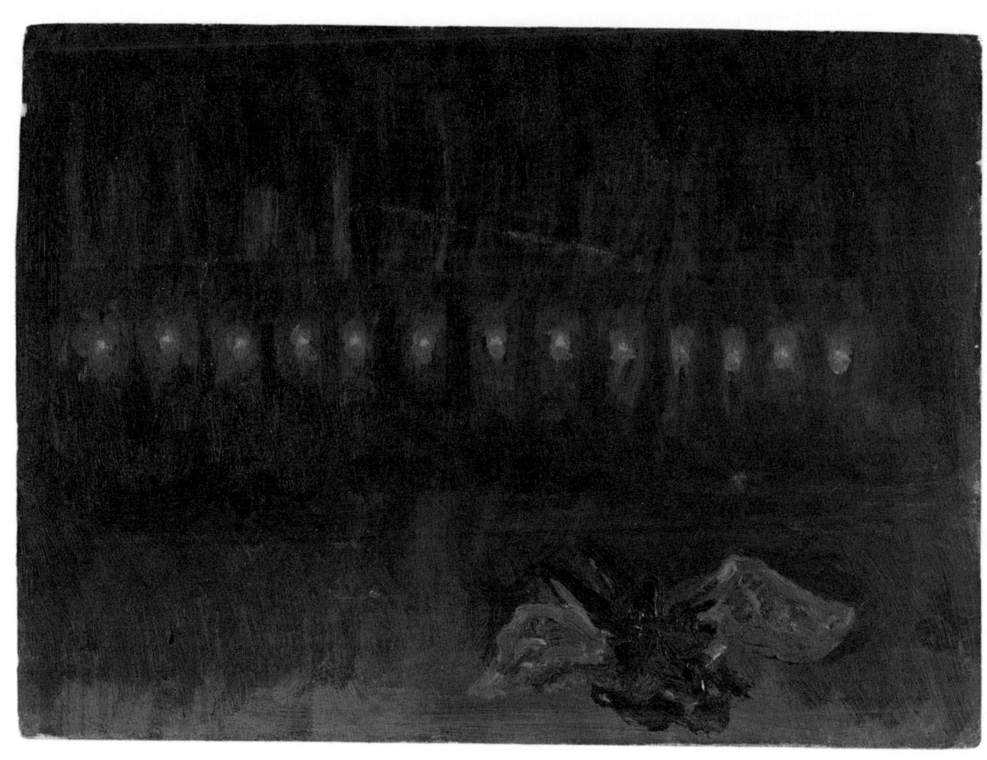

Arnold Schönberg

b.1874 Austria–d.1951 U.S.A.

The Lucky Hand, Scene 2
(Die glückliche Hand)
1910
oil on cardboard
22 x 30 cm
Arnold Schönberg Center, Vienna

This sketch refers to the second scene of *The Lucky Hand*, in which Schönberg makes the following stage directions: 'In the left background a soft blue, sky-like backdrop. Below, left, close to the bright brown earth, a circular cut-out five feet in diameter through which glaring, yellow sunlight spreads over the stage.'

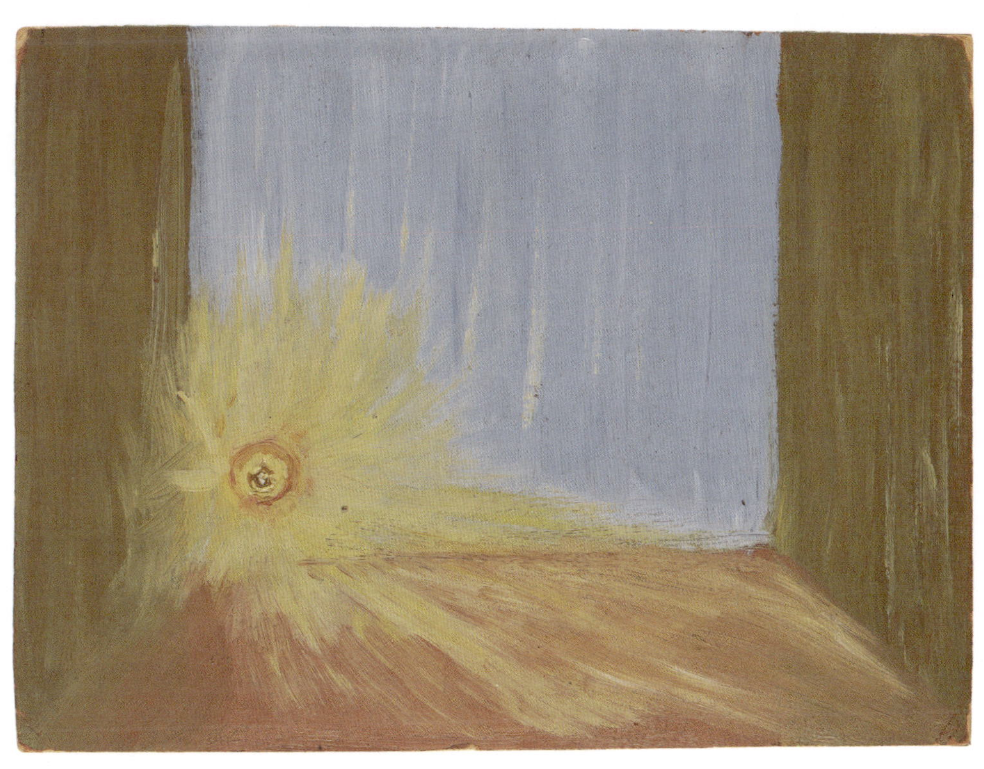

Wassily Kandinsky

b.1866 Russia–d.1944 France

Lyrically (Lyrisches) from 'Sounds' ('Klänge')
1913
book
30.5 x 23.8 x 2.5 cm
Victoria and Albert Museum

From 1909–14, Kandinsky exhibited his work in London as part of the Allied Artists Association, founded in 1908 by Frank Rutter, the art critic of the *Sunday Times* and director of Leeds City Art Gallery. In the 1911 exhibition Kandinsky showed a selection of *Improvisations* and *Compositions*, some woodcuts and the proofs for *Sounds*, an illustrated book of his own prose poems. These works caught the attention of Michael Sadleir, Rutter's friend and co-editor of the new art journal *Rhythm*, who wrote to Kandinsky to ask for permission to reproduce one of the woodcuts in the forthcoming edition of the journal. The ensuing correspondence ultimately led to the publication in English of Kandinsky's *Concerning the Spiritual in Art* in 1914 and the dissemination of his theories amongst the British avant-garde.

Sadleir wrote in the introduction to his translation of Kandinsky's treatise, 'Kandinsky is painting music. That is to say, he has broken down the barrier between music and painting, and has isolated the pure emotion which, for want of a better name, we call the artistic emotion.'

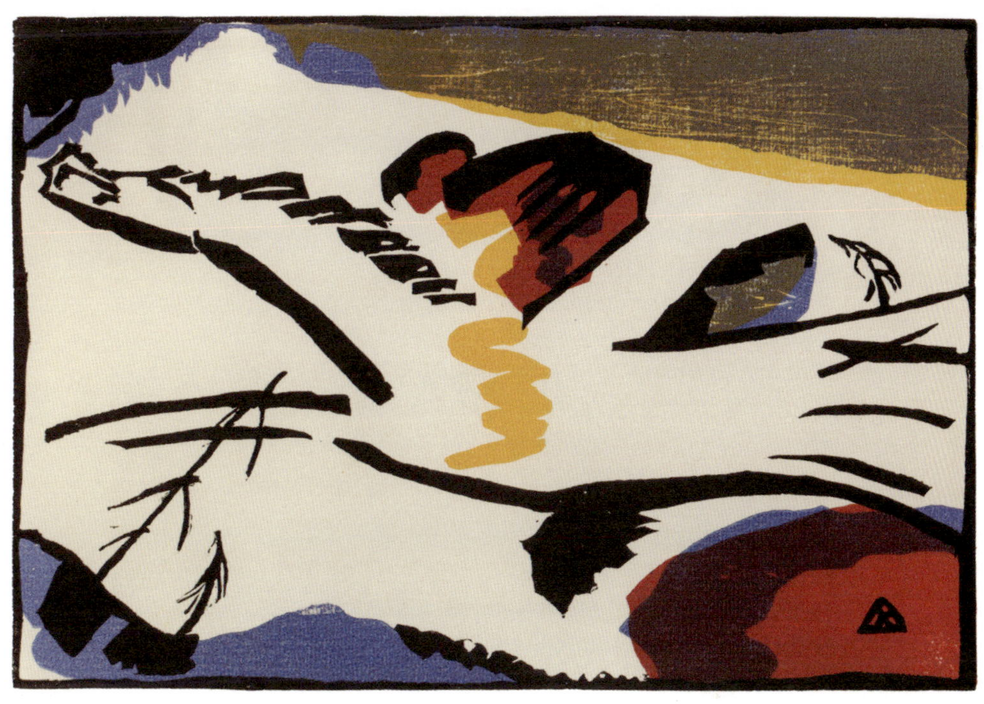

Wassily Kandinsky

b.1866 Russia–d.1944 France

Lyrically (Lyrisches)
1911
woodblock
14.6 x 21.8 x 2.5 cm
Private Collection, London

Woodcuts were a vital medium for Kandinsky in bringing about the transition from figuration to abstraction. Those in *Sounds* date from 1907 and include figurative images that resemble Kandinsky's early Jugendstil-inspired works as well as purely abstract forms. The woodcuts and accompanying prose poems were finally published as an album by Piper Verlag of Münich in 1912 and so span the most experimental era in Kandinsky's work.

The poems deal with transformation in nature and are themselves alternately narrative and expressive in content, reflecting the tension between representation and abstraction. Kandinsky wrote of the poems, 'This is, for me, a "change of instrument" – the palette to one side and the typewriter in its place. I use the word "instrument" because the force which motivates my work remains unchanged, an "inner drive." And it is this very drive which calls for a frequent change of instrument.'

On 11 July 1911, Kandinsky wrote to his partner, Gabrielle Münter about the making of the woodblock for *Lyrically*, one of few figurative images in *Sounds*, commenting how the print was 'better than the painting' of a horse and rider he had completed earlier the same year.

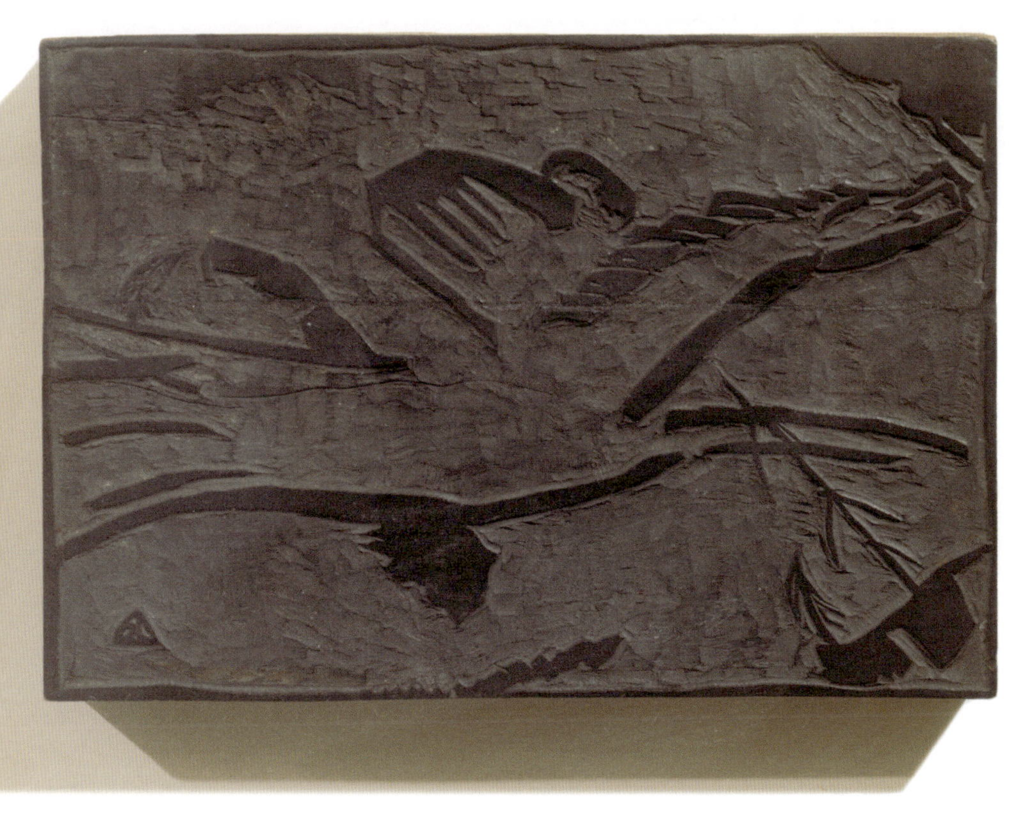

Wassily Kandinsky

b.1866 Russia–d.1944 France

**Study for Composition no. IV
from 'Der Blaue Reiter Almanac'**
1912
book
28.4 x 28.4 x 1.8 cm
Victoria and Albert Museum

Before their official resignation from the NKVM in December 1911, Kandinsky and Marc had already discussed a project for a book that would examine the status of contemporary art on an international level. It would be a compilation of writings from artists, theoreticians and composers highlighting the common goals in the arts, comparing works by contemporary artists with primitive art to demonstrate an innate spiritual kinship between them. In September 1911 the Almanac was named and Der Blaue Reiter was born, creating what would later become one of the most influential publications of the 20th century.

Der Blaue Reiter was never intended to be a movement but the artists associated with the project hurriedly organised an exhibition in opposition to the NKVM in December 1911. The exhibition included artists outside the group's immediate circle, such as Heinrich Campendonk, Robert Delaunay, Henri Rousseau and Schönberg. In the accompanying brochure, the aims of Der Blaue Reiter were condensed in the following sentence: 'Through this small exhibition we do not wish to propagate a *single* precise and special form; rather we intend to demonstrate through the *diversity* of the represented forms how the inner desire of the artists manifests itself multifariously.'

The first edition of *Der Blaue Reiter Almanac* materialised in May 1912. Marc contributed three essays tracing the history of modern German art. Kandinsky offered 'On the Question of Form', which expanded on aspects of *Concerning the Spiritual in Art*; a discussion of stage design, and the text for *The Yellow Sound*. Other contributions included Schönberg's discussion on the relationship between music

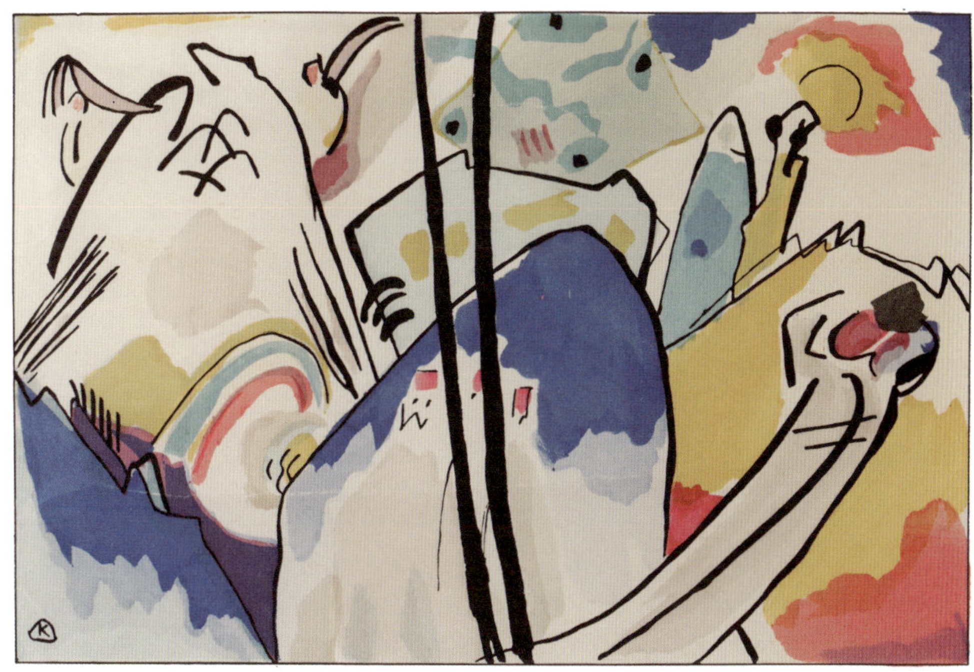

and text; the Russian composer Thomas von Hartmann's essay
'Anarchy in Music'; an appreciation of Robert Delaunay's work; and an
evaluation of Scriabin's *Prometheus*. The accompanying illustrations
included contemporary, non-European and medieval works and
excerpts from scores by Schönberg, Alban Berg and Webern.

The Almanac represented Kandinsky's and Marc's dream of an artistic
community united in a utopian goal. However, although a second
edition was produced and plans were made for a second publication,
the group's vision was shattered when war broke out in the summer
of 1914. Kandinsky returned to Russia and Marc was conscripted to the
German army where he was killed in action in 1916. When Kandinsky
eventually returned to Germany in 1921 and it was suggested that the
Almanac should be resurrected, he replied 'The Blaue Reiter – that
was the two of us: Franz Marc and myself. My friend is dead, and I do
not want to continue alone.'

Wassily Kandinsky

b.1866 Russia–d.1944 France

Untitled
1917
watercolour and ink on paper
27 x 22.2 cm
Private Collection, London

From the end of 1911, Kandinsky broke from figuration and painted almost purely abstract works in a free, expressive style. Although some of these paintings still allude to a subject, such as those based on the theme of the Last Judgement, and figurative elements can still be detected in the form of mountainous skylines or buildings, the majority of the large *Compositions* are experiments in the use of colour, developing his theories outlined in *Concerning the Spiritual in Art*. In his *Reminiscences*, Kandinsky wrote, 'I had little thought for houses and trees, drawing coloured lines and blobs on the canvas with my palette knife, and making them sing just as powerfully as I knew how.'

However, Kandinsky did not completely abandon figuration, reverting to it on occasion, particularly when painting works which related to his homeland of Russia where he returned with Münter after the outbreak of World War I. Moscow was a vital place for him and he made a series of watercolours of the city from 1916, producing stylised aerial views in which buildings, hills, church spires and rivers radiated out from the centre of the sheet. For Kandinsky, the iconography of old Russia had its own language of colour and symbolic shapes that he freely employed in his paintings.

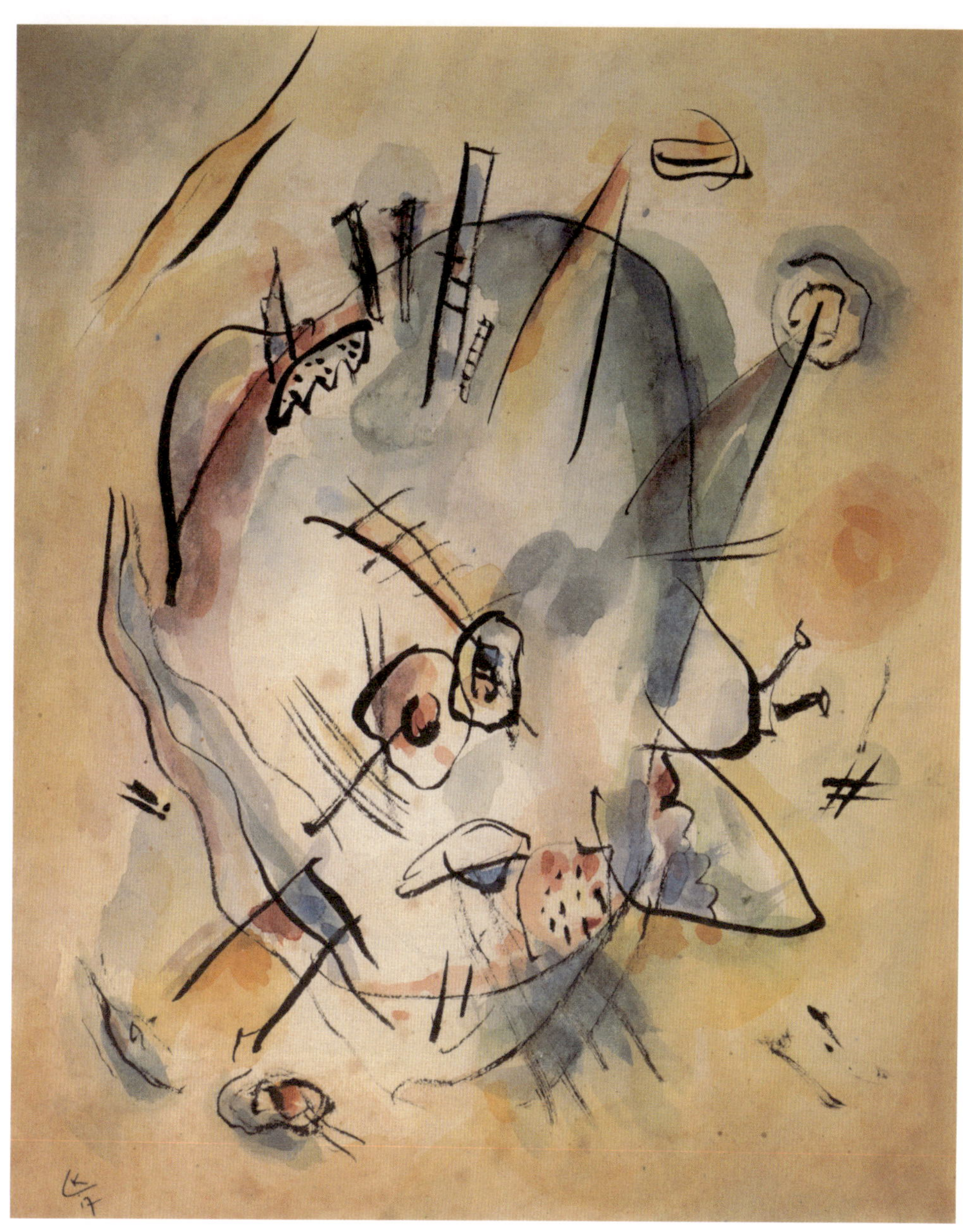

Alexej von Jawlensky

b.1864 Russia–d.1941 Germany

Variation: Soul Forces – Tryptych II
(Variation: Seelenkräfte – Triptychon II)
1919
oil on photographic paper with
linen texture, laid down on cardboard
36.2 x 27 cm
Private Collection, London

Jawlensky first met Kandinsky when he moved to Münich from
St. Petersburg with Marianne von Werefkin. Like his fellow Russian,
he studied with Anton Azbe and subsequently travelled to France
where he exhibited with the Fauves in 1905. He was influenced by
the artists Paul Sérusier and Jan Verkade who were members of the
Nabis, from whom he learnt about theosophy and the expression of
inner feelings through painting.

After leaving Germany on the outbreak of World War I, Jawlensky
and Werefkin rented a house near Lake Geneva where they lived
in cramped conditions. Jawlensky wrote, 'our flat was very small,
and I had no room of my own, just a window, and that was as it
were mine', and from this window he painted some 400 *Variations*
of the same landscape from 1914–21. The view of trees, the road
and the sky became increasingly abstract, rendered in patches of
colour that reflected the change in the seasons and mirrored the
artist's emotional state, reworking his subject in the manner of
musical variation.

Jawlensky was a founding member of the NKVM but did not split
from it after Kandinsky's resignation in 1911, much to the
disappointment of his friend. Although this precluded his involvement
in Der Blaue Reiter, Jawlensky did become one of Die Blaue Vier
(The Blue Four), along with Kandinsky, Klee and Lyonel Feininger in
1923, exhibiting and lecturing together in the United States in 1924.

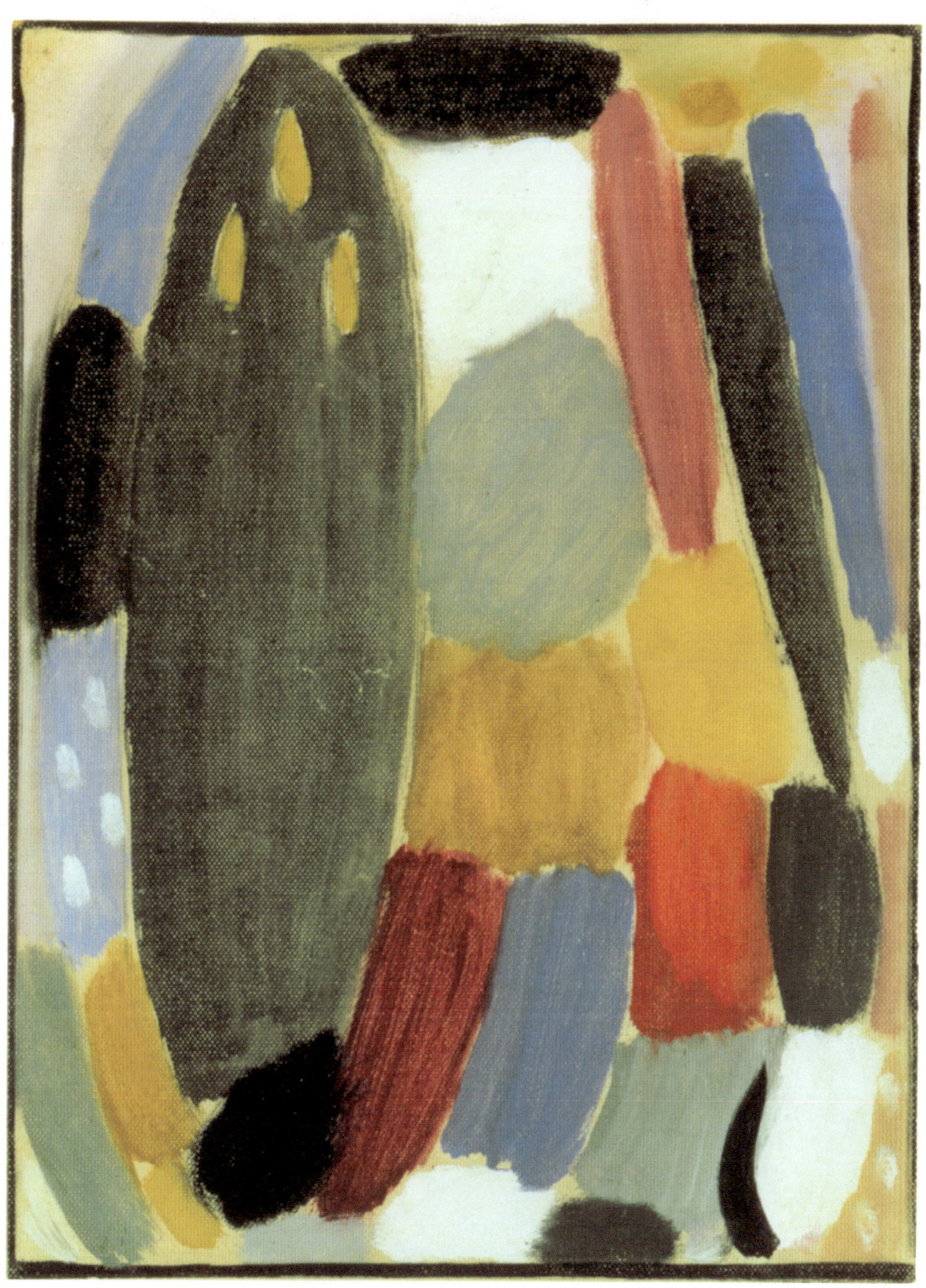

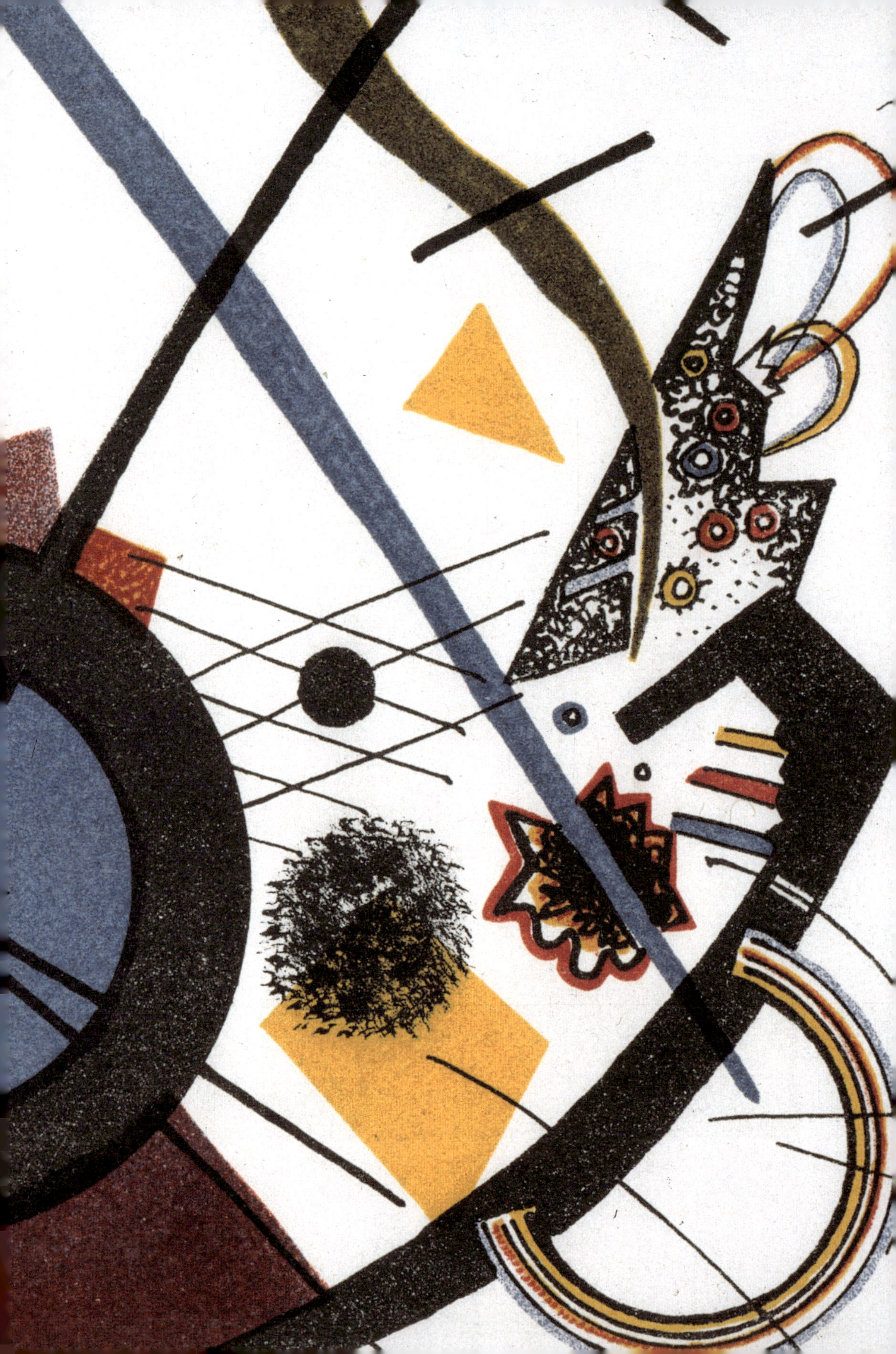

tones and colours

'Colour is the keyboard, the eyes are the hammers, the soul is the piano with many strings. The artist is the hand which plays, touching one key or another, to cause vibrations in the soul.'

Wassily Kandinsky, *Concerning the Spiritual in Art*, 1911

Kandinsky developed a theory of colours and their use in conjunction with form that underpinned his development of an abstract visual language and that, like music, would be able to speak directly to the soul: 'The composition arising from this harmony is a mingling of colour and form each with its separate existence, but each blended into a common life which is called a picture by the force of the inner need.'

Kandinsky's theory was also informed by his synaesthesia, his perception that colours resonated with certain sounds, even lending them particular 'physical' and 'psychic' characteristics that he felt caused a corresponding 'spiritual vibration'. He wrote, 'In music a light blue is like a flute, a darker blue a cello; a still darker a thunderous double bass; and the darkest blue of all – an organ.' Lemon yellow is a 'shrill trumpet-note', green 'the placid, middle notes of a violin', and light red 'the singing notes of a violin'. White and black were given the attributes of silence, the former being 'like many pauses in music that break temporarily the melody', and the latter 'represented by one of those profound and final pauses, after which any continuation of the melody seems the dawn of another world.'

Wassily Kandinsky, Violet (detail), 1923
colour lithograph, 34.1 x 27.1 cm
Bauhaus Archive, Berlin

Kandinsky and other artists associated with Der Blaue Reiter were particularly inspired by the theory of 'Simultaneity' which was developed by Robert and Sonia Delaunay. In the first exhibition organised by the group in 1911, Robert Delaunay was asked to participate and contributed two works from his 'windows' series, which were particularly admired for their modern Cubist composition and for their use of colour. The Delaunays' theory was the use of complementary colours that, when placed in opposition and viewed simultaneously, would give an appearance of movement, depth and light, and the very essence of the natural and spiritual world. Kupka, who worked closely with Robert Delaunay for a while, also used colour and light in a series of works based on spinning multi-coloured disks in simultaneous motion that were intended to convey their vision of the cosmos and spiritual truth.

Colour was a driving force in modern art, and through classes like those held by Percyval Tudor-Hart in Paris attended by artists representing the avant-garde from many different countries, its properties were exploited in innovative and exciting ways. Klee and Kandinsky both brought their perspective on colour to their teachings at the Bauhaus where Itten was already instructing students in colour theory based on the writings of Goethe who extolled its musical, emotional and spiritual properties.

The relationship between the seven notes of the musical scale and the seven colours of the colour scale had been proposed by Isaac Newton in the eighteenth century. The group of French artists called the Musicalists and the composer Messiaen with whom they were closely associated exploited this comparison to create works which aimed to provoke a synaesthetic response in those who encountered them.

tones and colours

catalogue entries

Robert Arthur Wilson

b.1884 England–d.1975 England

La Lumière (Light)
1917
watercolour over pencil on paper
15 x 12 cm
Private Collection, Andrew C. Bunce

Wilson's artistic career began in Sunderland where he was
apprenticed to a firm of sign-writers, subsequently being awarded a
government scholarship to attend the Royal College of Art and then
a bursary to study in Paris in 1911. There he enrolled in the Académie
Julian as a pupil of Jean-Paul Laurens whose students included
C. R. W. Nevinson, William Roberts, Matthew Smith and Edward
Wadsworth. He was introduced to artists of the French avant-garde
and shared a studio with Modigliani.

The most influential figure he met whilst in Paris, however, was
Percyval Tudor-Hart, an American artist who led classes in colour
theory. His classes were widely attended and Wilson remembered
'He spoke a good deal about accentuation and rhythm saying
that art should be the expression of human emotion.' Tudor-Hart
believed in a correspondence between colour and musical tones,
which would also influence his American students Morgan Russell
and Stanton MacDonald-Wright who developed a theory of
'Synchromy' based on his teachings. To Tudor-Hart, light and
colour were the foundation of harmony and rhythm in life.

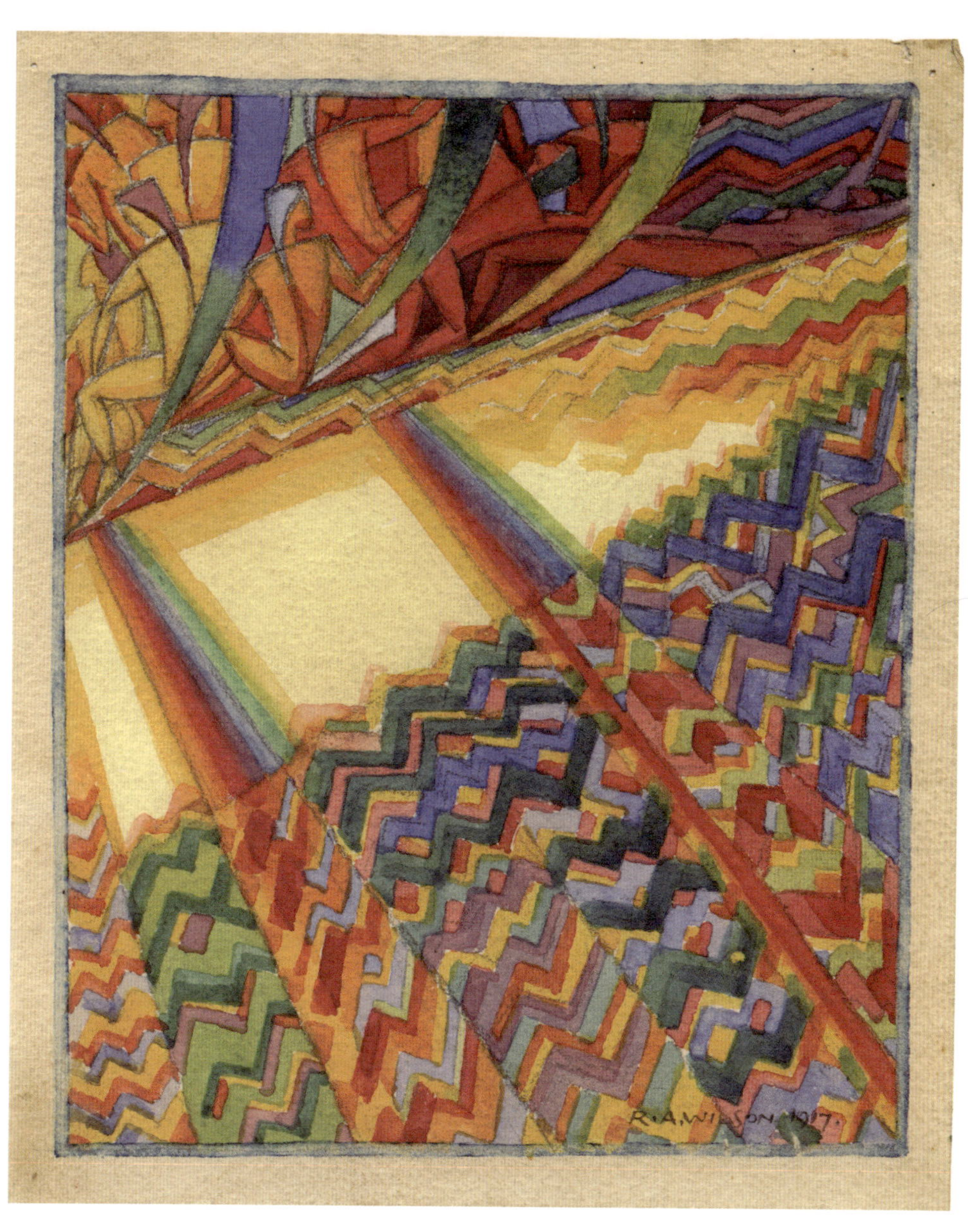

R. A. Wilson. 1917.

Robert Arthur Wilson

b.1884 England–d.1975 England

Abstraction of Music
1922
watercolour over pencil on paper
22 x 27 cm
Private Collection, Andrew C. Bunce

Wilson attended Tudor-Hart's studio in Montparnasse from 1912–16
and then taught with him both in Paris and in Hampstead during
World War I where Tudor-Hart, as a pacifist, secured Wilson's
time to help him manage his studio. In 1920 Wilson had his first
one-man show and exhibited watercolours, which he described as
'semi-abstract decorative subjects based on the analogy of colour
and music.' The BBC broadcast his talk on 'Colour, its meaning and
use, logic, mystery, symbolism and power' and in 1922 he gave
a lecture on 'Colour and Music' as part of his exhibition in South
Kensington, where he was helped by the pianist Edward Mitchell
who played chords to correspond with colours in the paintings and
also gave a recital of music by Scriabin.

In Wilson's *Memoirs of an Individualist*, written in 1972, he describes
his colour theory of 12 standard hues to which he ascribed descriptive
and emotional characteristics and related them to the notes of
the chromatic scale. He wrote 'Both feeling and knowledge are
essential and needed by would-be good colourists in search of purity,
luminosity and harmony in their artistic creations.' However, Wilson
experimented with abstraction for a brief period only before
returning to a more representational style in the mid 1920s.

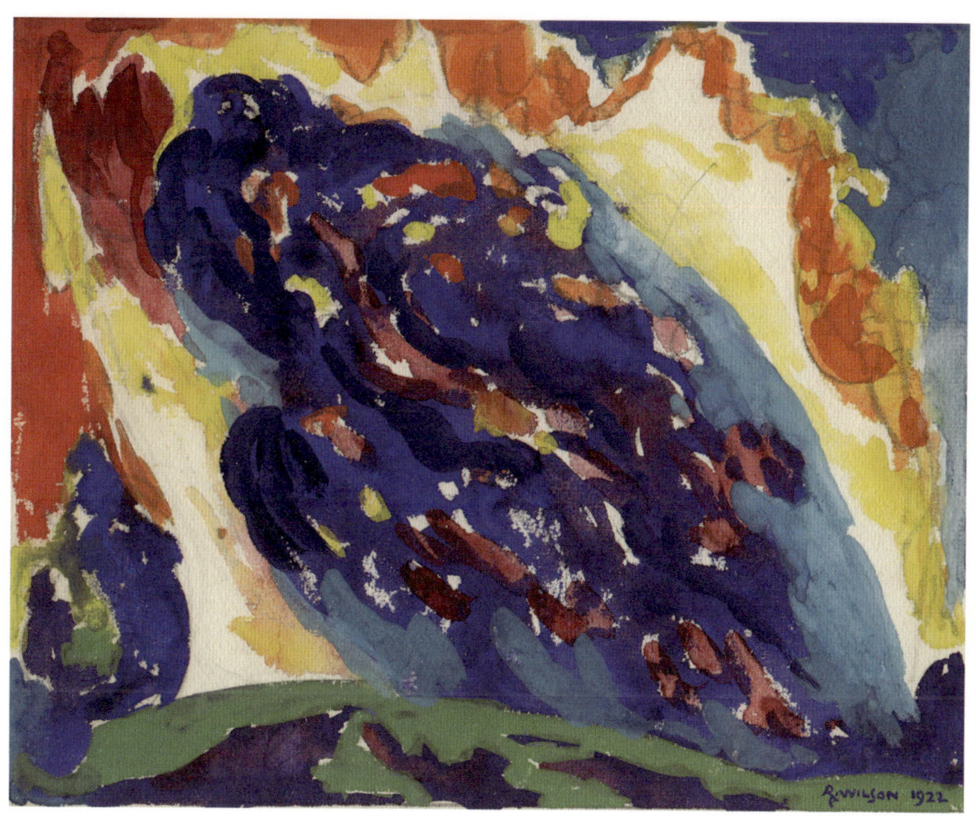

František Kupka

b.1871 Czechoslovakia (Czech Republic)–d.1957 France

Study for 'Amorpha, Fugue in Two Colours'
and 'Amorpha, Warm Chromatics'
1911–12
oil on canvas
84 x 128 cm
Centre Pompidou, National Museum of Modern Art, Paris,
gift of Eugenie Kupka in 1963

This study is one of many preparatory works for the two
paintings exhibited at the Salon d'Automne in 1912. It is derived
from various sources, such as Kupka's studies of church interiors,
his studies of complementary colours to produce an illusion of light,
and his drawings of his step-daughter Andrée playing with a ball
that he reduced to a series of ellipses to convey the dynamics
of movement.

Kupka was developing his aesthetic between 1910–13, which he
expressed in a handwritten treatise. In 1913 he wrote to his friend
Arthur Roessler, the Viennese art critic, 'Paintings I exhibited
recently are called *Planes by Colours*, *Amorpha, Fugue in Two
Colours*, *Warm Chromatics*, etc. All in all what I am seeking now
are symphonies.' In the same letter, Kupka wrote of the
unfavourable reception his work had received in Paris and his
response to viewers who queried the subject of the works,
'Must then a work of art represent something?'

Kupka eventually published his theories in *Creation in Art and
Sculpture* in 1923. They were similar to those of Kandinsky, although
Kupka did not read *Concerning the Spiritual in Art* until 1913, long
after he had formulated his own approach to abstraction.

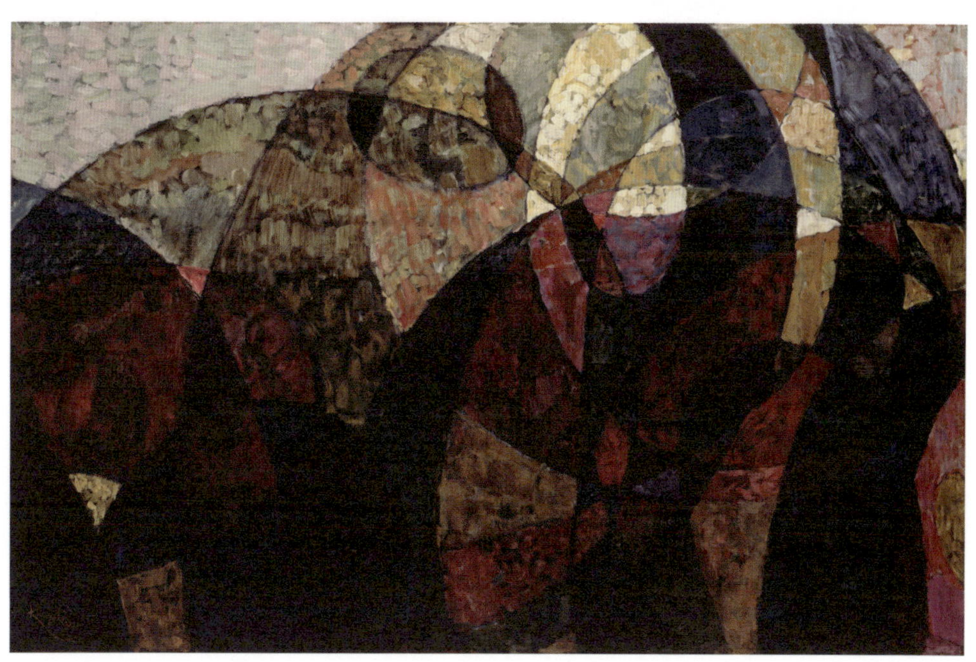

František Kupka

b.1871 Czechoslovakia (Czech Republic)–d.1957 France

Study for 'The Cathedral'
1911–12
gouache on paper
68.2 x 50.4 cm
Museum Kampa, the Jan and
Mada Mladek Foundation

Kupka was inspired by stained glass, admiring the 'vertiginous musicality of colour' of windows in Gothic cathedrals and commenting that painting on glass would be the ultimate medium with which to express his cosmic vision. In his painting *The Cathedral* (1913), for which this is a study, the same complementary colours of red and blue predominate that also appear in *Amorpha, Fugue in Two Colours*, in part inspired by the stained glass of Notre Dame in Paris and Chartres Cathedral which he used to visit with his pupils. Kupka found both Gothic architecture and that of the Viennese Secession intensely spiritual, and wrote 'both architecture and music are superior because they are able to express the inexpressible, to which we are sensitive.'

Not only were the colours and luminosity of stained glass appealing, but their vertical linearity also. In 1913, Kupka exhibited *Vertical Planes* at the Salon des Indépendants, prefiguring the rectilinear compositions of Kasimir Malevich, Jean Arp and Mondrian.
He believed that 'the ceremonial perpendicular line is the backbone of life within space.'

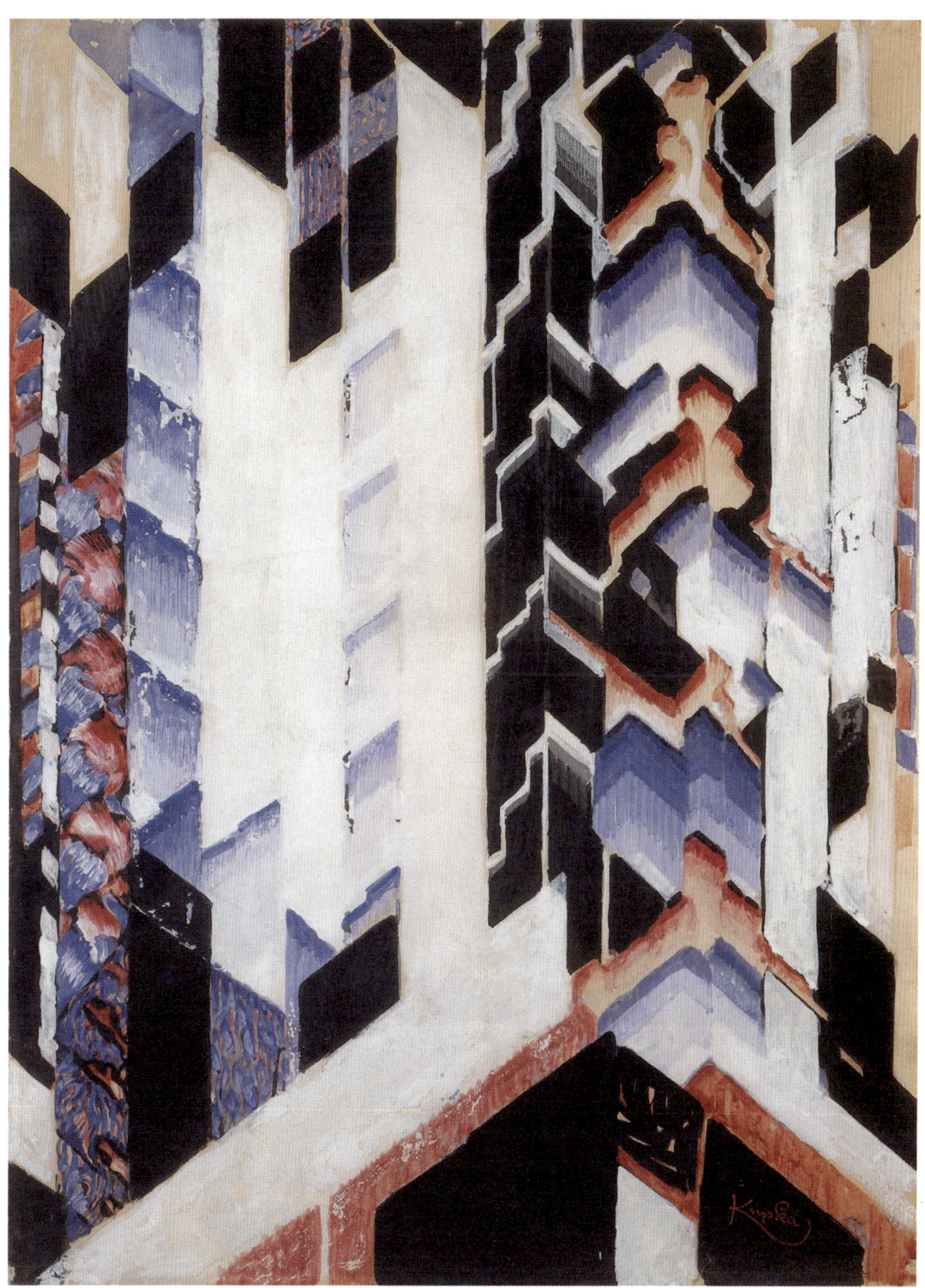

František Kupka

b.1871 Czechoslovakia (Czech Republic)–d.1957 France

Discs of Newton, study for 'Fugue in Two Colours'
1911–12
oil on canvas
66 x 66.5 cm
Centre Pompidou, National Museum of Modern Art, Paris,
gift of Eugenie Kupka in 1963

Guillaume Apollinaire, the influential poet, writer and critic, grouped
Kupka with other artists such as Robert Delaunay, Francis Picabia
and Fernand Léger, practising what he termed 'Orphic Cubism'.
Of Delaunay's 'window pictures' of 1912, Apollinaire wrote
'This art will have so many links with music as only an art that
is the opposite of music can have. This will be pure painting.'
Similarly he used musical terms to describe Kupka's work,
although the artist derided such analogies despite utilising them
himself throughout his career. Kupka acknowledged his debt to
Delaunay and likewise to colour theorists from Isaac Newton in
the seventeenth century to Michel Chevreul in the first half of
the nineteenth century and the more contemporary Ogden Rood,
who wrote his theory of *Modern Chromatics* in 1879.

Kupka was closely associated with Delaunay at the time of painting
Discs of Newton. They were both members of what was known as
the Puteaux Group although in 1913, Kupka left the group to work in
relative isolation. The concentric bands of complementary colours
in *Discs of Newton* pre-empt the solar discs Delaunay began to
paint in 1912. Underpinning Kupka's composition was his belief
that colour equalled light and was an expression of the essence
of nature. He used it to introduce a spiritual dimension to his work
akin to the sensation of musical harmony.

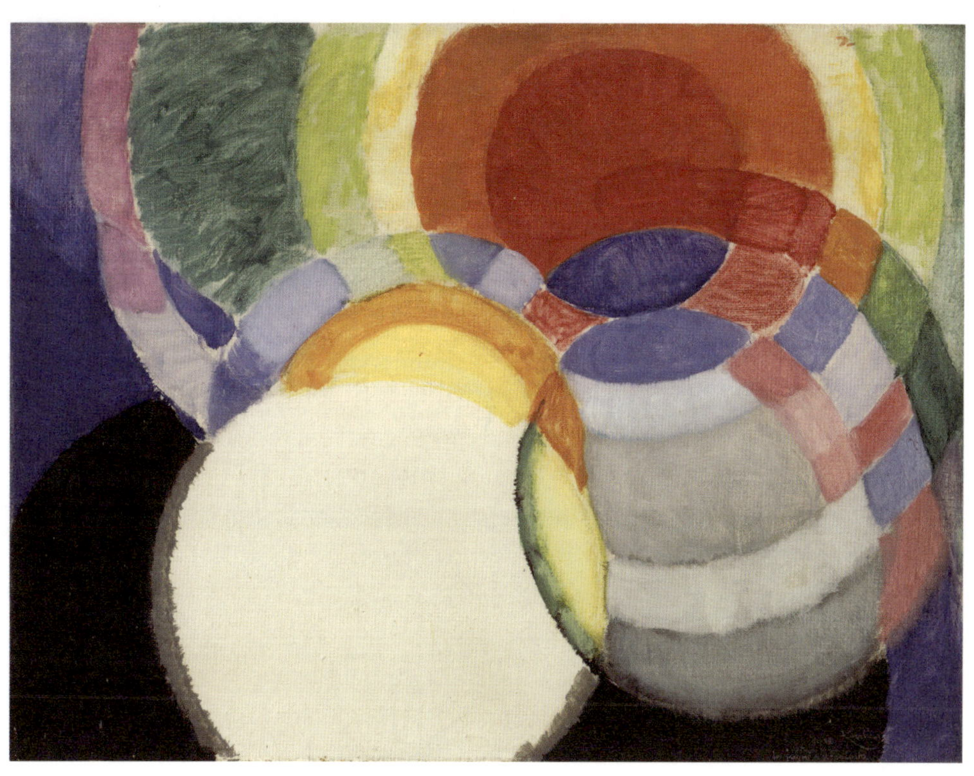

Sonia Delaunay (née Terk)

b.1885 Ukraine–d.1970 France

Project for a cover for 'Vogue', work no. 443
1916
gouache and pencil on paper
34.5 x 23.3 cm
University of East Anglia,
Collection of Abstract and Constructivist Art,
Architecture and Design

Sonia Delaunay studied art and design in Germany before moving to Paris in 1906 where she made textiles, and met and married Robert Delaunay in 1910. Their shared aesthetic of Simultaneity, the use of contrasting colours to convey movement and depth and the very rhythms of nature as opposed to its material appearance, was the foundation of what came to be called Orphism. Robert Delaunay described the theory as combining colour in a manner relating to the relationship of harmonic intervals within a chord: 'Colour is both form and subject... Colour is self-referential, its entire effect is present at every moment in time, just as in a musical composition of Bach's age, or in a good jazz work in our own age.'

During the war the Delaunays travelled to Portugal and Spain, and during this period Sonia undertook a series of projects for *Vogue* magazine. The discs of contrasting colours in this design relate to her husband's paintings of solar discs, both aiming to convey the simultaneous interchange of colour and light in the interpenetrating compositions.

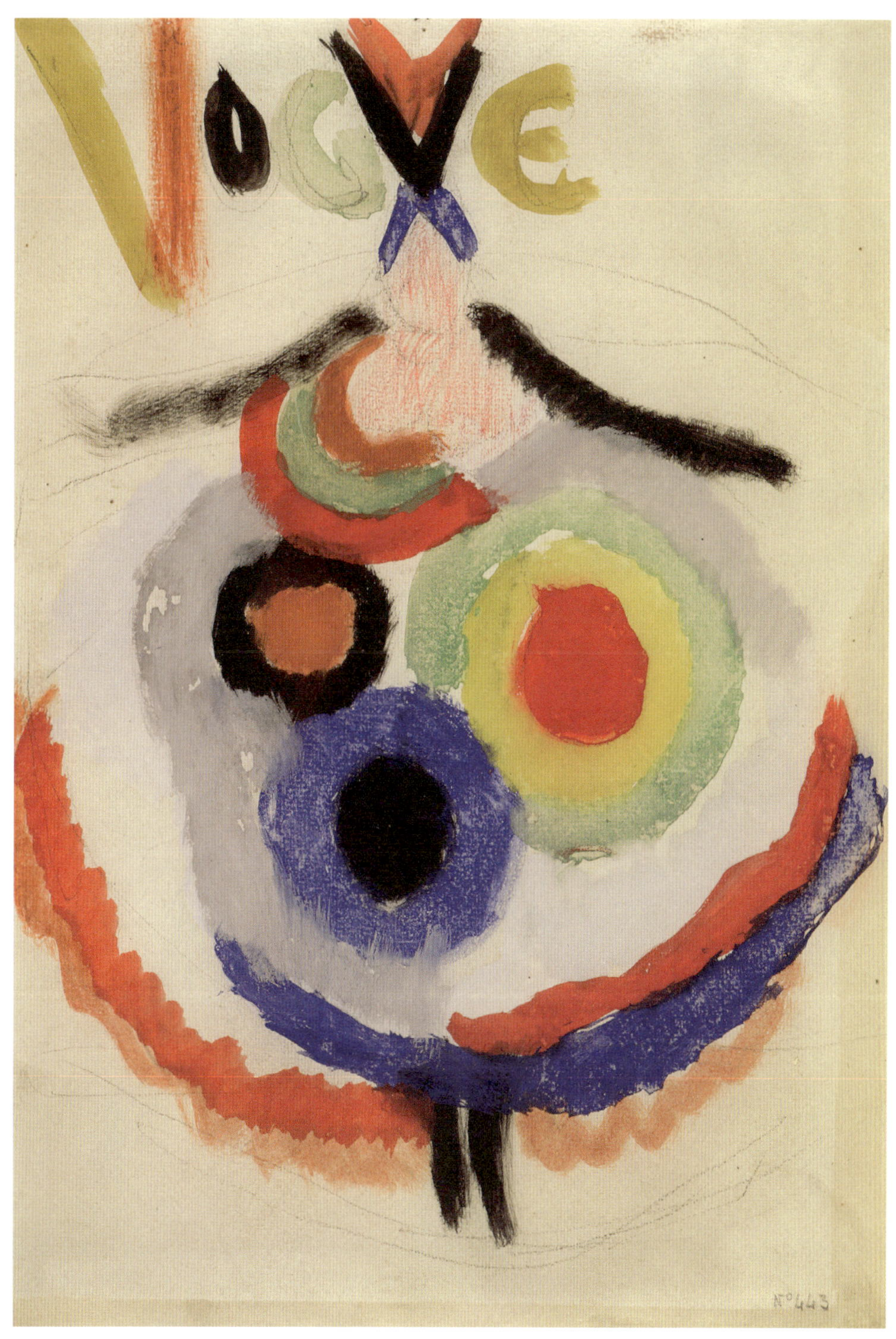
Vogue
N°443

Johannes Itten

b.1888 Switzerland–d.1967 Switzerland

Horizontal-Vertical
1917
oil on canvas
54 x 44.5 cm
Bauhaus Archive, Berlin

In 1919, Walter Gropius, the founder of the Bauhaus, appointed Itten as one of the first three Masters of Form along with Feininger and the sculptor Gerhard Marcks. Itten was responsible for teaching the preliminary course in which the colour theory he had learnt from his teacher Adolf Hölzel at the Stuttgart Academy, played an important part. Hölzel based his theory on the writings of Goethe and Runge and believed that harmonious paintings could be achieved by utilising the musical, emotional and spiritual properties of colour.

Itten was connected with the circle around Schönberg through his friendship with the composer Josef Matthias Hauer (1883–1959), who also wrote music according to a 12-tone system of composition. Itten and Hauer exchanged ideas, leading Itten to develop a 12-tone colour system in 1921, published as *The Art of Colour* in which he stated 'the quintessence of colour is a dreamlike chiming, is music become light.' His mystical beliefs lay behind Itten's teachings at the Bauhaus, in which he tried to liberate the creative potential of his students through meditation, physical exertion and drawing exercises that exploited the effects of contrast, tension and musical rhythm. His emphasis on craftsmanship and the individual as opposed to mass-production eventually led to differences with Gropius that forced him to leave the Bauhaus in 1923.

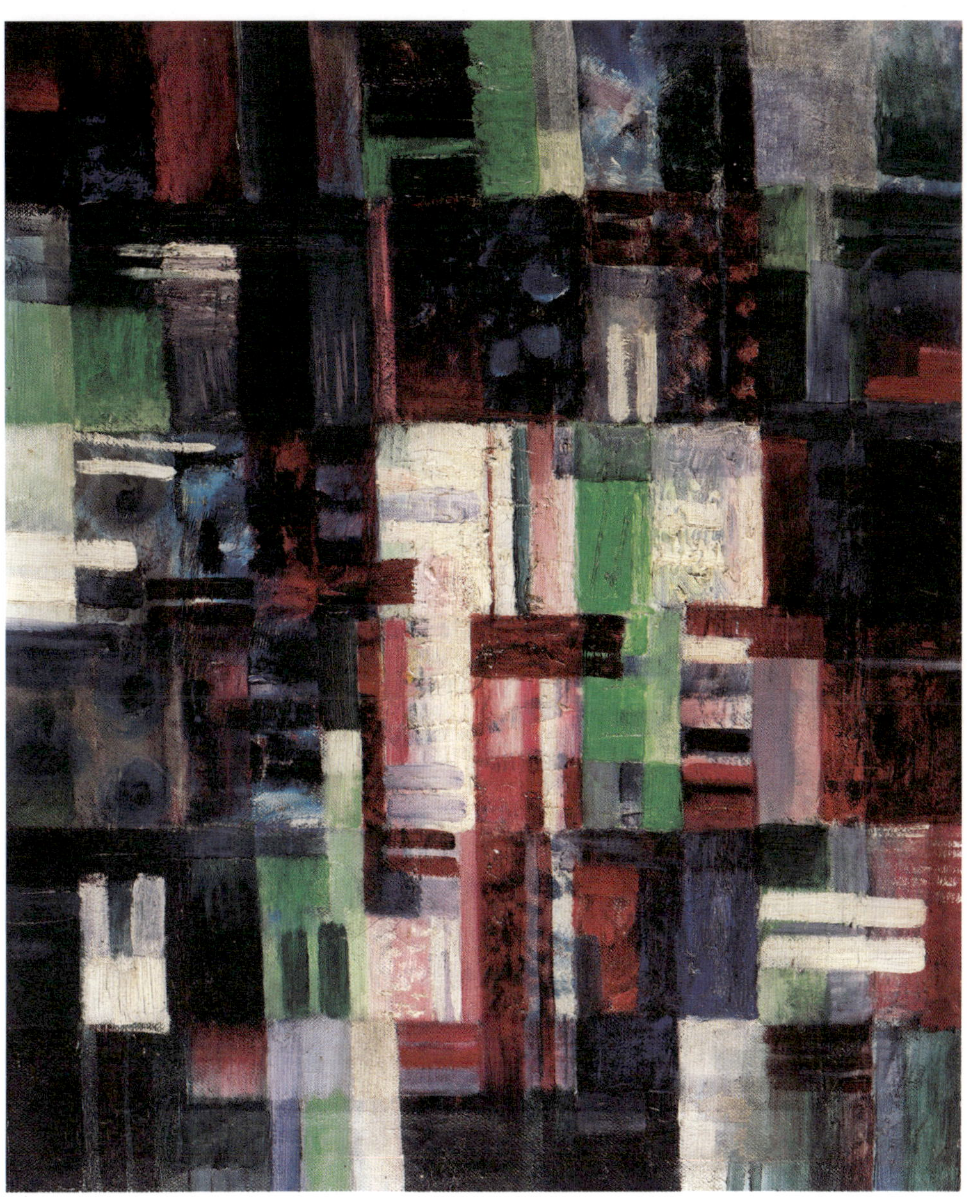

Lothar Schreyer

b.1886 Germany–d.1966 Germany

**Color Form 6 from Stage Work: Child Dying
(Farbform 6 aus Bühnenwerk Kindersterben)**
1921
Watercolour on paper
43.8 x 28.7 cm
University of East Anglia Collection of Abstract
and Constructivist Art, Architecture and Design

In 1921, Schreyer was appointed as the first Master of the theatre
workshop at the Bauhaus. Previously, he had been associated
with Der Sturm as an Expressionist painter and had taken part
in productions at an avant-garde theatre in Hamburg. Like Itten,
he adopted a highly mystical and esoteric belief system, which
found expression in his primitivistic and pseudo-religious theatre
productions at the Bauhaus.

Schreyer's productions were concerned with the integration of
sound, colour and gesture and were strongly Expressionistic and
emotional in nature. In a note to a production in 1922, Gropius
described its aims, presumably shared by Schreyer: 'In its origin
the stage derives from an ardent religious desire of the human
soul (theatre = show for the gods). It serves, then, to manifest
a transcendental idea. The power of its effect on the soul of the
spectator and auditor is therefore dependent on the success of
the transformation of the idea into (visually and acoustically)
perceivable space.'

This print was one of a group by Bauhaus Masters published in a
portfolio in 1921 and depicts a mystical spirit. Schreyer was later
forced to resign after Itten's departure and the introduction of
an anti-mystical element under the leadership of Moholy-Nagy.

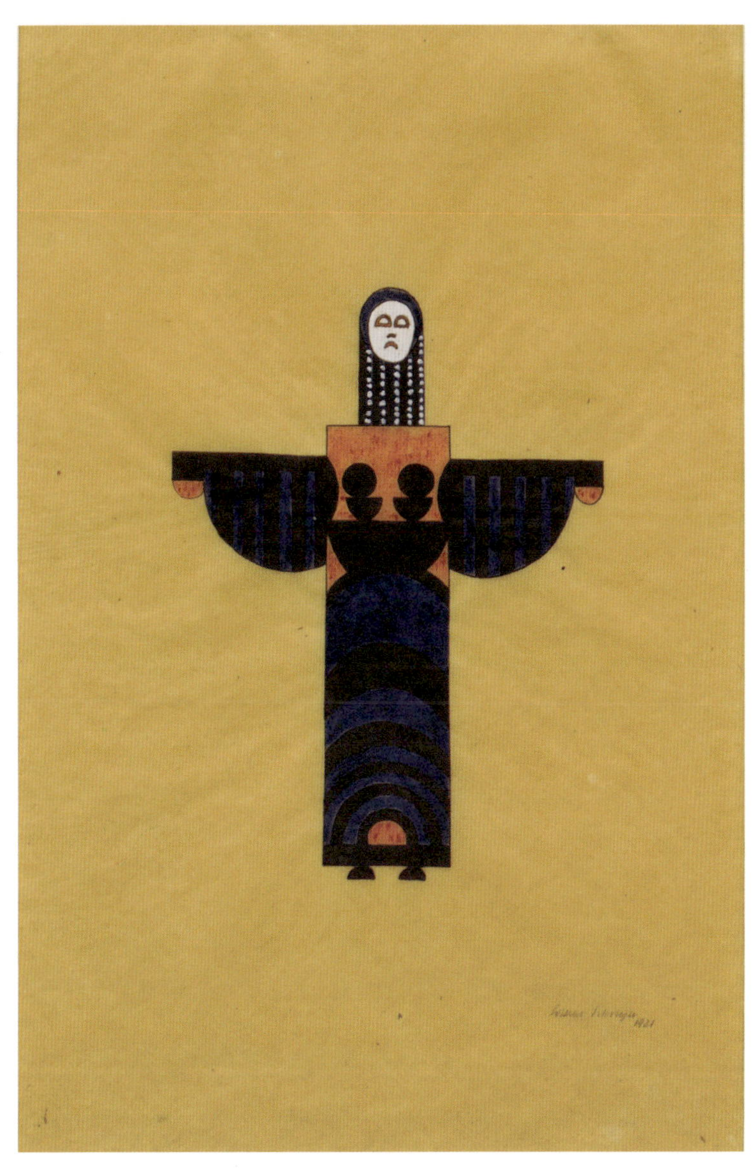

Paul Klee

b.1879 Switzerland–d.1940 Switzerland

Abstract Colour Harmony in Squares with Vermilion Accents
(Abstracte Farbenharmonie in Vierecken mit Zinnoberroten Akzenten)
1924
oil on lime primed paper on cardboard
framed with pen and ink and gouache
30.8 x 24.4 cm
Staatliche Museen zu Berlin, Nationalgalerie.
Museum Berggruen

'One day I must be able to improvise freely on the keyboard of
colours: the row of watercolours in my paint box.'

Klee's use of the keyboard as a metaphor in this diary entry stems
from Isaac Newton's experiments in optics and the development
of a scale of seven colours that paralleled the seven tones of
the musical octave. Klee, however, unlike other artists, was not
concerned with equating colours to specific tones but rather with
developing harmonious relationships between colours in terms of
their expressive content. This approach developed through his
admiration of the Delaunays' theory of Simultaneity. He would have
seen their work at the first exhibition of Der Blaue Reiter, and later
at the exhibition organised in Berlin by the expressionist gallery and
journal Der Sturm for which Klee translated Robert Delaunay's essay
'On Light' in 1913.

Whilst at the Bauhaus in Weimar, Klee started on a series of paintings
of rectangles, which he continued to develop after the school
moved to Dessau in 1925. Informed by Simultaneity, they are also
a development of the paintings of townscapes Klee had made in
response to his trip to Tunis with the artists Macke and Louis Moilliet
in early 1914. Klee was also interested in the chessboard pattern,
using it as a basis for his lectures on structural rhythms.
It allowed him to experiment with colour, achieving a harmonic
balance in which no single colour dominates, like musical chords.

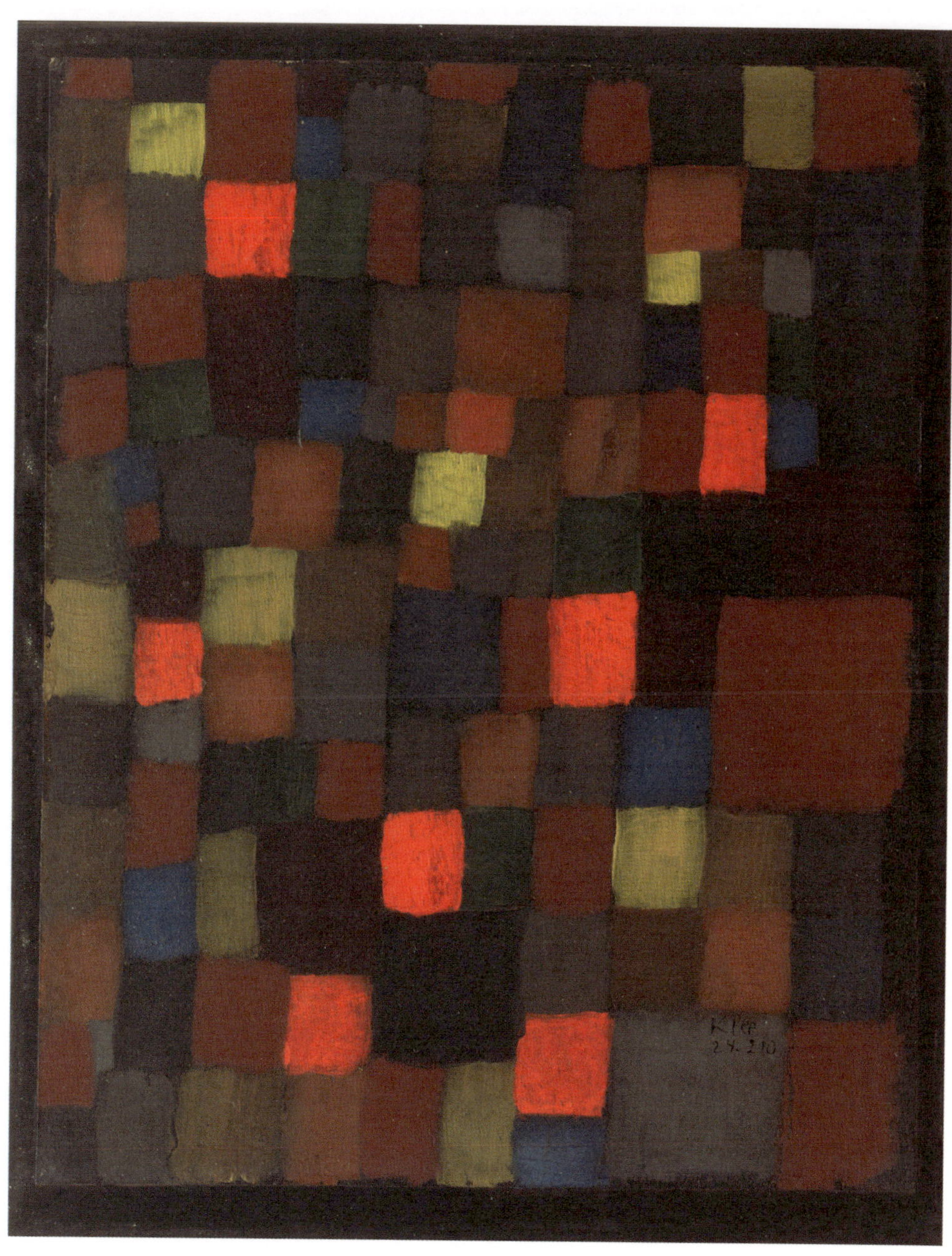

Wassily Kandinsky

b.1866 Russia–d.1944 France

Violet
1923
colour lithograph
34.1 x 27.1 cm
Bauhaus Archive, Berlin

In 1922, shortly after his return to Germany following his exile to Russia during World War I, Kandinsky received an invitation to teach at the Bauhaus from Gropius. He and his wife Nina, whom he had met and married in Russia in 1917, moved to Weimar where he was reunited with his friends Klee and Feininger.

Through his teachings at the Bauhaus, Kandinsky developed his theories of colour and form first outlined in *Concerning the Spiritual in Art*. His course in 'primary artistic design' included colour classes that associated primary colours with the basic forms of the triangle, square and circle. He also further defined the psychological effects of colour and the properties of the non-colours, black and white. Kandinsky possessed the phenomena of synaesthesia in which he could ascribe certain sounds and emotions to particular colours. In *Concerning the Spiritual in Art*, he wrote, 'Violet is therefore both in the physical and spiritual sense a cooled red. It is consequently rather sad and ailing. It is worn by old women, and in China as a sign of mourning. In music it is an English horn, or the deep notes of wood instruments (eg. a bassoon).'

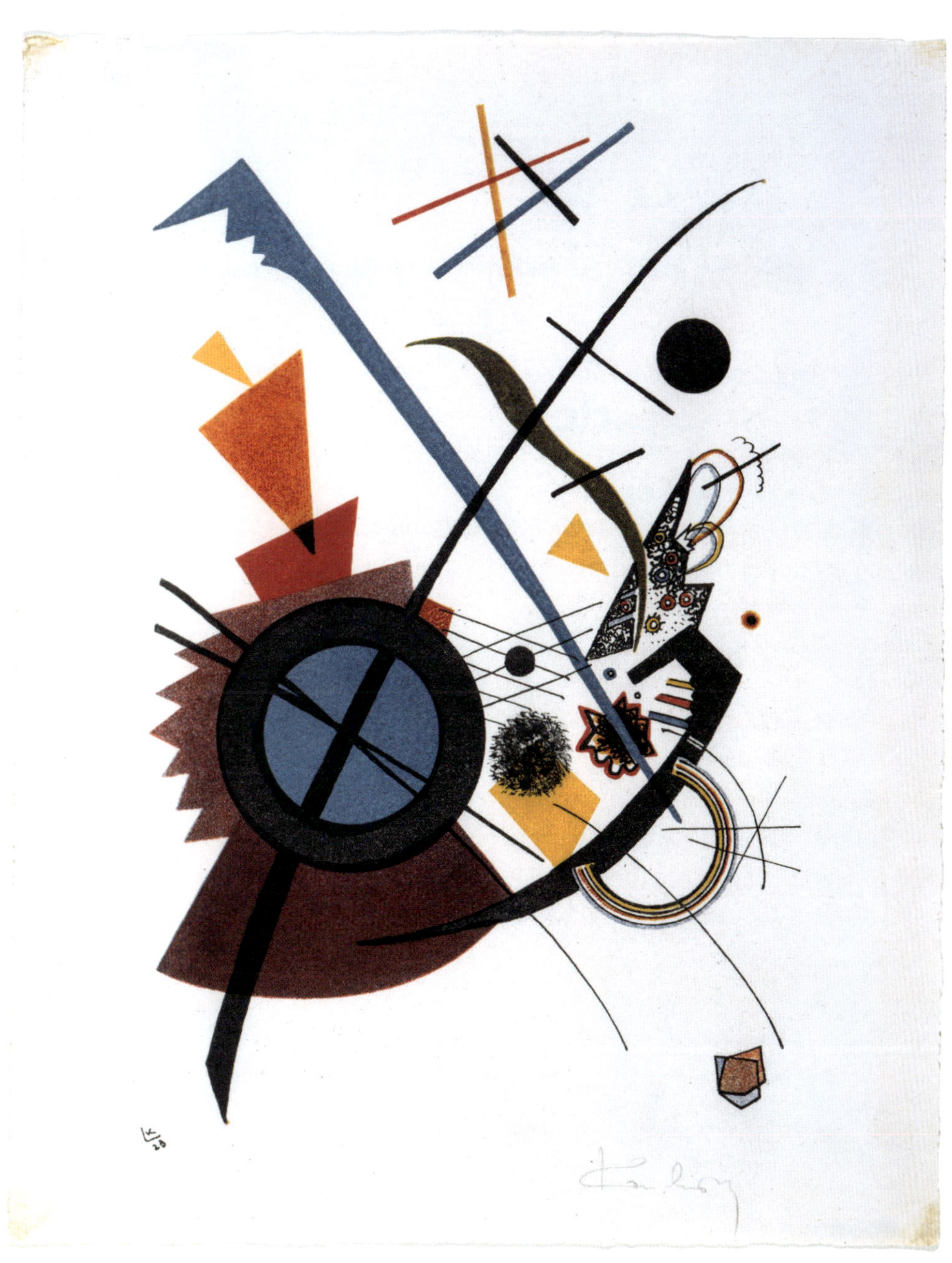

Wassily Kandinsky

b.1866 Russia–d.1944 France

Yellow-Pink (Gelb-Rosa)
1929
watercolour with pen and black ink on paper
40 x 48 cm
Private Collection, London

When the Bauhaus moved to Dessau in 1926, the families of Kandinsky and Klee were placed in a double house in the purpose-built housing colony. The two friends became closer than ever before and, despite the fact that Klee was thirteen years younger than Kandinsky whom he had regarded as his mentor and teacher, gradually the relationship shifted so that Kandinsky fell increasingly under the influence of Klee.

This painting by Kandinsky was made in December 1929, shortly after the two families had holidayed together at Hendaye-Plage. Klee had been leading experiments in the glass-painting workshop at the Bauhaus where he had been using stencils and applying paint with a spray since 1924. Here, Kandinsky uses the same technique.

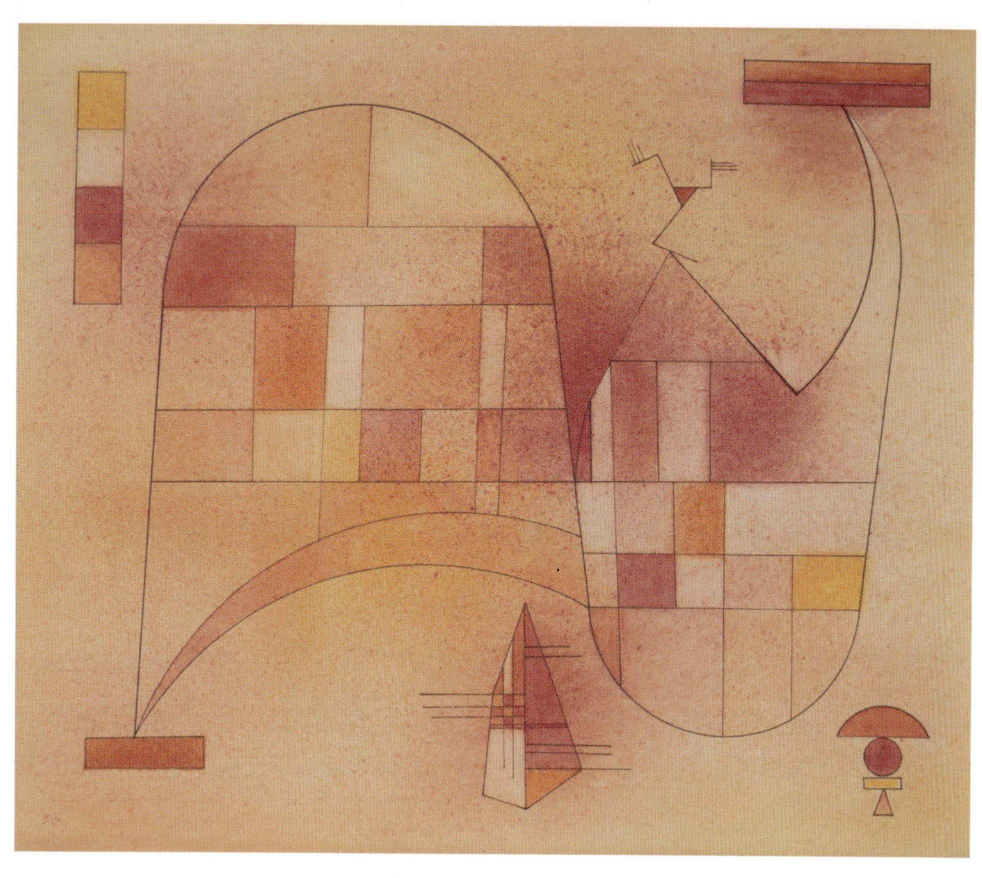

Henry Valensi

b.1883 Algeria–d. France 1960

Green Symphony (Symphonie Verte)
1935
oil on canvas
95 x 131 cm
Centre Pompidou, National Museum of
Modern Art, Paris, purchase of the State, 1949

In 1932, Valensi, Gustave Bourgogne, Charles Blanc-Gatti and
Vito Stracquadaini founded the group of 'Musicalist' artists.
The Musicalists were not concerned with replicating musical pieces
through painting, but each artist did adopt an individual approach to
the correlation between art and music. Valensi believed that music
would be the dominant art form in the twentieth century due to its
ability to surmount material representation and achieve a spiritual
essence. One of his concerns was to express dynamism and rhythm
and to introduce real time into his work, a project which was to
culminate in a film based on his painting *Spring Symphony* of 1932
which lasted 20 minutes and required 64,000 paintings.

Colour was also vital to the Musicalists, all of whom admired
Robert Delaunay and found inspiration in his theory of Simultaneity
and the works of the Orphists. Valensi stated 'Why not then conceive
a "pure painting"? Just as a musician has his notes, why not suppose
that colour, by its intrinsic force, can express the painter's thought?'.
The composer Olivier Messiaen (1908–92) was associated with the
group through his friendship with Blanc-Gatti. Both Blanc-Gatti and
Messiaen, to a greater or lesser degree, possessed the neurological
condition of synaesthesia and the resulting interaction of colour
and sound was intrinsic to their respective artistic and
musical compositions.

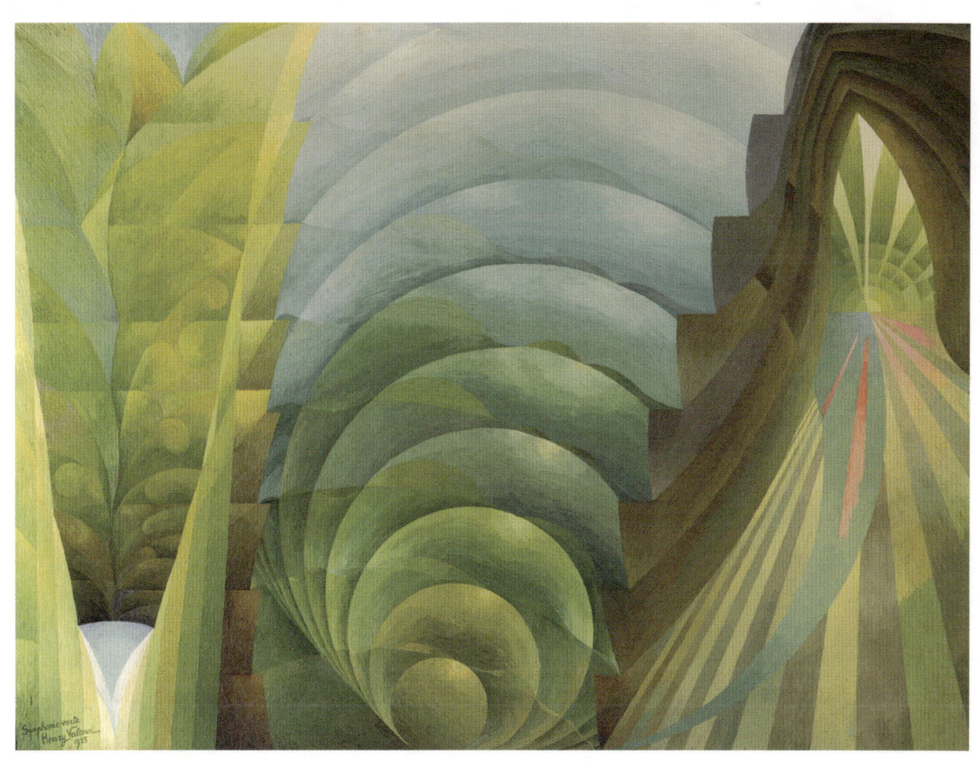

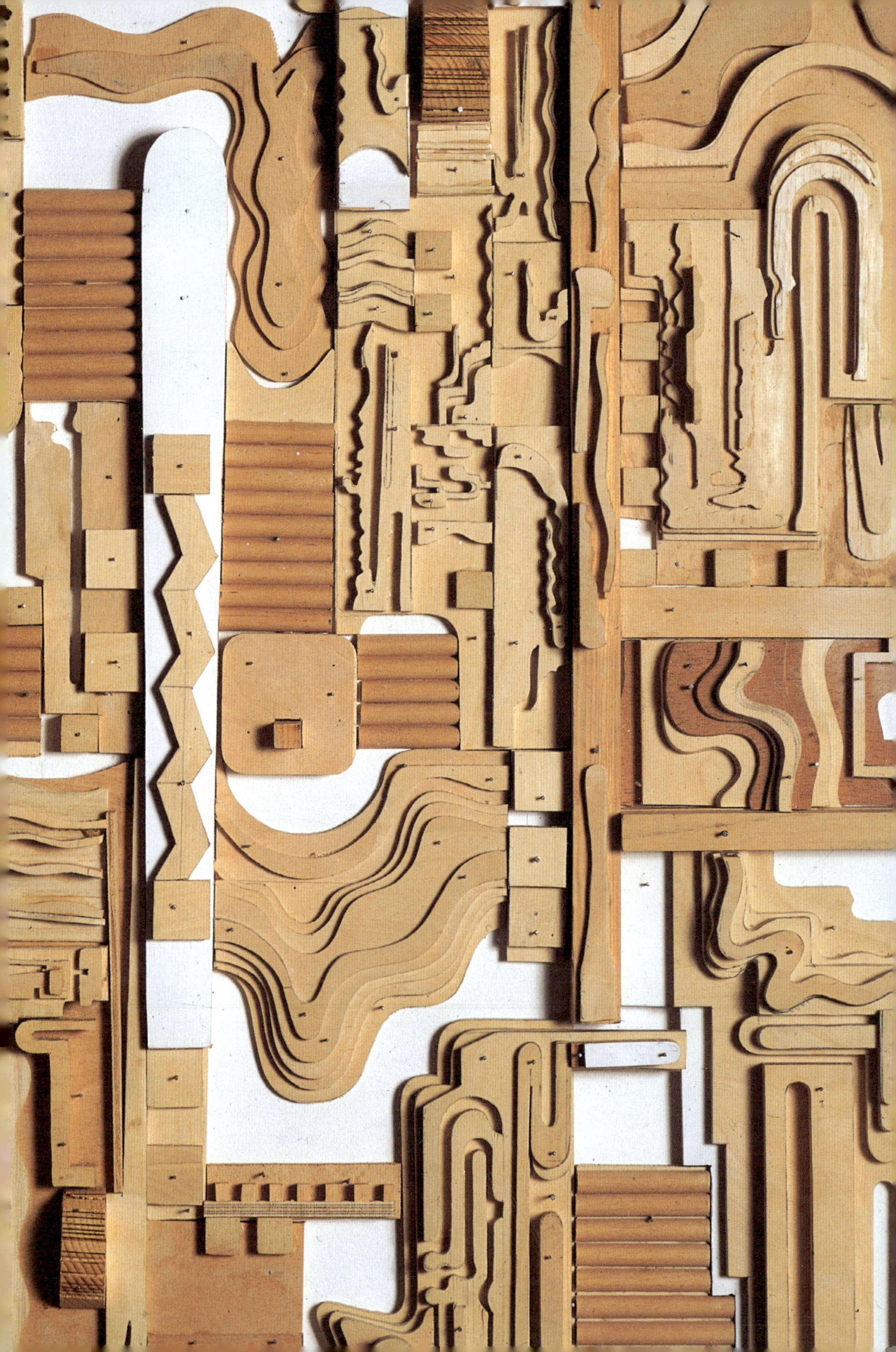

rhythm and time

'The swing of a curve, the even flow, the radiation, or the forceful clashing of lines, as well as the plastic relations of planes, may have an effect as soothing or exciting, as stimulating to the imagination, as those purely abstract combinations of sound we speak of as music.'

P. G. Konody in *'Abstract Art in England 1913–15'*

The flurry of exhibitions from 1910–14 organised by artists, art critics and entrepreneurs such as Roger Fry and Frank Rutter, introduced the work of the Parisian avant-garde to Britain and had a huge impact on individuals and art movements. The critical reaction and artistic response to these works often focussed on their rhythmic qualities, as illustrated above. Grant and Vanessa Bell, who had both been creating abstract designs for furniture and textiles made in Fry's Omega workshops, began to include rectangular forms in their paintings, producing some of the most innovative British art of the period. However their experimentation was cut short by World War I and later, these forms became purely decorative backdrops in their work. Nevertheless, Grant left one extraordinary work, *Abstract Kinetic Collage Painting with Sound*, which can be seen as forerunner of early abstract film in its intention to combine moving images and sound.

The relative merits of space versus time in the debate about the superiority of one art form over another were an important issue for abstract artists. Many wished to introduce a temporal element to their work to emulate that particular quality of music and for Robert Delaunay, Kupka and others, the fugue was yet again the model with which to experiment, using new formats, large canvases and complex interweaving of form and line to lead the eye over their compositions.

Eduardo Paolozzi, Small study for Cleish Panel (detail), 1972
wood and white paint, 89.4 x 88.6 x 8.4 cm
Scottish National Gallery of Modern Art

Both Kandinsky and Klee, for whom the relationship between form and line was a rhythmic component in their abstract compositions, published theoretical works whilst teaching at the Bauhaus outlining their ideas. Klee's *Pedagogical Sketchbook (Pädagogisches Skizzenbuch)* published in 1925, is based on his lectures at the Bauhaus as head of the bookbinding and glass workshops. In this book he visualises his idea of a 'line on a walk, moving freely, without goal. A walk for a walk's sake' and defines his theory of active and passive lines and forms and structural rhythms. Similarly, Kandinsky's *Point and Line to Plane (Punkt und Linie zu Fläche)* (1926) presents a detailed analysis of the inner dynamics of abstract art which centres on the point (representing rest) and its antithesis the line, thereby creating tension by movement.

In the same way as Kandinsky, Klee and others had developed a new vocabulary of line and form for their compositions, Paolozzi also searched for a visual language of his own in the 1970s. Like them he turned to music, or more specifically to an earlier artist's visual interpretation of organ music he found in a junk shop in Germany whilst teaching in Hamburg. This abstract work of interweaving lines became the basis of many of his subsequent works, whether in prints, sculpture or other designs. He wrote of his method of composition at this time, 'Similar motifs juxtaposed to create a cluster might suggest a chord of music, to be repeated elsewhere at a different scale with a different surround. Spaces suggest a silent pause. The viewer's mind may be engaged in making varied connections between form and music – an activity well recorded in the history of art.'

rhythm and time

catalogue entries

František Kupka

b.1871 Czechoslovakia (Czech Republic)–d.1957 France

Study for Around a Point
1911–30
gouache on paper
38 x 40.7 cm
Museum Kampa, the Jan and
Mada Mladek Foundation

This study is part of a series that Kupka made from 1911 onwards for a painting that was finally realised in 1930. The studies are perhaps more dynamic and innovative than the final painting because they convey a natural energy and dynamism that is compromised in the finished, more formal work. With the series, Kupka was attempting to introduce the temporal quality of music to his painting. He wrote in 1910, 'By using a form in various dimensions and arranging it according to rhythmical considerations, I will achieve a "symphony", which develops in space as a symphony does in time.'

Around a Point is a mixture of different elements including the lotus flower, symbolic of mystical evolution and cosmic space that was embraced by the theosophical movement in which Kupka was involved, and the colour discs from his earlier compositions. The centrifugal spiralling motif was one that occurred regularly in Kupka's work. It is the ultimate expression of Kupka's vision of natural rhythms and form, and the chromatic juxtapositions that made up his vision of the cosmos.

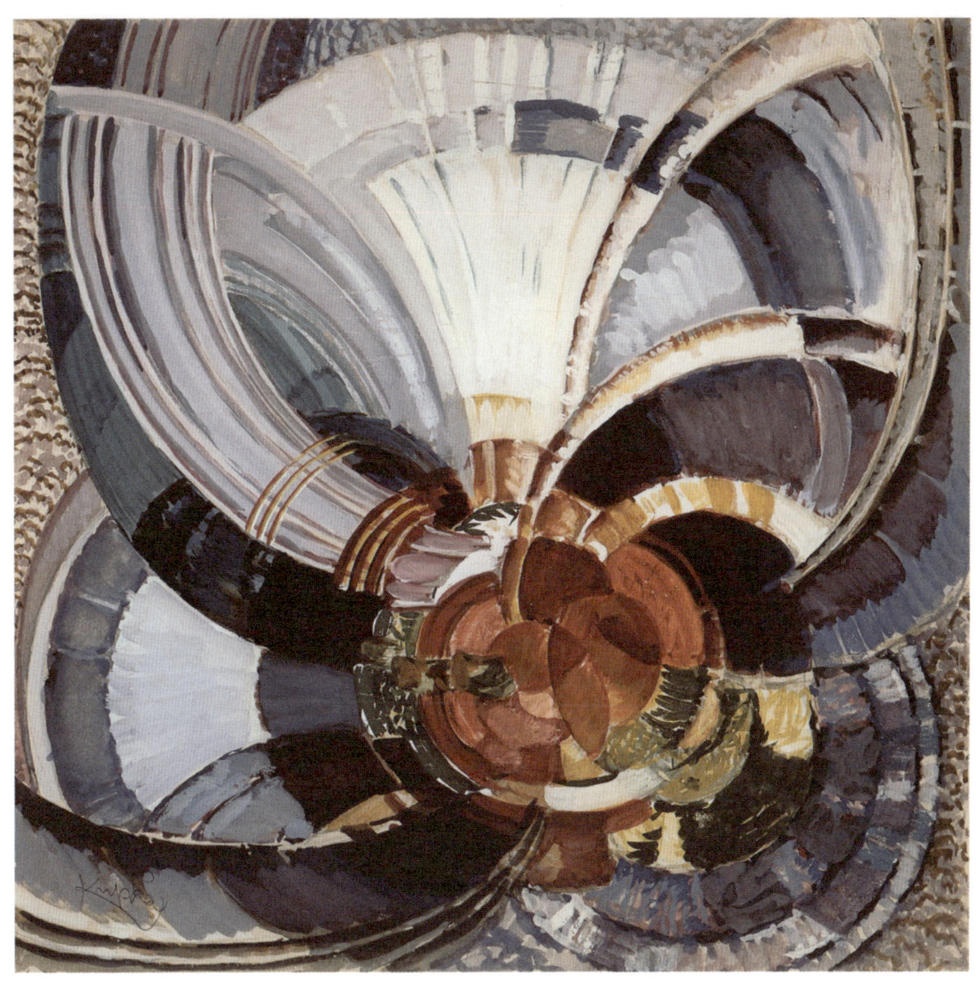

Duncan Grant

b.1885 Scotland–d.1978 England

Abstract Kinetic Collage Painting with Sound (detail)
1914
gouache, watercolour, ink and collage of painted and cut papers,
on sheets of paper laid on unpainted canvas support
27.9 x 450.2 cm
Tate, London, purchased 1973

In a letter sent to Roger Fry from Asheham House in Sussex in August 1914, Vanessa Bell wrote, 'Duncan and I do nothing here but paint. He has started on a long painting which is meant to be rolled up after the manner of those Chinese paintings and seen by degrees. It is purely abstract.'

Grant, Bell and Fry, who had established the Omega Workshops in 1913, travelled to Paris the same year where it is likely that they would have seen Kupka's *Vertical Planes*, consisting of groups of narrow, vertical rectangles, exhibited at the Salon des Indépendants. Shortly after, both Grant and Bell began experimenting with architectonic abstract forms in their paintings, although mostly in a decorative role influenced by their work for Omega. Grant had also been experimenting with *papier collé*, the medium used in *Abstract Kinetic Collage Painting*, as a means of preparing designs for marquetry.

Grant planned to mount the scroll on a mechanism that allowed his painting consisting of groups of coloured rectangles to be viewed through an aperture, passing in a slow continuous motion whilst accompanied by music. The mechanism was never made and the painting was rolled up and stored for nearly sixty years, but Grant later collaborated with Tate to make a film of it to be shown alongside the artwork in an exhibition marking his 90th birthday. He selected the slow movement from J.S. Bach's *Brandenburg Concerto no.1* as relating most closely to the work's musical concept.

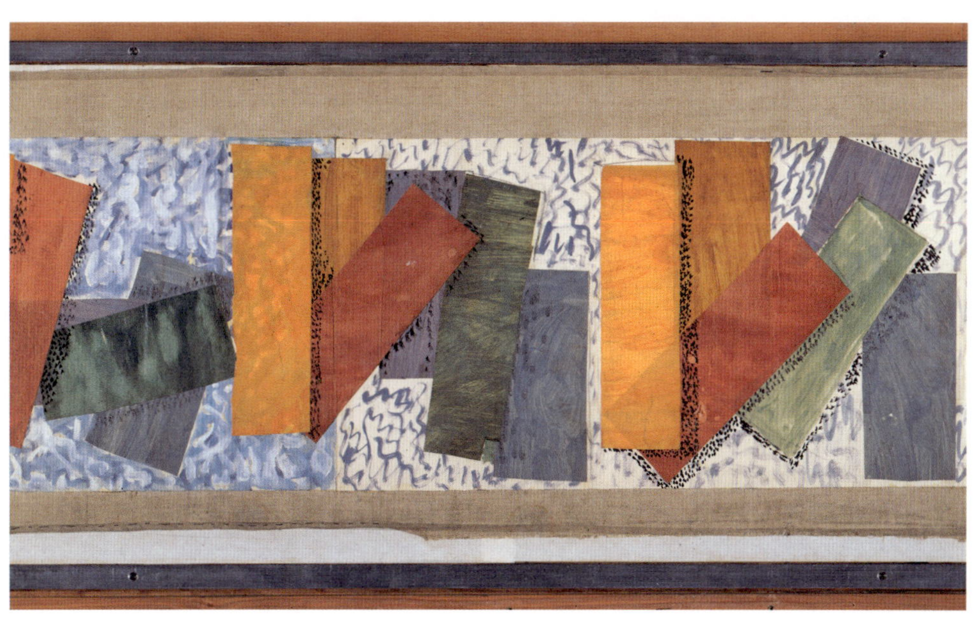

Wassily Kandinsky

b.1866 Russia–d.1944 France

Towards Pink (Zum Rosa)
1926
oil on board
71 x 27 cm
Private collection, London.
On loan to Courtauld Gallery, London

Whilst teaching at the Bauhaus, Kandinsky wrote his second treatise on art entitled *Point and Line to Plane*, published as the ninth in a series of fourteen Bauhaus books. By 1923, Kandinsky had formed a new abstract vocabulary of geometrical forms comprising arrows, circles, squares, zigzags and curves. The circle was a particularly potent cosmic symbol for Kandinsky, to which he ascribed 'inner potentialities'. When combined strategically with colour according to his theories, the resulting compositions were intended to exhibit a dynamic tension (see also Cat. 30).

In his introduction to *Point and Line to Plane*, Kandinsky wrote, 'Only by means of a microscopic analysis can the science of art lead to a comprehensive synthesis, which will extend far beyond the confines of art into the realm of the "oneness" of the "human" and the "divine".'

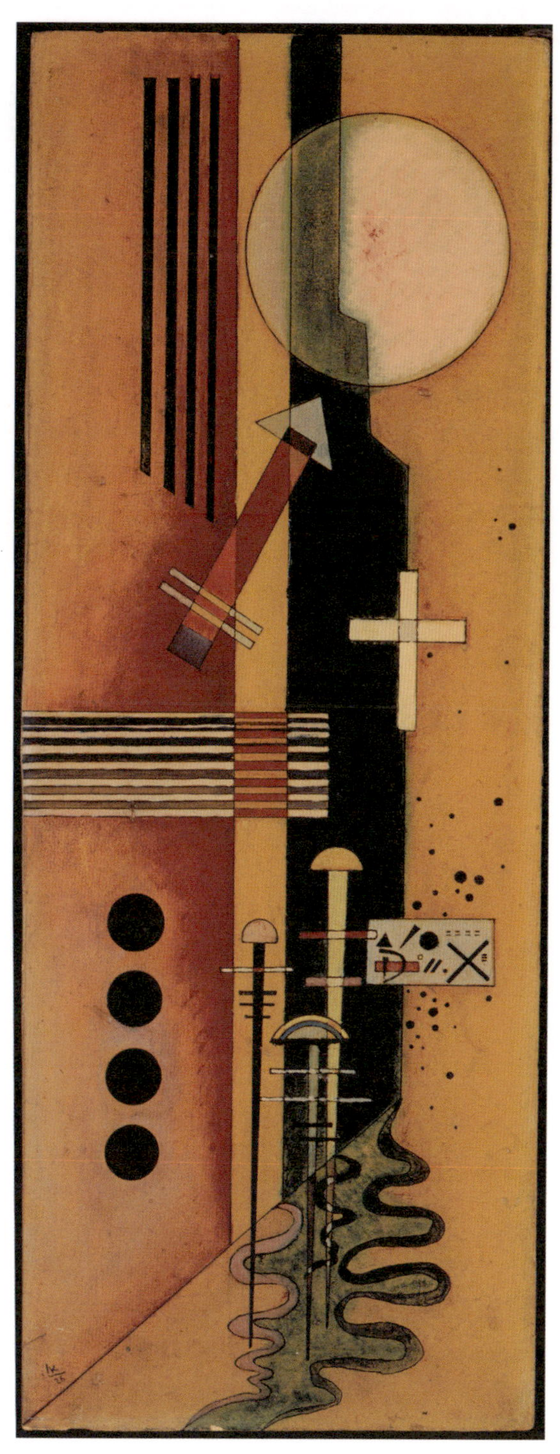

Heinrich Bormann

b.1909 Germany–d.1982 Germany

**Analysis of a piece of music from
Kandinsky's teaching class at the Bauhaus**
1930
ink and coloured inks, gouache over pencil on heavy paper
48 x 61.5 cm
Bauhaus Archive, Berlin

Many of Kandinsky's theories in *Point and Line to Plane* concern music since, as he observed, 'the graphic musical representation in common use today – musical notation – is nothing other than various combinations of point and line.' He went on to write, 'It is instructive to note that the concision and simplicity of the means of transcription manage to convey to the initiated eye (and indirectly the ear), in an explicit manner, the most complicated sonorities.'

Kandinsky attempted to render music graphically, as can be seen in his transcription of the opening bars of Beethoven's *Symphony no.5* in *Point and Line to Plane*. He placed points and varied their disposition according to the pitch of the given sound and their volume in terms of intensity or duration. These exercises also informed his teaching, as is evident in this analysis of a piece of music undertaken by a student in one of his classes. This common vocabulary was then used to inform his increasingly geometric compositions to give them both a metaphorical and metaphysical 'inner sound'.

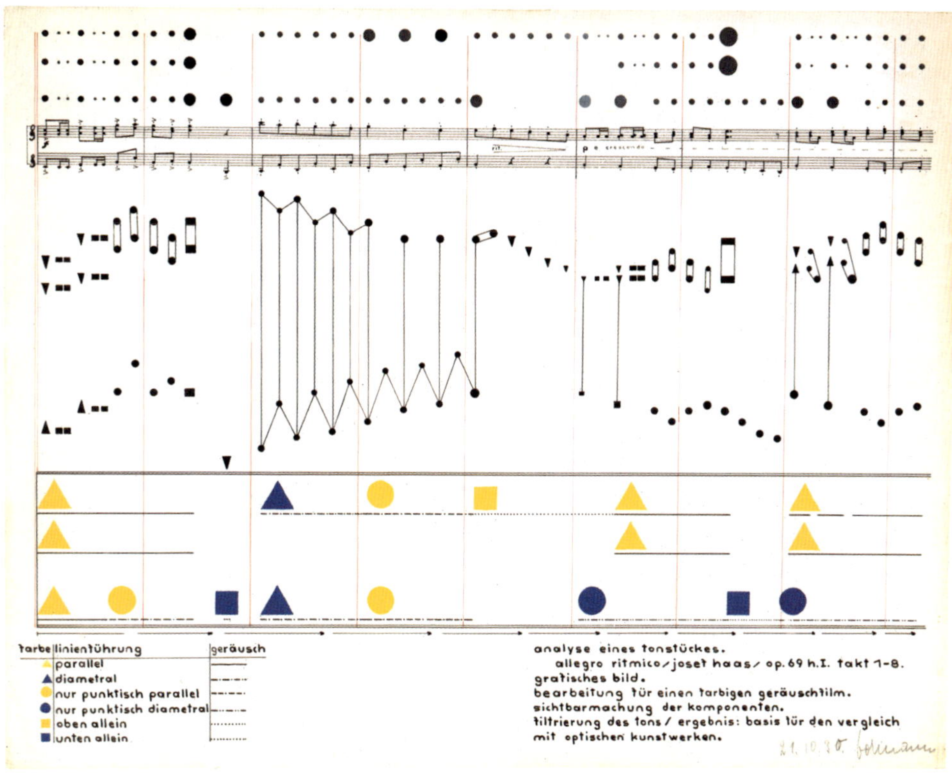

farbe | linienführung | geräusch
parallel
diametral
nur punktisch parallel
nur punktisch diametral
oben allein
unten allein
analyse eines tonstückes.
allegro ritmico / josef haas / op. 69 h.I. takt 1-8.
grafisches bild.
bearbeitung für einen farbigen geräuschfilm.
sichtbarmachung der komponenten.
filtrierung des tons / ergebnis: basis für den vergleich
mit optischen kunstwerken.

Wassily Kandinsky

b.1866 Russia–d.1944 France

Woodcut in Red and Blue
1939
woodcut, edition of 1200
22.9 x 31 cm
University of East Anglia, Collection of Abstract and
Constructivist Art, Architecture and Design

This woodcut was made as an illustration for an article Kandinsky
wrote for the journal *XXe Siècle* in 1939. In it, he commented on the
parallel compositional problems in painting and music. Kandinsky
often made woodcuts in order to explore ideas and problems,
and this image probably relates to what that artist was addressing
in his text:

> *'...music organises its means (sounds) in time, painting its
> means (colours) in the plane... the "organic difference"
> between time and plane is generally exaggerated.
> The composer takes the listener by the hand, makes him
> enter into his musical work, guides him step by step and
> lets him go when the pieces is finished. The parallel is exact.
> It is not so exact in painting. But the painter is not deprived
> of his power to "guide" – he is able, if he wishes, to make
> the spectator start here, follow a precise route through
> his painting and "exit" over there.'*

Elements of the woodcut are taken from musical notation including
a treble clef, parallel lines that relate to the musical stave, and
figures and dots that resemble notes.

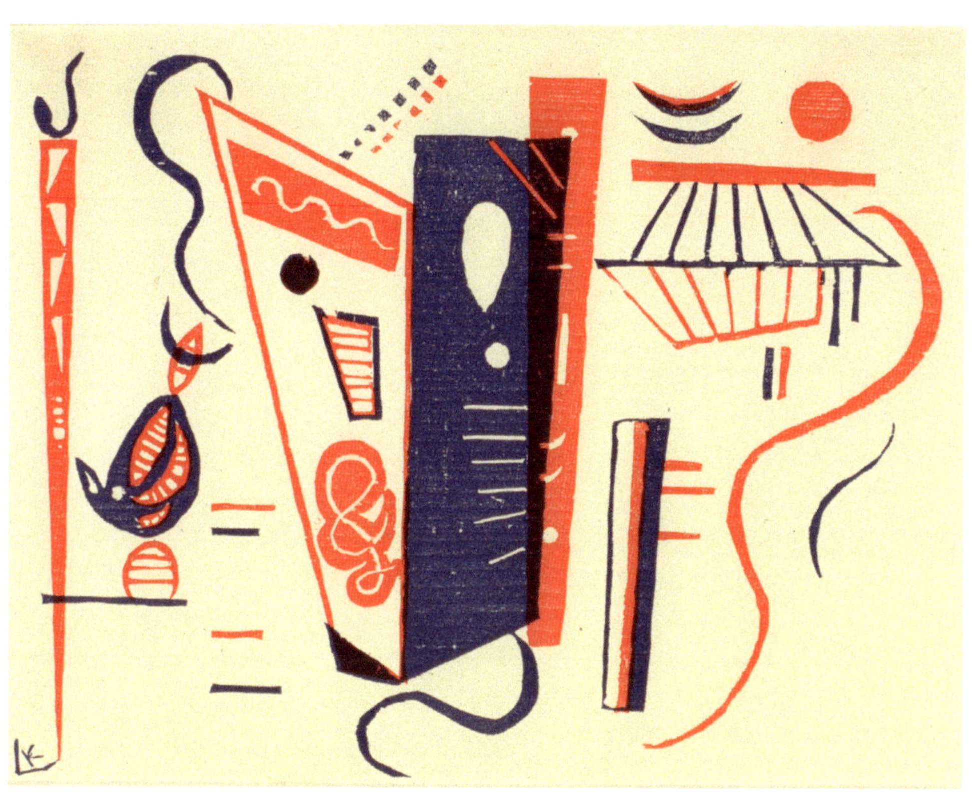

Paul Klee

b.1879 Switzerland–d.1940 Switzerland

Wandering Soul (Anima Errante)
1934 (162)
scratched drawing in wax on paper on board
18 x 26 cm
Dublin City Gallery, The Hugh Lane

In this work from the 1930s, Klee is attempting to create a dimension of time within his work using parallel lines. In an essay 'Creative Credo' of 1918, he wrote 'There are paths laid out in an art work for the eye to follow as it scans the ground rather like a grazing animal… the image is created from movement, is itself fixed movement and is recorded in movement (eye muscle).' This movement was a basic tenet of his theory of polyphonic painting.

At the Bauhaus, Klee first worked in the bookbinding workshop and then in the glass-painting class with Joseph Albers. He taught the theory of form and analysis of line until he left in 1931. He also gave lectures on rhythm, showing how parallel lines combine to form 'structural rhythms' which he compared to musical notation, and these theories were published in the *Pedagogical Sketchbook* in 1925. In his classes, as well as in those of Kandinsky, he analysed musical compositions and devised a graphical system for marking the pitch of notes, structuring a bar of music into qualitative and quantitative groupings. The combination of these elements resulted in what he called a 'linear counterpoint', which he related to that of music.

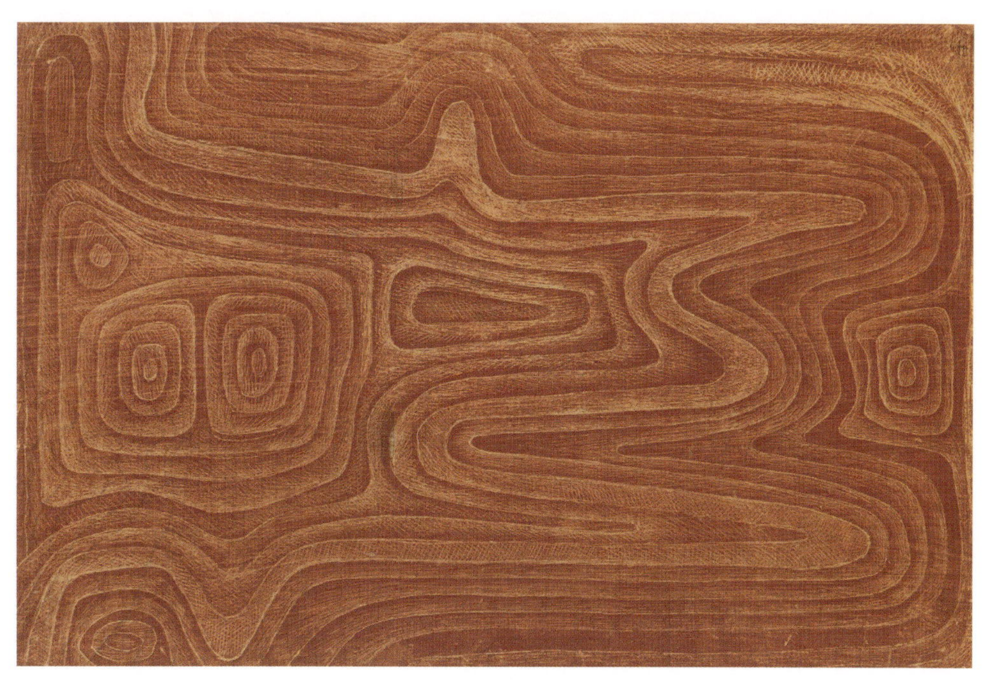

Joseph Albers

b.1888 Germany–d.1976 USA

Homage to the Square No. 5
1964
seriograph, 90/125
35.5 x 35.5 cm
University of East Anglia, Collection of Abstract and
Constructivist Art, Architecture and Design

Albers proved himself to be a gifted student at the Bauhaus where
he enrolled in Itten's preliminary course in 1920. He remained
as a junior member of staff and, following the school's move to
Dessau in 1925, he was made a 'Young Master', subsequently
taking responsibility for the preliminary course in 1928 when László
Moholy-Nagy resigned. At the Bauhaus, he devised a theory of
systematic composition and serialisation based on control and
order, which can perhaps be seen to parallel the serial technique
that Schönberg and his pupil Webern developed for music. This
resulted in works such as the sequence based on the treble clef and
the glass-paintings that were based on repeated rectangular units,
some of which were given musical titles such as *Fugue* of 1925.

Following the closure of the Bauhaus in 1933, many of its staff,
including Albers, made a mass exodus to the United States. Albers
taught at the Black Mountain College in Carolina until 1949 and then
at Yale. Here Albers began the series *Homage to the Square,* which
he called 'a space-time arrangement that is comparable to the beat
in music.' By subtly altering the colour gradations in each work,
Albers achieved different moods and rhythms: 'Only by alterations
in colour can a completely different climate be engendered... Every
colour gives and takes from the others... What I envisage is playing
"staccato" or "legato" – and all the other musical terms.'

Eduardo Paolozzi

b.1924 Scotland–d.2005 England

Small Study for Cleish Panel
1972
wood and white paint
89.4 x 88.6 x 8.4 cm
Scottish National Gallery of Modern Art

In the 1970s, Paolozzi was interested in developing a visual language that could be used across all media and which resulted in works such as the nine ceiling panels designed for Cleish Castle in Kinross and the doors for the Hunterian Art Gallery in Glasgow. These were the first projects in which Paolozzi utilised the stylised interpretation of organ music he had discovered whilst on one of his many visits to second-hand bookshops in Hamburg to search for raw material to use in his teaching classes. The work referred to is *Stille Nacht* by Hugo Meier-Thur, which was published in the journal *Kosmos* in 1927. Writing in an article in 1983, Paolozzi recalled:

> 'There was a strong metaphysical, esoteric side to German art in the twenties in which a kind of visual imagery was ancillary to, or attendant on, certain musical signs. I found by accident in one book an anonymous artist's concept of organ music, made in about 1922. I have used this image – done tracings of it, enlarged it, coloured it, twisted it – for quite a long time.'

Cleish Castle in Kinross was renovated by the architect Michael Spens, who commissioned the panels and also three tapestries from Paolozzi. Of these the artist said, 'I was able to do something I had wanted to do for a long time which was to have a set of images like music but reinterpreted through reasons of material and different kinds of disciplines.'

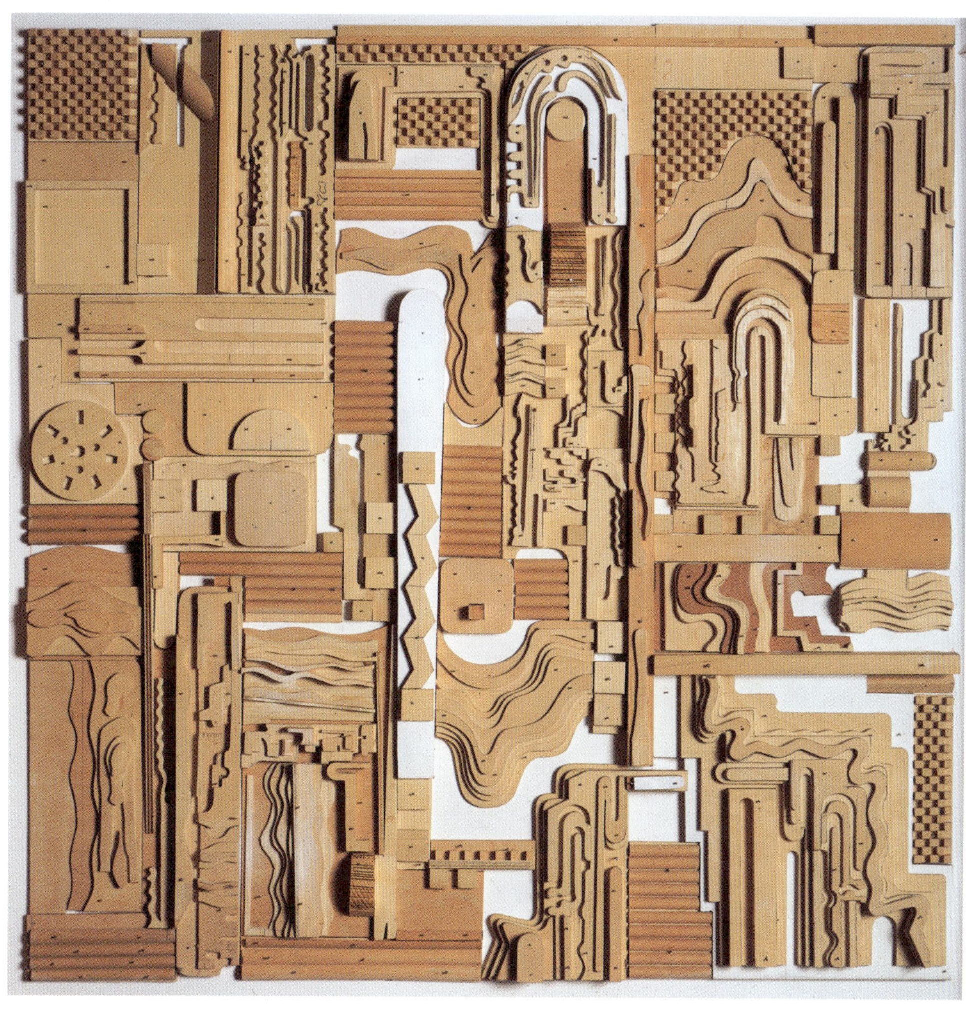

Eduardo Paolozzi

b.1924 Scotland–d.2005 England

Plaster Study for Homage to Bruckner
1977
plaster
6 x 19.6 x 13 cm
Scottish National Gallery of Modern Art

In 1977, Paolozzi was invited to go to Linz in Austria where he was commissioned to design a sculpture next to the Bruckner Concert House. Using a casting technique using polystyrene moulds in sand developed by a Professor in Linz, Paolozzi worked on a design that lay flat along the ground, perhaps evolving from his recent experience of working on children's playgrounds. The work was a dedication to the composer and was not intended as an illustration to Bruckner's music:

> *'I wanted to make some kind of connection with Bruckner,
> even a poetical connection, so that by certain of the forms,
> and by being flat, and being shaped in a particular way, it
> could become allied, rather in a Japanese way, with nature,
> and parts of it would be filled with water, and this is what
> actually happens and the sky is reflected in the water...
> When people come out during the interval they are able
> to lean on it or sit on it, so that the actual sculpture is
> part of the landscape.'*

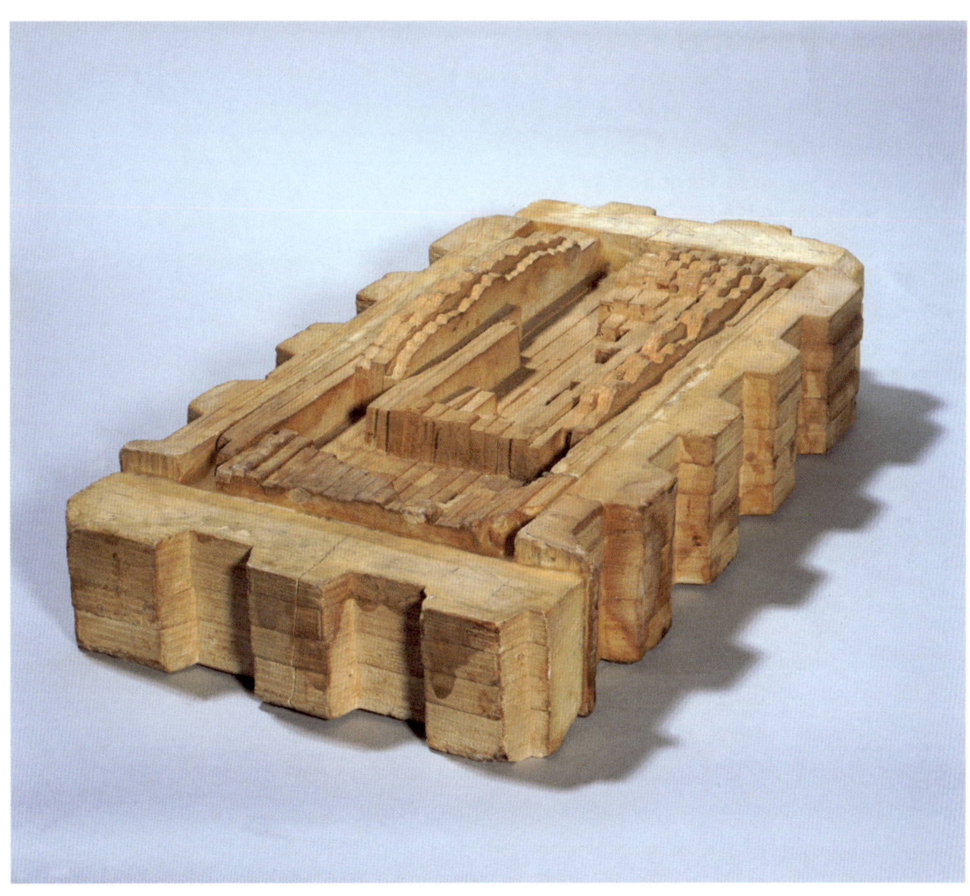

Eduardo Paolozzi

b.1924 Scotland–d.2005 England

Calcium Light Night
i. The Children's Hour, ii. Largo to Presto,
iii. Central Park in the Dark Some 40 Years Ago
iv. Allegro Moderato Fireman's Parade, v. Aeschylus and Socrates,
vi. From Early Italian Poets vii. Four German Songs,
viii. Calcium Light Night, ix. Nettleton
1974–76
series of 9 screenprints, edition of 200
99 x 69 cm
Pallant House Gallery (Wilson Gift through The Art Fund)

Paolozzi dedicated this series of nine screenprints to the American composer Charles Ives (1874–1954). Born in Conneticut the same year as Schönberg, Ives was an insurance agent who, working in relative isolation, had developed ideas in composition comparable to those of the European avant-garde. Many of his works feature layers of musical sources in a collision of symphonic and popular sounds. In the orchestral piece of circa 1906 referred to in the title of Paolozzi's print series, the composer represents the sensation of hearing, from a fixed point, the songs of a group of fraternity brothers as they approach, pass by and retreat. Paolozzi saw in Ives' use of material a similarity to his own technique of visual composition based on collage:

'In the series I also wanted to look at the idea of the relationship between collage and making images. With Chris Betambeau, who did the printing, I was able to use a variety of printing techniques in each print including adding colours photographically, handpainting some photographic areas on the screens, mechanical tints, under and over exposing photographically, hand-stippling and embossing. In the series between six and twelve screens were used for each print. The overall theme in addition to the dedication to Charles Ives is an attempt to find some visual comparison between music and drawing.'

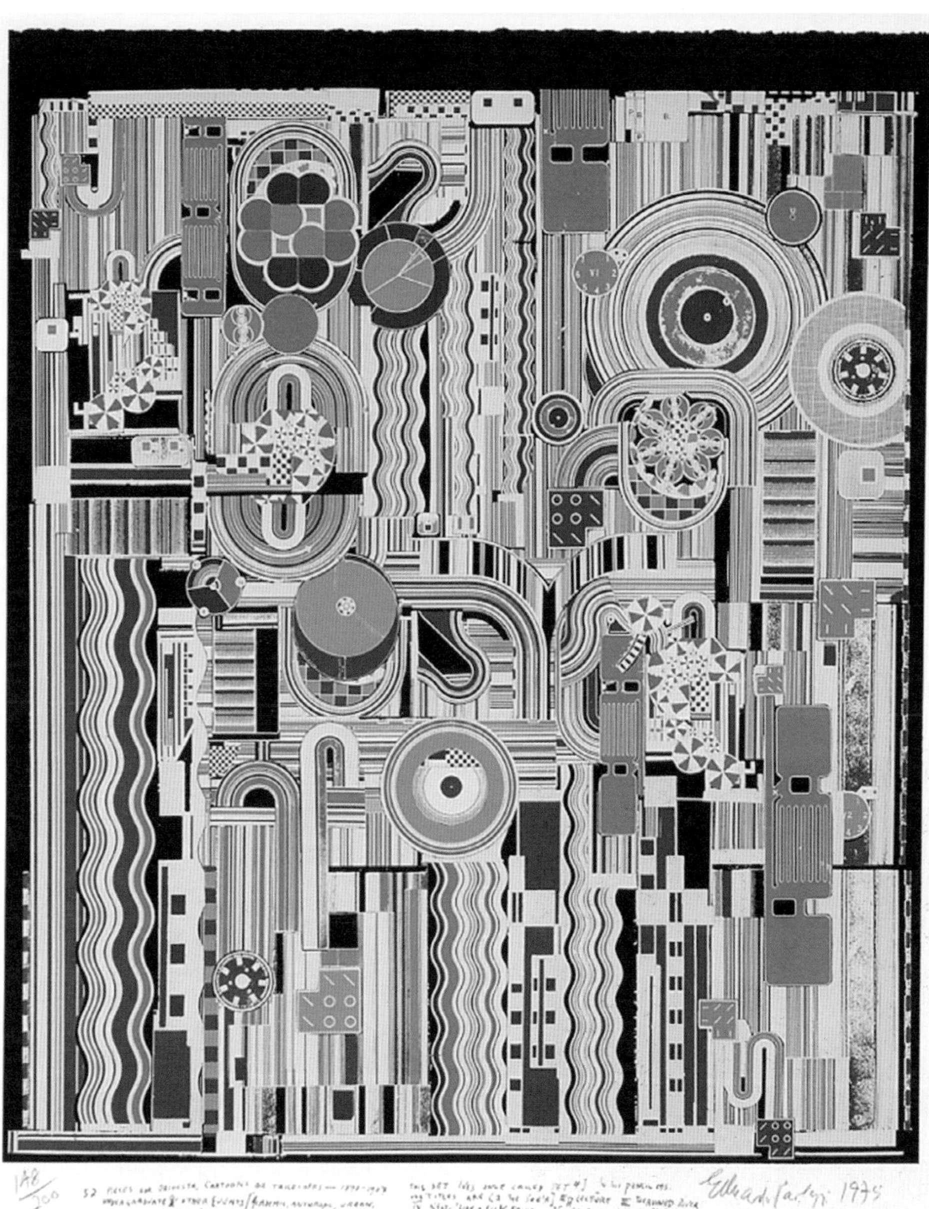

viii. Calcium Light Night

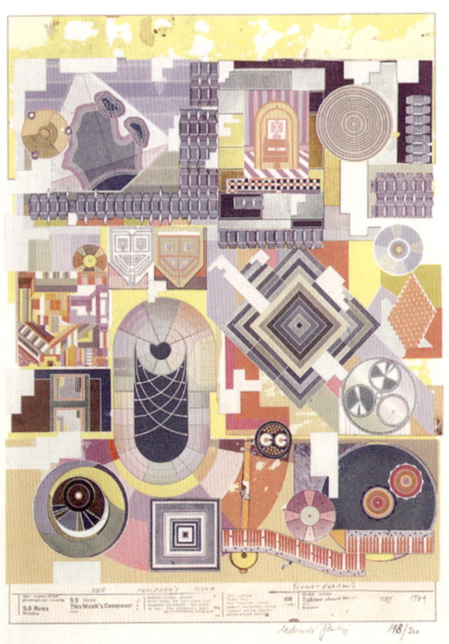

i. The Children's Hour

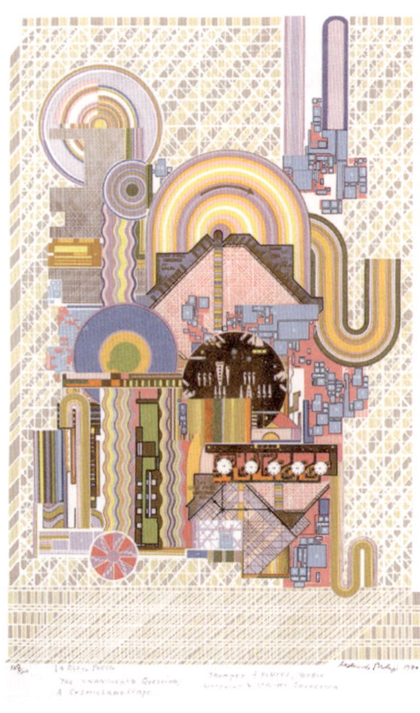

ii. Largo to Presto

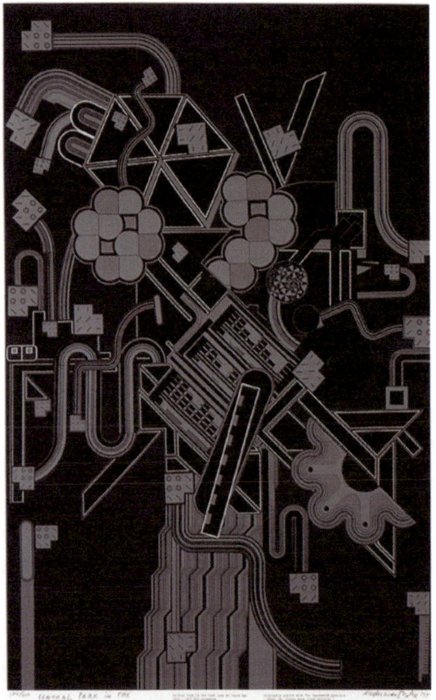

iii. Central Park in the Dark Some 40 Years Ago

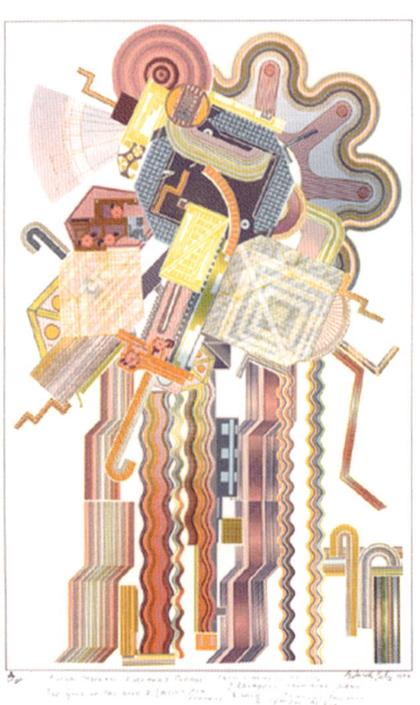

iv. Allegro Moderato Fireman's Parade

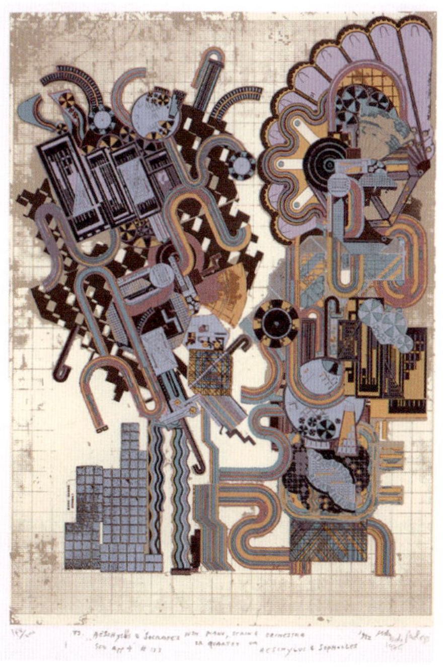

v. Aeschylus and Socrates

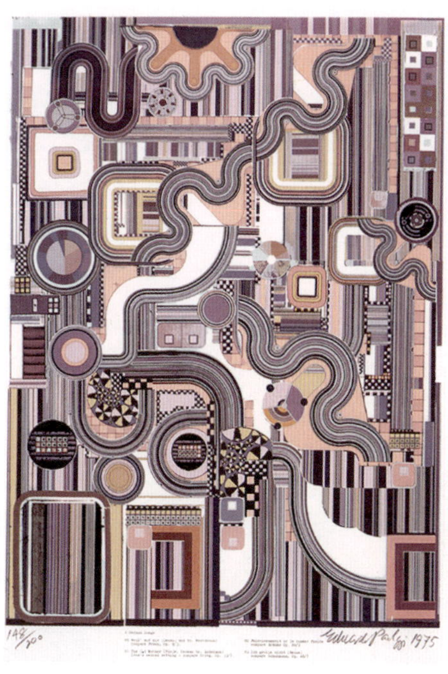

vii. Four German Songs

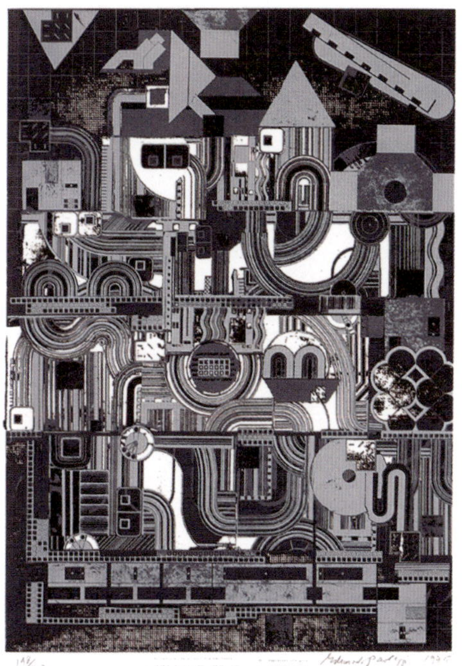

vi. From Early Italian Poets

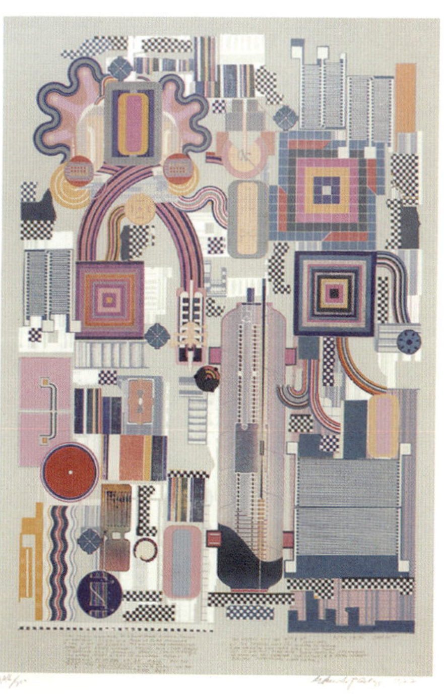

ix. Nettleton

Jack Smith

b.1928 England

Musical Painting Touching no.2
1992
oil on canvas
89.5 x 89.5 cm
Jack Smith, courtesy of Flowers, London

After leaving the Royal College of Art, Smith was associated with early 1950s realism and what came to be dubbed the 'Kitchen Sink' school. However, a decade later his work had become almost entirely abstract, partly through his admiration for Mondrian and also for Jackson Pollock, whose work he had seen in the 1958 exhibition at the Whitechapel. Another important influence in his work was the music of Anton Webern, Schönberg's pupil who also wrote music according to the 12-tone system. He also loved Erik Satie's music for its clarity and economy of expression, which he related to the inner necessity of nature. In his *Notes of Paintings* of 1965, Smith wrote:

'I think of my paintings as diagrams of an experience or sensation. The subject is very important. The sound of the subject, its noise or its silence, its intervals and its activity. When I talk about the sound of the music of the subject, I'm not always thinking in terms of a symphony, but groups of single notes. The closer the painting is to a diagram or a graph, the nearer it is to my intention. I like every mark to establish a fact in the most precise, economical way.'

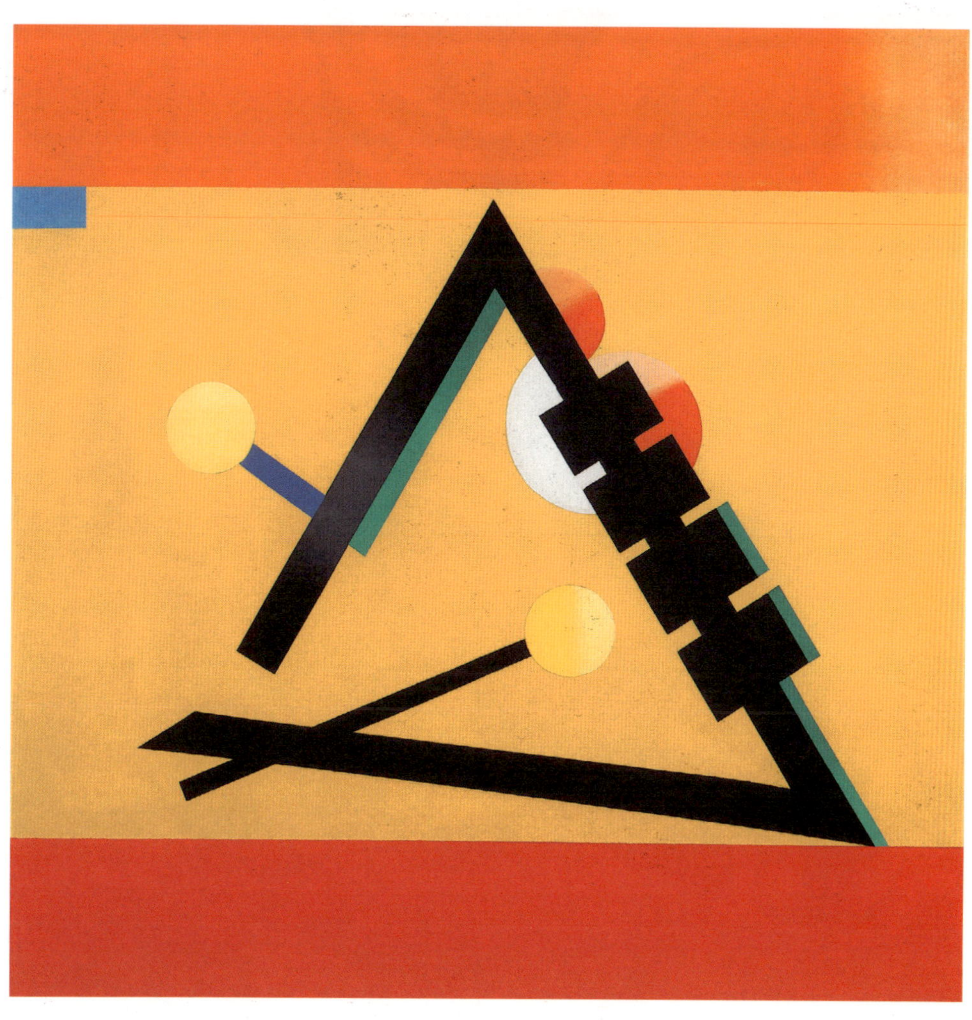

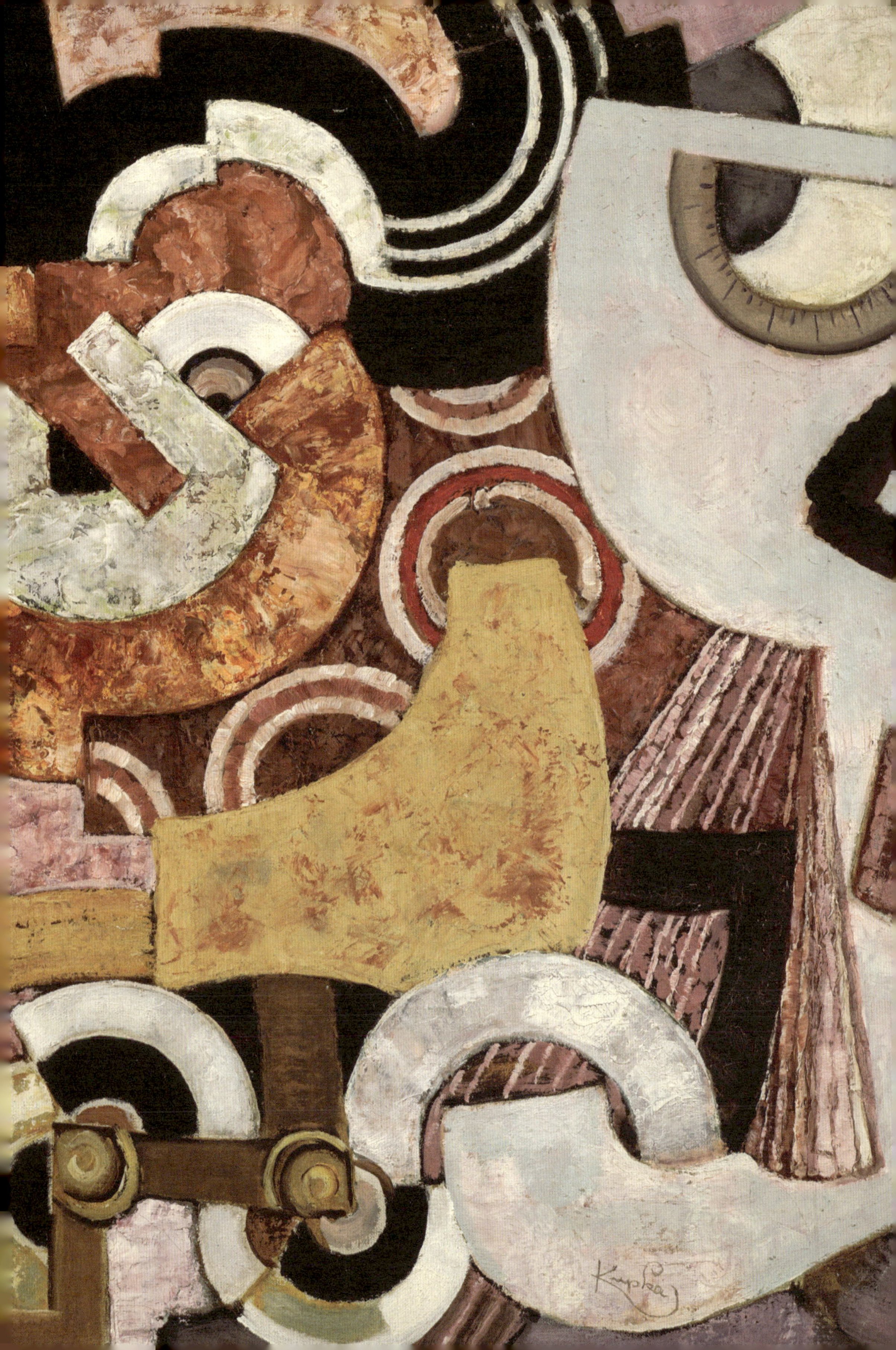

dance and jazz

'The eye was led with varying velocity from one group of colour gradations to the next. Simultaneously, and in contrast to the endless mutability of the smaller motifs, the image was dominated by a constant repetition of the right-angle theme, which droned like an incessant double-bass rhythm through a sprinkling of rapid arpeggios and lissom clarinet note.'

James Johnson Sweeney, in the catalogue of a posthumous exhibition of Mondrian's work, New York, 1948

The theme of dance in twentieth century art would be deserving of an exhibition in its own right, but it is worth noting that both ballet and popular dance and the music associated with it were an inspiration to many artists at the beginning of the century. Diaghilev's productions with the Ballets Russes combined modern music with set designs by avant-garde artists and provoked outrage with their revolutionary choreography, most notably with Stravinsky's *Rite of Spring* in 1913. Both these productions, and the craze for popular dance such as tango and ragtime which swept through the music-halls and cafes in the early 1900s, captured the imagination of many artists, particularly those associated with the Vorticist Group in London who viewed modern dance as a metaphor for modern living in its dynamism and rhythmic qualities.

For van Doesburg, van der Leck, Mondrian and other artists who were associated with the new art journal and movement De Stijl, founded in 1917, dance was not only a leisure pursuit, with van Doesburg and Mondrian in particular frequenting Dutch dance-halls, but also an important element in

František Kupka, Jazz Hot no. 1 (detail), 1935
oil on canvas, 60 x 92 cm
Centre Pompidou, National Museum of Modern Art,
Paris, gift of Eugenie Kupka in 1963

their work as a means of conveying the movement and essential rhythm of nature. Mondrian wanted to see 'Neo-Plasticism' (the group's principle of reducing painting to its basic elements of colour, line and form used in their purest state) realised in music, and in modern dance music and jazz, where the descriptive elements and emotions of melody are secondary to the rhythm, he recognised an equivalent to what they were trying to achieve.

In New York, Mondrian was entranced by the sights and sounds of the city, epitomised for him by boogie-woogie music. Although he strongly countered any suggestion that his paintings of this period were visual equivalents of boogie-woogie, or that painting could indeed be visual music, there is undoubtedly an increased syncopation and rhythmic quality to these works.

Jazz music in its many forms was a liberating influence on many artists from the 1920s onwards as it spread from America to Europe and Britain. In France, Kupka found inspiration in jazz to revitalise his paintings in the 1930s, and Matisse used jazz as a metaphor for improvisation in his 'cut-out' prints of 1947. Miró's paintings of the late 1940s onwards increasingly draw on music, associating jazz with the improvisatory techniques and creative freedom of Surrealist art and poetry.

For Davie, the experience of becoming a professional jazz musician after the war gave him a particular liberation which informed his active painting technique of 'the joys of spontaneous improvisation, the losing of the ME, and the active audience participation, the fire of the heart and the belly, and the marvellous abandon.'

dance and jazz

catalogue entries

David Bomberg

b.1890 England–d.1957 England

Russian Ballet Lithographs
1919
booklet, 6 lithographs, 6 pages text, sewn paper binding
14 x 22 cm
The University of East Anglia Collection of Abstract
and Constructivist Art, Architecture and Design

Although Bomberg's six lithographs of the Ballets Russes are dated
1919, they are based on drawings he made prior to World War I
and exhibit the stylistic attributes of the Vorticist group to which
Bomberg was allied but not a member. The booklet was published
by Hendersons, known as The Bomb Shop, in Charing Cross Road,
London. Each lithograph was accompanied by a brief poem in
blank verse written by Bomberg and printed by the artist himself.
Bomberg wrote of his Vorticist style works, 'I appeal to a sense of
form. In some of the work ... I completely abandon Naturalism and
Tradition. I am searching for an intenser expression. In other works
... where I use Naturalistic Form, I have stripped it of all irrelevant
matter ... My object is the construction of Pure Form.'

Serge Diaghilev's company performed in London from 1911, their
productions including Stravinsky's *Rite of Spring* choreographed
by Nijinsky, which premiered in 1913. When first performed in
Paris earlier the same year it caused outrage for its percussive
and intense music matched by the barbaric and sexual dancing
of the troupe, a radical departure from classical ballet. As such,
the performance was an inspiration to many artists who tried to
capture its elemental qualities and rhythm in their own work.

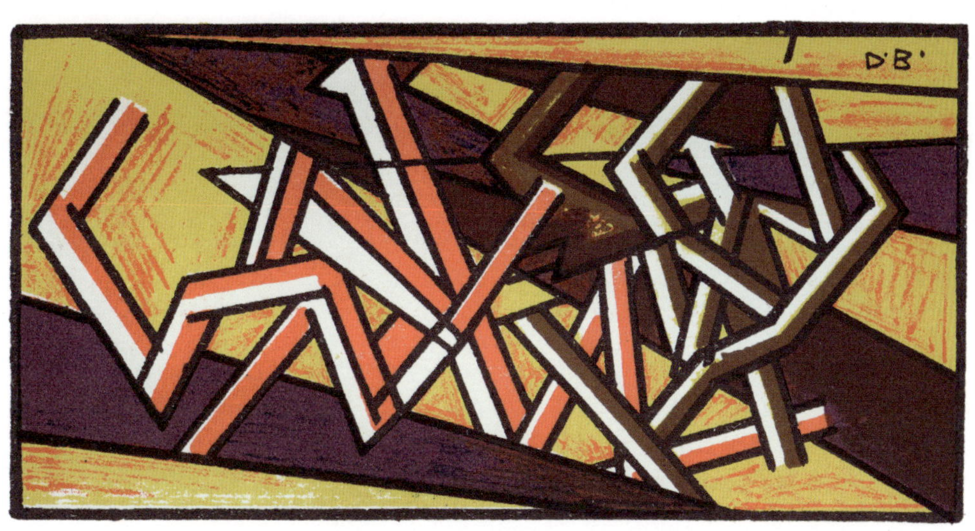

Natalia Goncharova

b.1881 Russia–d.1962 Russia

Portrait of Diaghilev
1919
lithograph on paper
49.4 x 31.3 cm
University of East Anglia Collection of Abstract
and Constructivist Art, Architecture and Design

Goncharova trained as a sculptor at Moscow School of Painting,
Sculpture and Architecture from 1898–1902 but started to
exhibit paintings from 1900. Her first contact with Diaghilev,
the impresario of the Ballets Russes, came in 1900 when he
organised an exhibition of works by Russian artists at the Salon
d'Automne in Paris to include work by Goncharova and her fellow
student and future husband, Mikhail Larionov. In 1914, Diaghilev
commissioned Goncharova to design sets and costumes for
the Paris production of Rimsky-Korsakov's opera *Le Coq d'Or*,
choreographed by Michel Fokine, and she chose to base her
designs on Constructivist principles, where the set became part
of the action. Diaghilev deemed the designs such a success that
he continued to commission modern artists to work with him,
inviting Larionov to create designs for his production of
Rimsky-Korsakov's *Soleil de Nuit* the following year.

After this venture into theatre design, Goncharova continued
to paint, alternating between naturalistic and abstract styles.
This portrait of Diaghilev was commissioned for a book *L'Art
Decoratif Theatre Moderne* published in Paris in 1919.

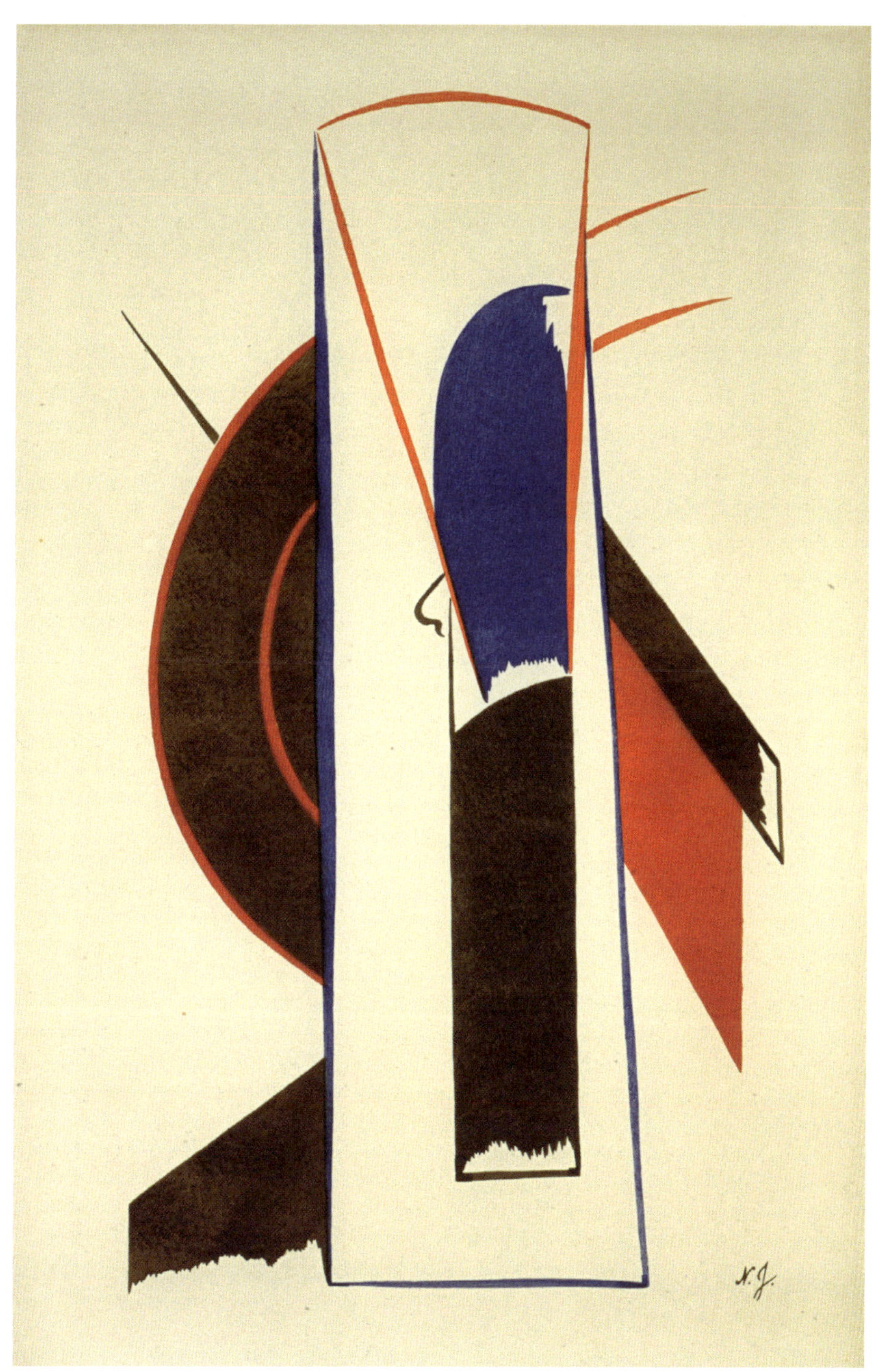

Robert Arthur Wilson

b.1884 England–d.1975 England

Dance
1919
watercolour over pencil on paper
15 x 10 cm
Private collection

On his return from Paris, Wilson was associated with, and exhibited alongside, the vanguard of British art. From 1919–20 he exhibited at the Allied Artists' Exhibition, the London Group, and the Decorative Art Group and also became involved with the Rebel Art Centre that had been established by Percy Wyndham-Lewis. It was not just the Ballets Russes that influenced artists at the beginning of the twentieth century but also popular dance and the music associated with it, such as ragtime. Wyndham-Lewis himself had been commissioned in 1912 to decorate the interior of the cabaret theatre club 'The Golden Calf' with designs featuring semi-abstract dancing figures, which in turn were based on his earlier paintings such as *Kermesse* of 1912, now lost but sketches and preparatory works survive which indicate the rhythmic movement he was aiming to capture.

This design by Wilson is very much in the same style as Lewis' figures and shows his concern to express dynamic movement through the juxtaposition of complementary colours.

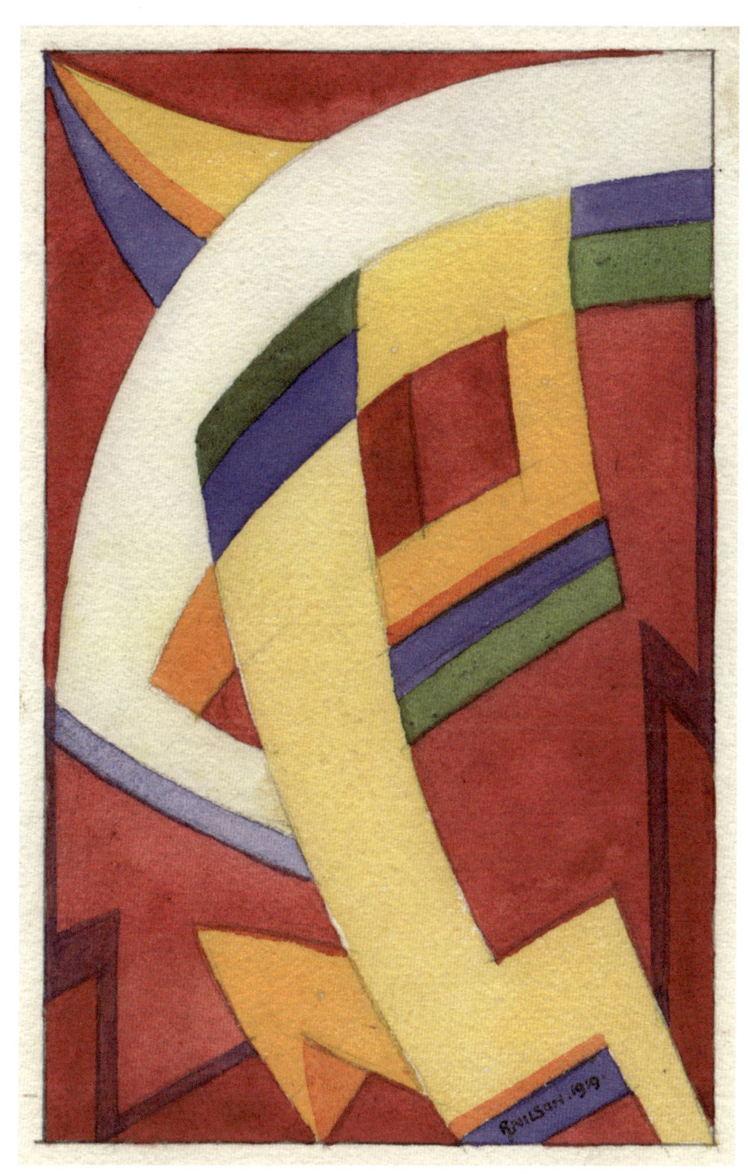

Bart van der Leck

b.1876 Holland–d.1958 Holland

Watercolour No. 390
1916–32
watercolour on paper
34 x 27 cm
University of East Anglia Collection of Abstract
and Constructivist Art, Architecture and Design

Due to its neutrality in World War I, Dutch artists were not able to
leave Holland after 1914 and were therefore isolated from the rest of
the art world and its current capital, Paris. The artist van Doesburg
wanted to establish an art movement and journal in his homeland
and began looking for other artists with whom to collaborate. In 1915
he met Mondrian who, although he had moved to Paris, had been
visiting Holland on the outbreak of war and was staying in the artistic
community of Laren, which included van der Leck amongst others.
These artists and the architect Gerrit Rietveld formed the core of
De Stijl, whose artistic tenets they called 'Neo-Plasticism', or the
non-figurative arrangement of right-angled lines and primary colour
to express a utopian ideal of spiritual harmony and order.

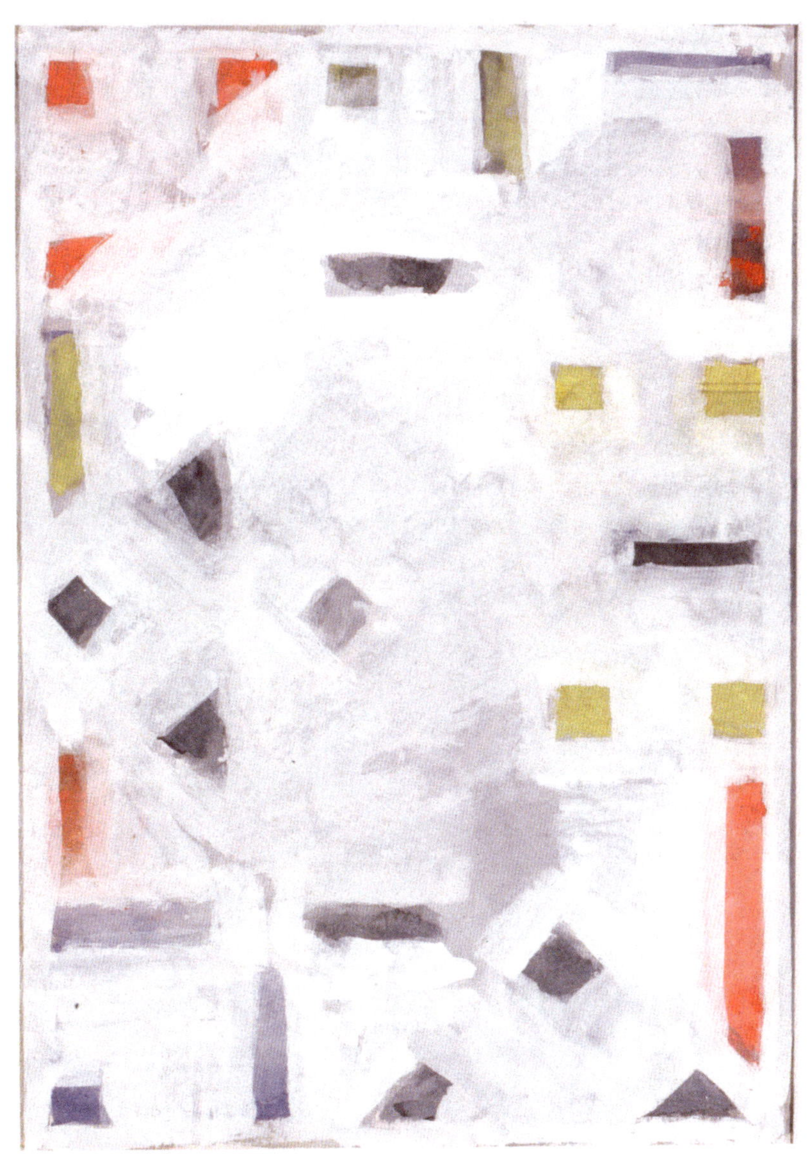

Theo van Doesburg

b.1883 Holland–d.1931 Switzerland

Composition in Grey (Rag-Time)
1919
oil on canvas
96.5 x 59.1 cm
Peggy Guggenheim, Venice
(Solomon R. Guggenheim Foundation, NY)

Van Doesburg shared with Mondrian a love of dance, regarding
it as 'the most dynamic expression of life and it is therefore the
most important subject for a pure plastic art.' He composed a
series of works based on dance from 1916 in which he explored the
potential of rendering movement and rhythm in pure pictorial form.
Composition in Grey (Rag-Time) was probably based on a drawing
of a couple dancing which he then reduced to its essence according
to the principles of De Stijl. In 1921 van Doesburg took this painting
to Weimar where he taught at the Bauhaus. The work hung in his
studio and was used to illustrate the principles of Neo-Plastic art
to his pupils.

It is likely that the ragtime piece that inspired van Doesburg's
painting is a piano composition by Erik Satie. Nelly van Doesburg
recalls her first meeting with her husband when, on learning that she
was a pianist, he enthusiastically extolled the music of Stravinsky,
Schönberg and Satie: 'He was especially mad about Satie.
I had not even heard the name, but I dared not confess it...
I just mumbled that modern music was extremely hard to play.
The next day he sent me a package of music by Erik Satie, with -
among other things - "Ragtime" and "Pièce en forme de poires" etc.'

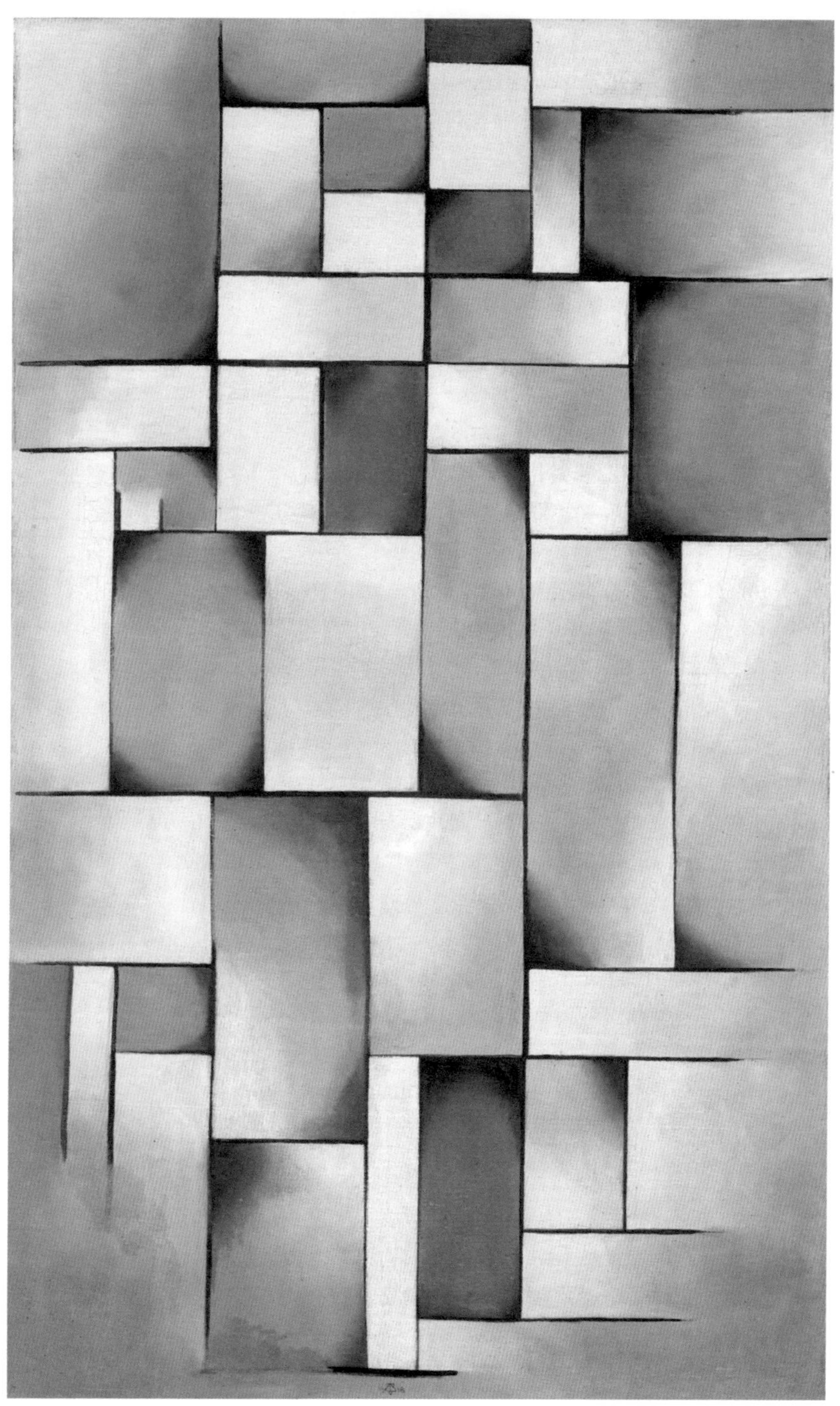

Sophie Taeuber-Arp

b.1889 Switzerland–d.1943 Switzerland

Collage
c.1928
paper collage with watercolour
30.8 x 21.7 cm
University of East Anglia Collection of Abstract
and Constructivist Art, Architecture and Design

Taeuber-Arp studied applied arts in Germany and was later
appointed Professor of Textile Design and Techniques at the School
of Arts and Crafts in Zürich where she lived during the war. She also
studied dancing with Rudolf von Laban and became involved with
the Zürich Dadaists through her husband Jean, whom she married
in 1922. Her interest in performance and her skills in craft and
design led her to try to capture movement in her work, in particular
in collages she produced in collaboration with her husband that
attempted to replicate the choreography of Laban.

In 1926, Taeuber-Arp, Arp and van Doesburg were commissioned
to redecorate the interior of a large restaurant and nightclub, the
Café de l'Aubette in Strasbourg (now re-constructed). The designs
included wall paintings, reliefs, stained glass and light fittings,
united in rhythmically spaced rectangles of colours. This experience
affected Taueber-Arp's future work and in the following decade
she produced a series of reliefs based on the same basic forms
of rectangles and circles in harmonious arrangements, and then
designed the house she shared with Jean at Meudon-Val Fleury
near Paris.

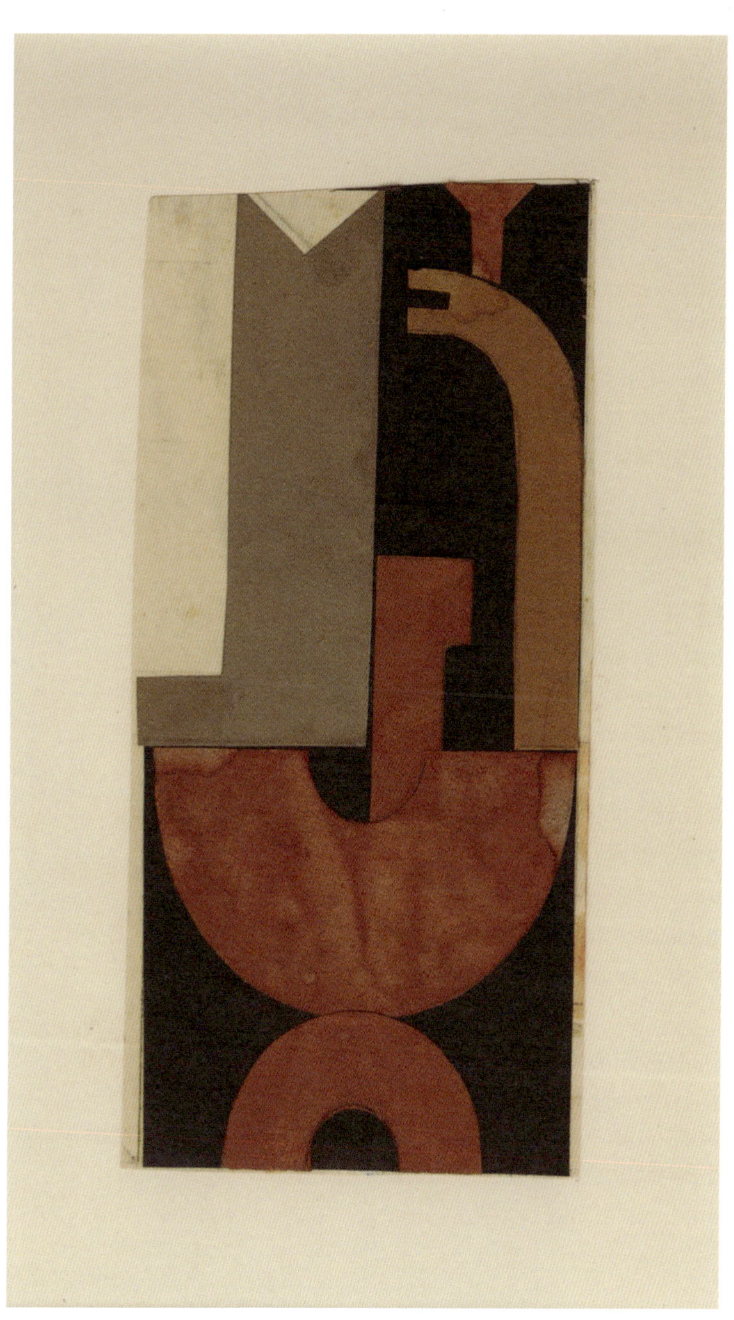

César Domela

b.1900 Holland–d.1992 France

Lithographic Print
1926, replica by the artist, 1970
lithograph on paper
75.5 x 52 cm
University of East Anglia Collection of Abstract
and Constructivist Art, Architecture and Design

In 1924 Domela became an active member of De Stijl, shortly
before van Doesburg and Mondrian fell out due to the former's
introduction of diagonal line and forms into his paintings.
Van Doesburg had developed the theory of 'Elementarism'
following his teachings at the Bauhaus where he came under
the influence of Moholy-Nagy and Russian Constructivism.
In his Elementarist works he sought to exploit the quality of
time by rejecting the static nature of the juxtaposition of the
horizontal and the vertical. Mondrian felt this was a rejection
of his Neo-Plastic principles and the essence of his paintings,
which he believed already contained movement and dynamism
in their configuration.

Initially Domela became a disciple of Mondrian but, once Mondrian
had left the group in 1925, he became more influenced by van
Doesburg and began to compose paintings based on the diagonal.
This lithograph is a replica of one of Domela's Neo-Plastic paintings
of 1926. Later he worked in Berlin where he made Elementarist
constructions out of Perspex, metal and painted surfaces and then
returned to Paris where he founded the *Review Plastique* with
Hans Arp and Sophie Taueber-Arp.

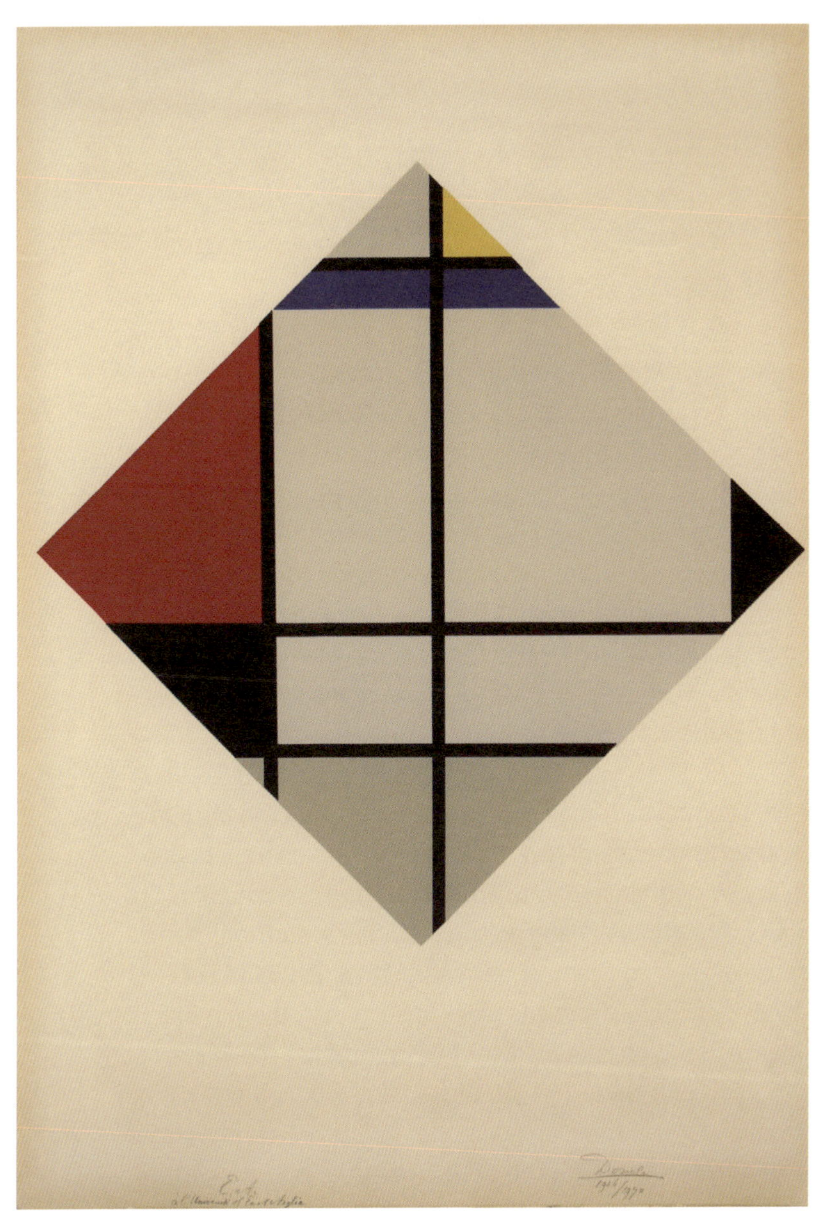

Piet Mondrian

b.1872 Holland–d.1944 USA

Composition with Yellow, Blue and Red
1937–42
oil on canvas
72.7 x 69.2 cm
Tate, purchased 1964

In September 1938 Mondrian left Paris for London on the invitation of Ben Nicholson as the situation in Europe worsened. His friend Harry Holtzman obtained a visa to the United States on his behalf and, in 1940 Mondrian sent his paintings ahead of him and departed for New York. On his first night in Manhattan, Holtzman played the dance-loving artist some boogie-woogie records to which Mondrian responded, in his broken English, 'Enormous! Enormous!' He would spend time in Greenwich Village cafés listening to the music of Albert Ammons, Pete Johnson, Meade 'Lux' Lewis and other greats of the American wartime music scene.

In the 'transatlantic' paintings that Mondrian worked on both in Europe and subsequently in New York, a profound change began to take place. Mondrian began to add blocks and bars of colour to these works, sometimes changing the black lines, shifting them, adding more or making them longer and thinner. He would often release blocks of colour from the black lines, giving them more independence in the picture plane. When comparing this painting to a photograph of it taken in Mondrian's Paris studio in 1937, it has two additional vertical lines, an additional yellow area and a larger red area. In an interview with the critic Sidney Janis in 1941, Mondrian said that the new colour elements gave his paintings 'more boogie-woogie'. However, he also stated that his work was not to be seen as an interpretation of music, despite the fact that the Valentine Gallery, where he exhibited, offered their audience the opportunity to experience his paintings to the sound of boogie-woogie music.

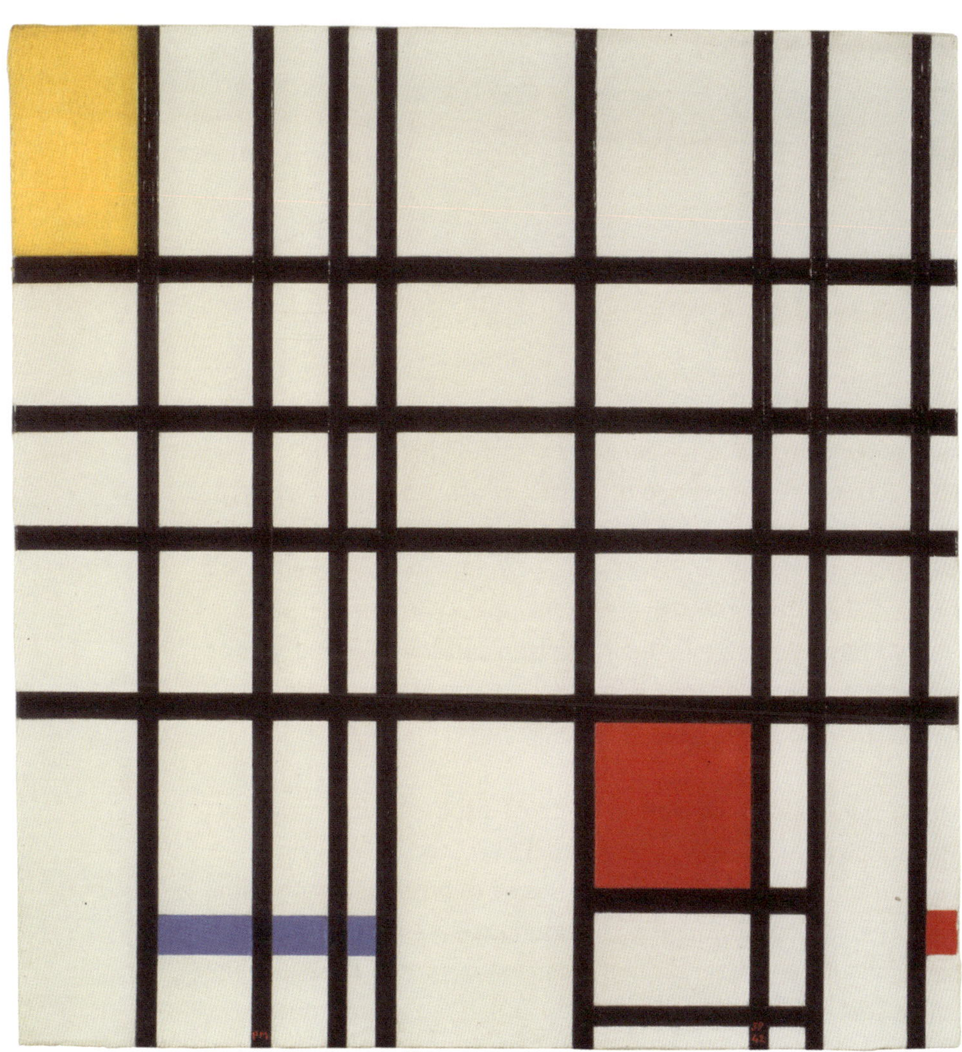

František Kupka

b.1871 Czechoslovakia (Czech Republic)–d.1957 France

Jazz Hot no. 1
1935
oil on canvas
60 x 92 cm
Centre Pompidou, National Museum of Modern Art,
Paris, gift of Eugenie Kupka in 1963

In his later life, after ill health and a period of crisis in his work,
Kupka found inspiration again in his involvement with the
Abstraction-Création group of artists, which started in Paris in
1931 and of which he was a founding member. The group included
Mondrian, van Doesburg and Georges Vantongerloo from De Stijl,
Kandinsky and major British artists including Barbara Hepworth,
Henry Moore, John Nash, Ben Nicholson and John Piper. It was an
extremely influential group in promoting abstract art during the
five years of its existence.

Kupka still found music a vital source of inspiration in his work.
Towards the end of the 1920s, he had executed an increasing
number of paintings based on the theme of jazz and 'machinism',
which he associated together to emphasise the dynamism of his
paintings. They contain allusions to piano keys and utilise jagged
forms that emulate the rhythmic syncopations of jazz music.
In the two works entitled *Jazz Hot*, both executed in 1935, Kupka
includes mechanical elements such as gears and cogwheels that
are intended to describe a perpetual motion in the works and
give an impression of movement and speed.

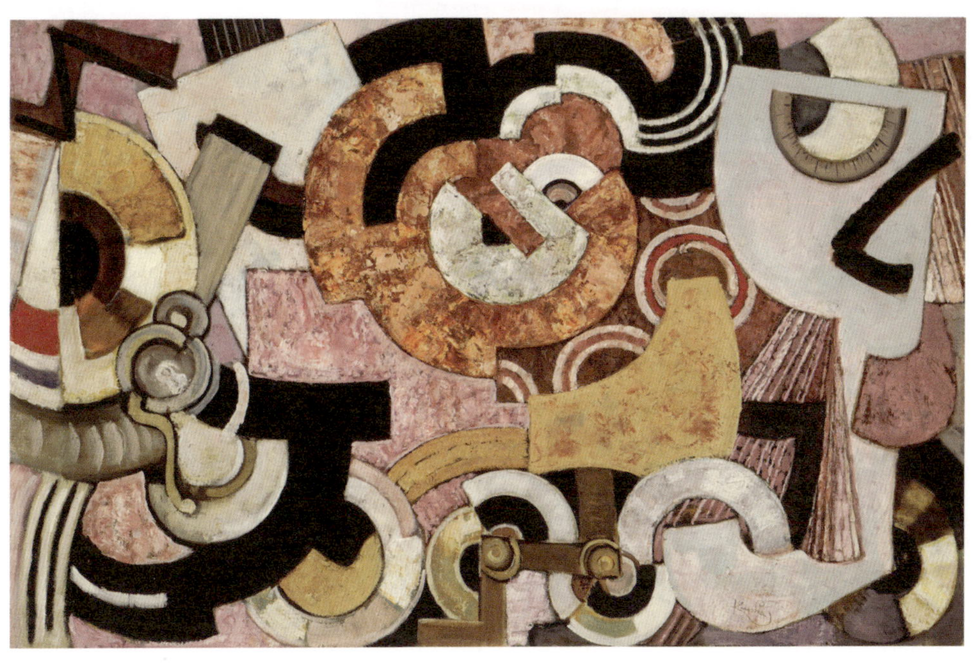

Henri Matisse

b.1869 France–d.1954 France

Jazz
c.1947
book
42.5 x 37.2 x 4.5 cm
Victoria and Albert Museum

In 1943, while convalescing from a serious operation, Matisse once more returned to the medium of collage and 'cut-outs' as a means of expression, feeling it to be more compatible with his now deteriorating eyesight. The resulting suite of twenty images, translated into prints by the stencilling of gouache paint, became known as *Jazz*, considered one of his most ambitious and important works. The themes in *Jazz* fall into four categories: the music hall and circus; mythology and legends; allegories symbolising World War Two; and memories from his life and travels. Of *Le Tobogan (The Toboggan)*, among the first images completed, Matisse wrote 'He who loves, flies, runs, and rejoices; he is free and nothing holds him back.'

For Matisse, the title *Jazz* signified 'chromatic and rhythmic improvisation' and 'rhythm and meaning.' The artist wrote to a friend in late 1947, 'There are wonderful things in real jazz, the talent for improvisation, the liveliness, the being at one with the audience.' Matisse enhanced the feeling of syncopation in the book by breaking its flow with rhythmically ordered sequences of text. As the Curator of Prints at the Museum of Modern Art in New York commented, 'Few artists have added to their pictorial work words that have been equally important in form and meaning. The precise equilibrium of these elements in *Jazz* is Matisse's unique achievement. The dark rhythms, roiling counterpoint, happy staccatos, and jolting dissonances of this *Jazz* will sound forever. Matisse has taught the eye to hear.'

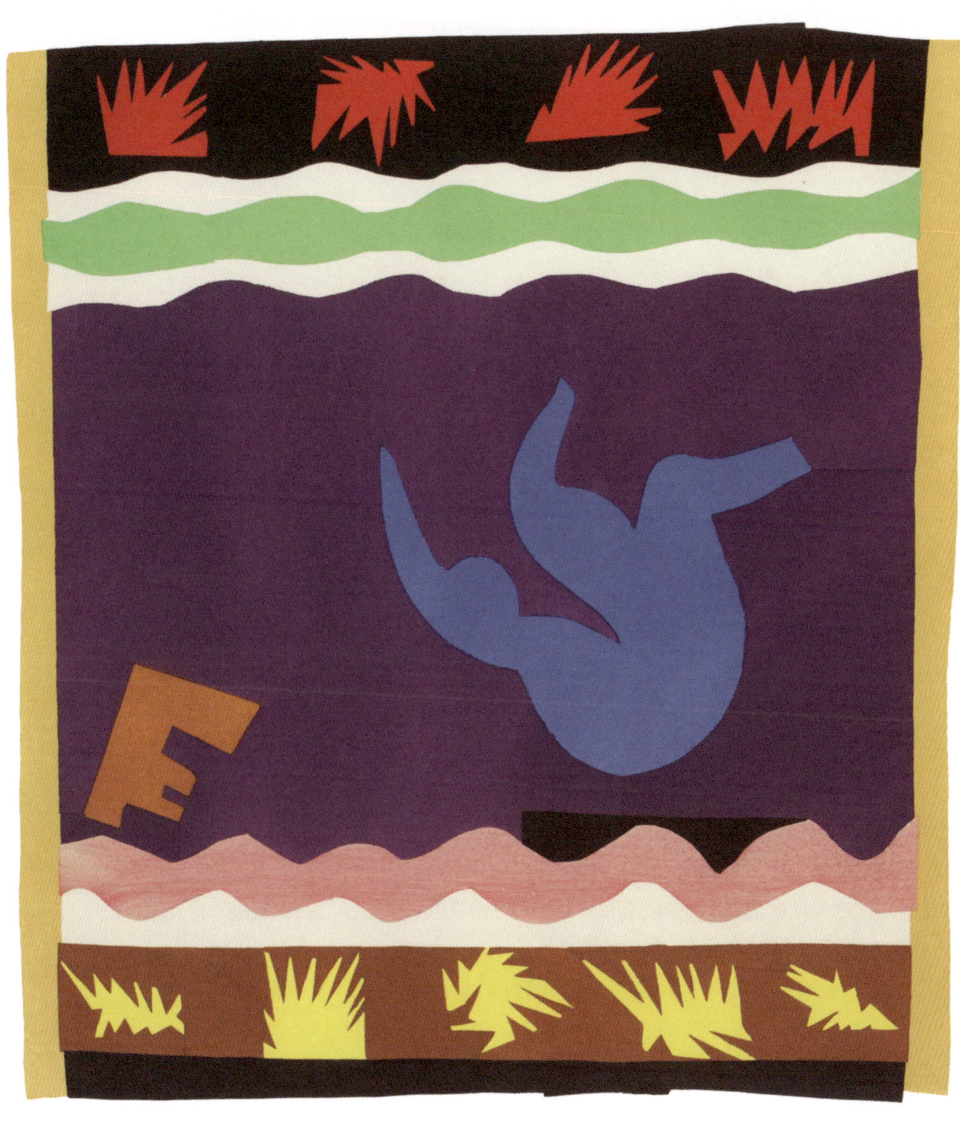

John Tunnard

b.1900 England–d.1971 England

Frequency
1943
gouache on paper
35 x 55 cm
Private collection, Professor Brian Whitton

'One day a marvellous man in a highly elaborate tweed coat walked into the gallery. He looked a little like Groucho Marx. He was as animated as a jazz-band leader, which he turned out to be. He showed us his gouaches, which were as musical as Kandinsky's, as delicate as Klee's, and as gay as Miro's.'

This is Peggy Guggenheim's account of her first meeting with Tunnard at her gallery Guggenheim Jeune in New York in 1939. Tunnard had been the drummer in a four-piece band founded whilst studying at the Royal College of Art from 1919–23 and during the 1920s he continued to play as a drummer in semi-professional bands. He had exhibited with Mondrian whilst the Dutch artist was living in London in the late 1930s and shared with him a passion for jazz and dancing. According to an article in 'Everybody's Weekly' in 1939, 'Invariably Tunnard paints to an accompaniment of swing music – the hotter the record the better the inspiration flows.'

Tunnard's passion for jazz music continued throughout his life. In the 1950s he was renowned for his jazz parties where he would frequently perform a 'soft-shoe' dance or a top hat and cane routine for the entertainment of his guests.

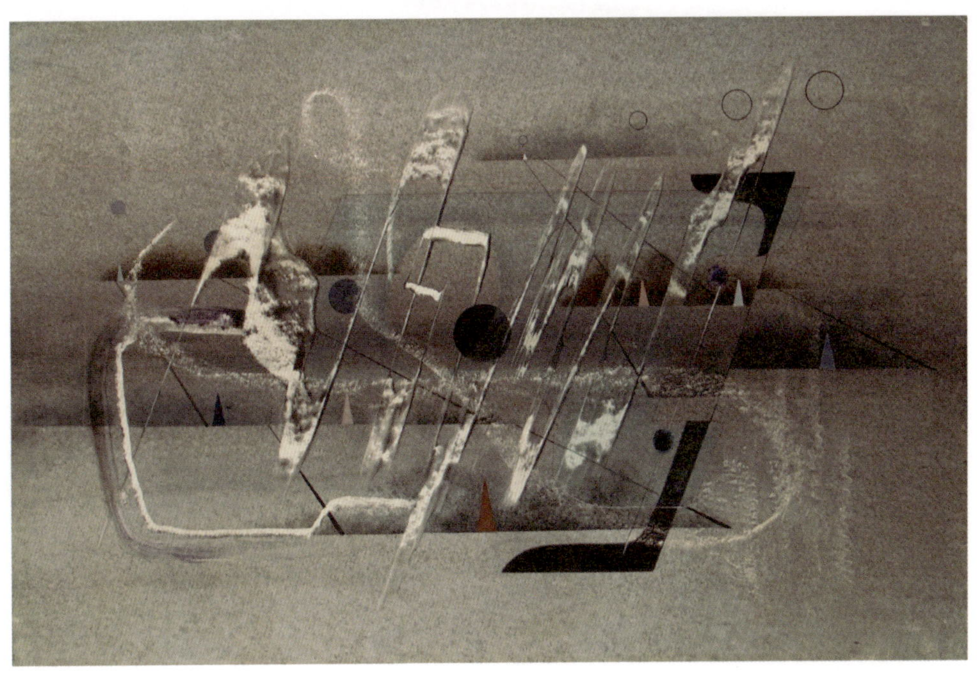

John Tunnard

b.1900 England–d.1971 England

Ascension
1945
gouache on paper
33 x 55 cm
Private collection, Professor Brian Whitton

From 1938 onwards Tunnard was introducing a sense of depth to his abstract works and incorporating elaborate stringed elements that had the appearance of musical staves or guitar strings.

Julian Trevelyan reviewed these works for an article in the *London Bulletin* in 1939: 'Another thing Tunnard does is to make musical instruments, but musical instruments that won't make a sound! They are tightly strung with delicate wires in red and blue; sometimes on of the strings lies broken and wiggly across the whole work. Occasionally he even leaves a bow beside to tempt the meddlesome amateur and then shuts it all away in a glass box, so that the music can only be apprehended with the eye. And to my mind music, like children, should be seen and not heard.'

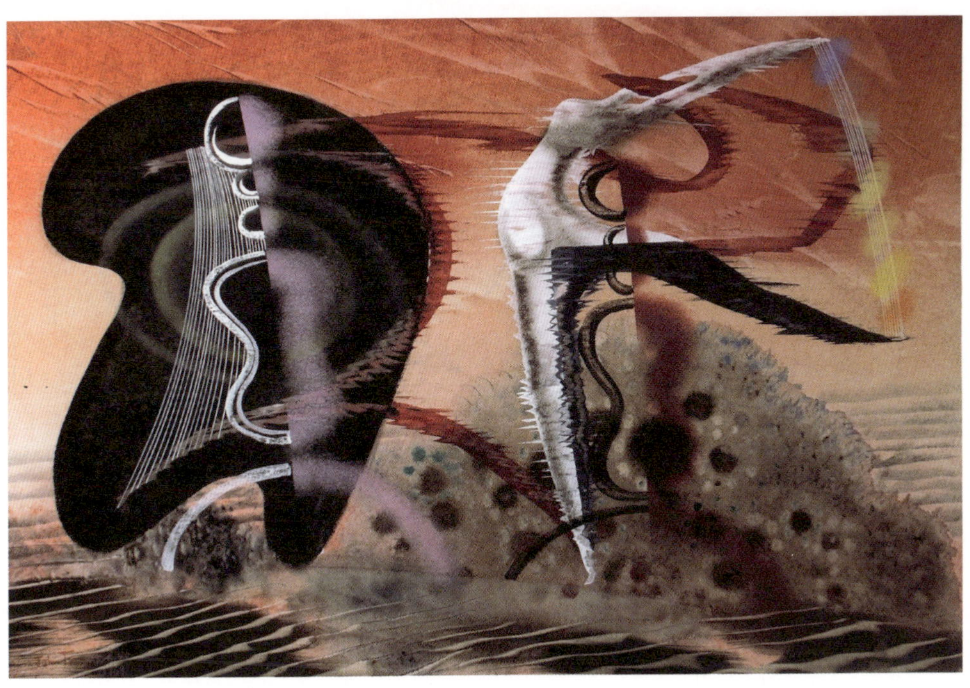

Alan Davie

b.1920 Scotland

Jingling Space
1950
oil on masonite
122 x 152.5 cm
Collection Scottish National
Gallery of Modern Art

Davie studied piano at an early age and was passionately
interested in playing all kinds of musical instruments. He went
to the Edinburgh College of Art from 1938–40 but became
disillusioned when his tutors told him he would find painting
difficult. He spent much of his time learning the saxophone and
the clarinet and, after he left college and following World War II,
he became a professional jazz musician for a time, playing with
groups such as the Tommy Sampson Orchestra in London. Despite
enjoying considerable success, Davie took up painting once more
after being awarded a travel scholarship in 1948. He went to Venice
where he met Peggy Guggenheim who was exhibiting works by
Jackson Pollock and the New York abstract expressionists, whose
improvisatory techniques were another vital influence in his work.
He described his method of work in the following way:

*'It's never the case in my work of having an idea first and
then putting it on paper. The idea comes out of working. I do
a whole series of drawings on an idea which has presented
itself. I might do about twenty variations using that idea and
developing it. It is very much like improvising on a piano –
sitting down and playing, an idea will appear out of putting
one note against another, which leads to other notes and,
before you know where you are, a melodic line has appeared
and a harmonic structure presents itself.'*

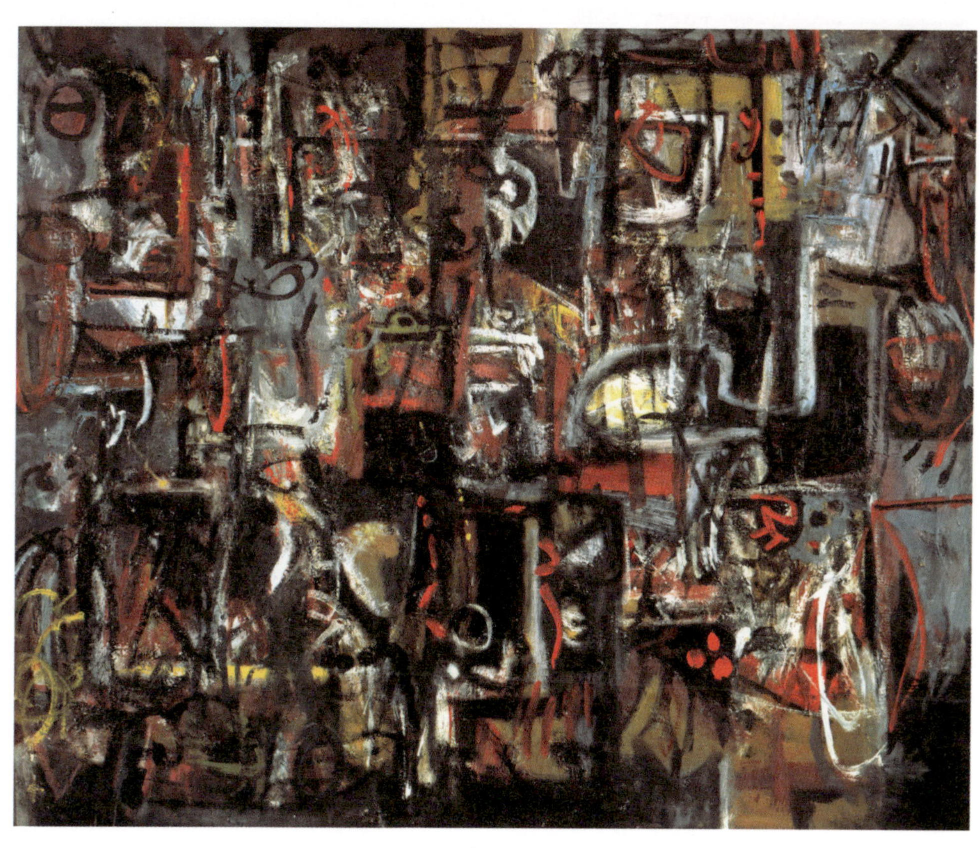

Alan Davie

b.1920 Scotland

Jazz by Moonlight no. 3
1966
oil on canvas
48 x 60 cm
Private collection, courtesy of Goldmark Gallery, Uppingham

In his essay 'Notes on Colour' of 1992, Davie wrote about the affinity between colour and music: 'Perhaps colour is impossible to talk about. Colour is like scent – indescribable; or like a chord struck on a harp in the darkness. The mysterious element of colour, perhaps the most important element in my painting (and indeed my life) is something utterly magical to me, filling my life and surrounding me with wonder... The colours must sing together very much like the notes in music; a mingling in wave lengths; in light as in sound... A certain conjunction of colours cannot be of real meaning until there is a working of inner movement and subtle interplay of space and proportion.'

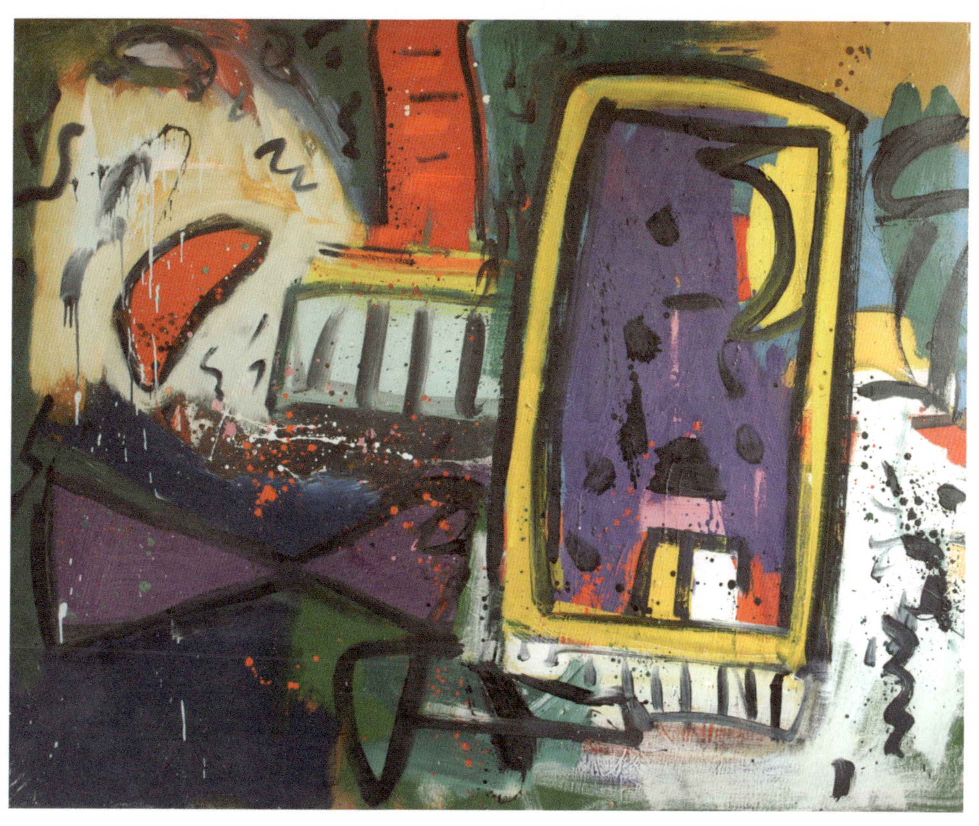

Joan Miró

b.1893 Spain–d.Mallorca 1983

Sonatine 1
1966
etching and aquatint on paper, edition 19/30
31 x 24.5 cm
Private collection, England

There is an oft-quoted remark the Spanish artist Miró made about his work: 'I try to apply colour like words that shape poems, like notes that shape music. What I am looking for… is an immobile movement, something which would be the equivalent of what is called the eloquence of silence, or what St. John of the Cross, I think it was, described with the term "mute music".'

In the 1920s when Miró was living in Paris, he immersed himself in the artistic milieu, enjoying in particular the company of Surrealist poets, writers and artists such as André Breton, Paul Eluard, Michel Leiris and André Masson. His inspiration was the world of memory, fantasy and dreams, often generated through 'automatic' techniques of spontaneous drawing, which can be likened to the improvisation of free jazz. In the 1940s, Miró drew much more on music as inspiration for his work, ascribing it the same role that poetry had played earlier. He wished his paintings, 'might be invested with a high poetic and musical quality, executed without any apparent effort, like bird song, the beginning of a new world or the return to a purer world without any dramatic quality and with nothing theatrical about them.'

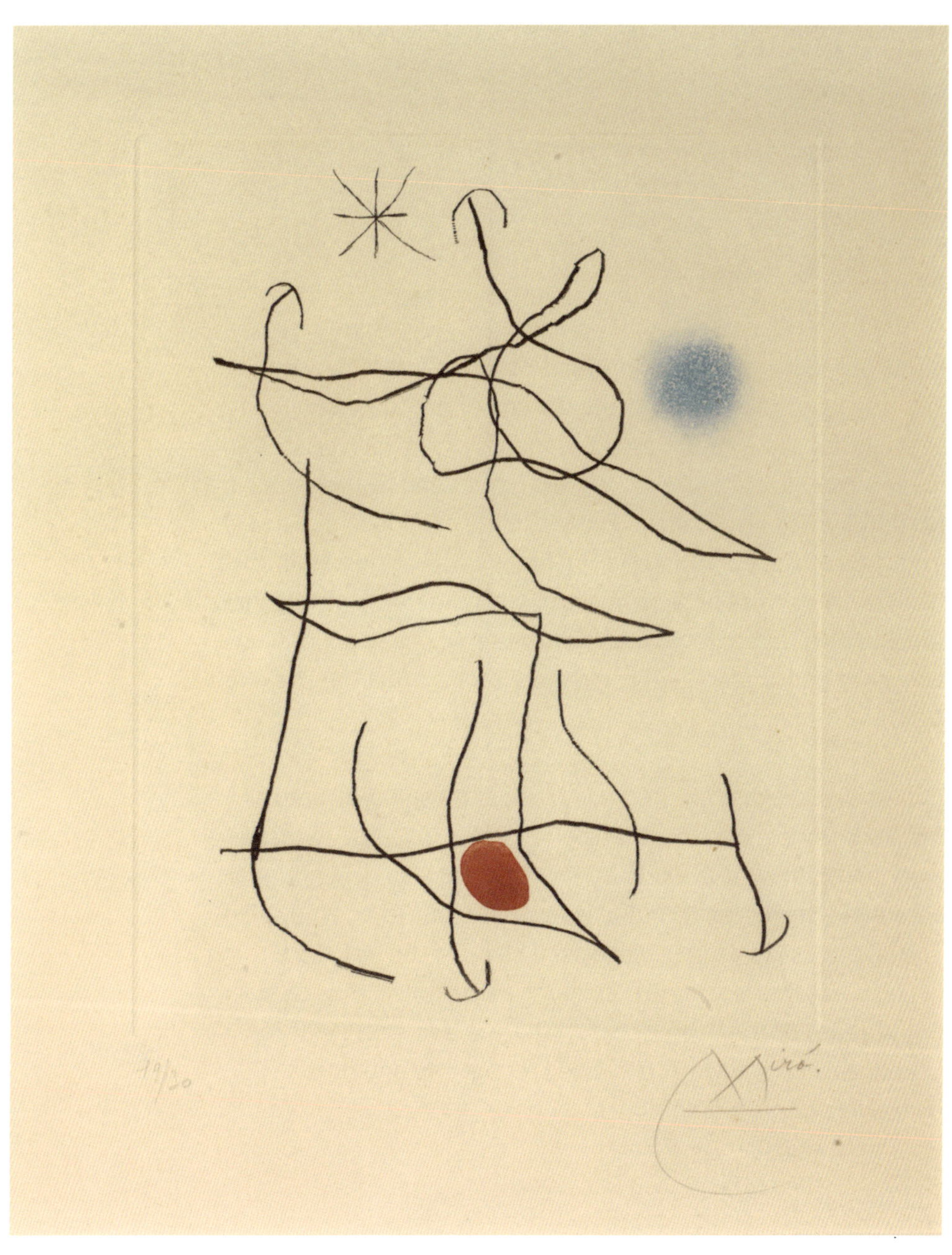

Harvey Daniels

b.1936 England

Lime to Orange
1991
acrylic on canvas
61 x 41 cm
Private Collection, England

Born in London, and with a long and continuing association with
Brighton where he taught at the College of Art (now University
of Brighton) since 1958, Daniels' work has often been related to
music, and especially jazz, by writers, critics and historians such as
Norbert Lynton and Michael Tucker. In the catalogue of Daniels'
exhibition at the Canaletto Gallery in 1965, the art historian John
Boulton Smith, making a comparison with the music of Matthew
Arnold wrote, 'A contemporary composer who was good; who
was witty and modern and could write tunes! I feel like this about
Mr Daniels's prints'.

Daniels himself has commented, 'Music is most important to
my work – not just in the listening but in the attempt to make
work that is musical in itself. By this, I don't mean descriptive or
schematic, and certainly not as a response, but as an equivalent.
The brightness of a viridian against a black or the structure using a
circle or a row of dots is just as much a part of the musicality as is
the vibrancy of the overall colour. There is also a sense of fun which
I need as a corrective. This is often recognised and noted
by viewers of my work.'

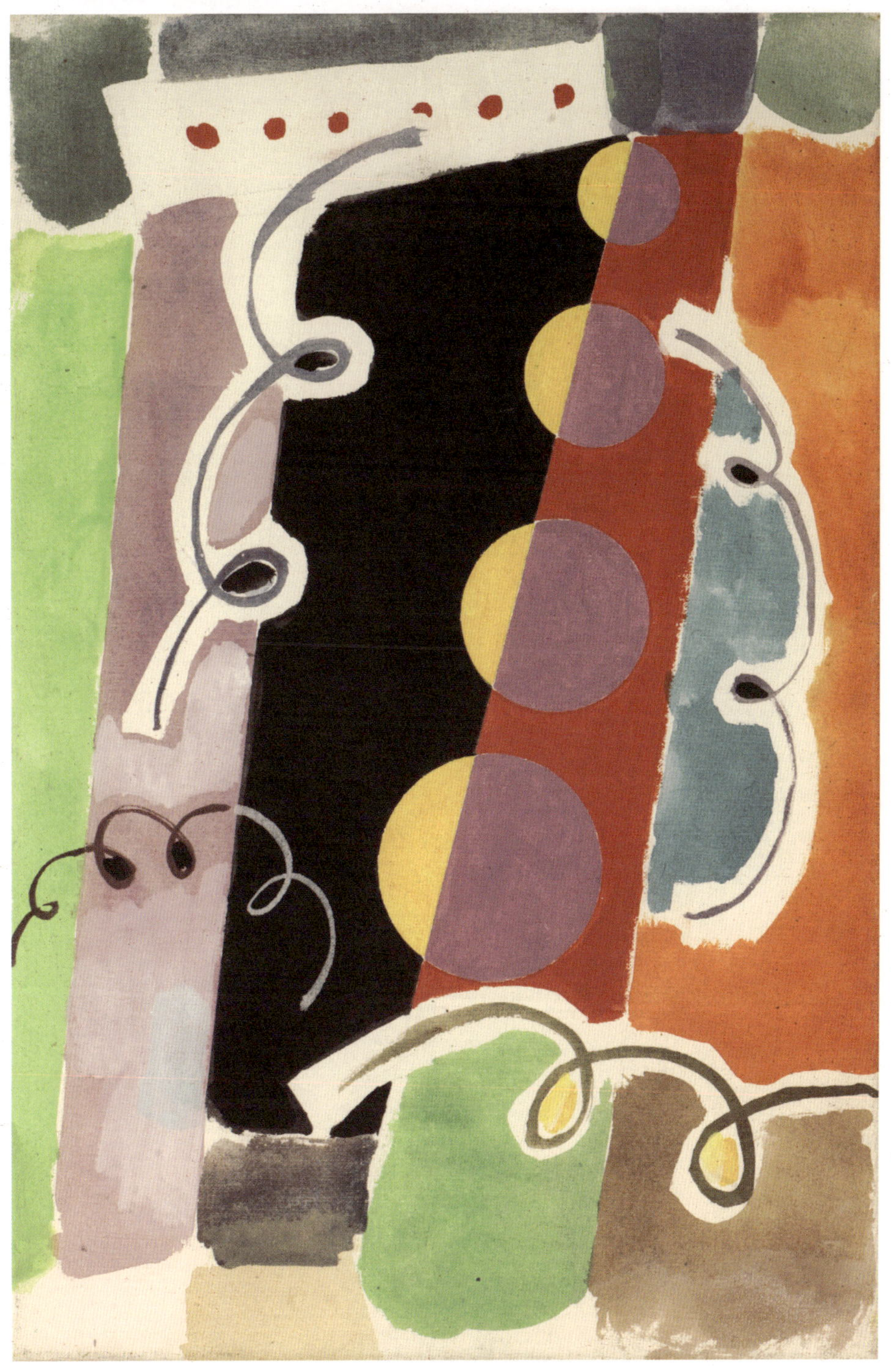

glossary of musical terms and select bibliography

Atonal

The term used to describe music which avoids the use of a central (tonic) note and allows the use of all 12 notes available on a keyboard. This means that **pitches** which are traditionally avoided or resolved in **tonal** music are liberated in atonal music. This type of music often involves the placing together of notes that jar or clash, resulting in a higher level of **dissonance**.

Bar

The division of music into short rhythmic (metrical) units, often 2, 3, or 4 beats long. Synonymous with the American term 'measure'.

Chord

A group of notes sounding simultaneously, creating **harmony** (colour).

Chromaticism

A chromatic scale is one in which all 12 semi-tones of a particular musical scale are played in sequence. Chromatic means 'colourful' and chromaticism is the effect achieved by extensive use of the notes of the musical scale interspersed with unrelated pitches of the chromatic scale.

Chromaticism and increased use of the chromatic scale became more widely used in the last half of the nineteenth century, especially in Wagner's operas such as 'Tristan and Isolde'.

Concerto

From the 17th century onward, the term used to describe an extended piece of music in which a solo instrument or instruments contrast with an orchestral ensemble.

Concerto Grosso

An orchestral form, especially popular in the 17th and 18th centuries, featuring the contrasting lines of a small group of players (the concertino) and the remainder of the ensemble (the ripieno). Bach's Brandenburg Concertos No. 1, 2, and 4 are concerti grossi.

Consonance

A concordant or agreeable combination of notes. The term which describes the essential feature of the clarity and perceived purity heard in **tonal** music. When chords do not fit into an accepted **harmony**, they are said to be unstable or **dissonant** (see dissonance).

Counterpoint

The relationship between two or more voices (musical lines) that are independent in contour and rhythm, but interdependent in **harmony**.
By definition, **chords** (harmony) occur when two or more voices sound simultaneously; counterpoint focuses on melodic interaction rather than the harmonic effects generated when melodic strands sound together.

Diatonic

Notes that occur naturally in a standard major or minor scale.

Dissonance

The placing together of notes which jar or clash.

Fugue

A composition, or compositional technique, in which a musical idea is extended and developed by imitation and repetition.

In musical terms, this is achieved by introducing the main idea (theme) at different **pitches** and weaving it against both itself and other themes. The music of Bach, in works such as Well-tempered Clavier and Art of Fugue, is often considered to be the apogee of fugal writing.

Harmony

The relationship between notes when heard together, often described as the vertical dimension in music, where **melody** and **counterpoint** is the horizontal. Harmony could be said to give a piece of music its colour or mood.

Improvisation

Musical improvisation is the spontaneous creative process of making music while it is being performed.

Improvisation exists in almost all music, but the term is most frequently associated with melodic improvisation as found in jazz.

Interval

The distance between a lower and higher note. How far apart two notes lie in **pitch** e.g. one octave.

Key (major/minor)

Music said to be in a certain key shows a strong pull towards a central (**tonic**) note. Both major and minor keys build scales from the tonic note but differ in their construction, leading to the difference in mood or colour that they evoke.

Legato
A musical term meaning 'smooth'.

Melody
A series of notes arranged in a
particular order to form a
recognisable unit.

Motif (leitmotif)
A fragment of music or succession of
notes that can be used to construct
the parts or entirety of complete
melodies and themes. A motif may
be harmonic, melodic (**pitch**) and/
or rhythmic (duration). A motif
thematically associated with a person,
place, or idea is called a leitmotif.

Nocturne
A moderately slow piece of music,
often of contemplative nature.
A work to be played after dark.

Notation
The method used to write down
music in a visual form. Western
music uses a five-line stave divided
into bars, on which notes are placed
to indicate pitch.

Octave
An octave is the interval between one
musical note and another, with half or
double its frequency. The human ear
tends to hear both notes as being
almost identical and, for this reason,
notes an octave apart are given the
same note name in Western notation:
the name of the note an octave above
A is also A.

Overture
A piece that acts as an introduction to
an oratorio, opera, play or ballet.

Pitch
The frequency of a musical note.
Currently, middle A on the piano is
defined as 440 cycles (vibrations of the
string) per second. Subjectively 'higher'
notes have a higher (faster) frequency;
'lower' notes, a lower (slower)
frequency.

Polyphony
Music with more than one part and
therefore simultaneous sounding
notes.

Scale
A collection of musical notes arranged
sequentially that provide material for
part or all of a musical work. The scale
required to define a particular key has
a fixed shape and set of notes. The C
major scale, for instance, contains the
notes C, D, E, F, G, A and B.

Sonata and Sonata Form

A piece of music, almost invariably instrumental and usually in several movements for a soloist or a small ensemble, or a structural principle: the sonata form.

Sonata form is a method of developing musical materials, taking themes through an initial presentation, transformation and then final re-presentation.

Staccato

A musical term meaning 'short' or 'detached'.

Symphony

An extended work for orchestra, usually in three or four movements, containing sonata form-type development of musical ideas. Often considered to be the high point of Western musical composition, symphony employs large orchestral forces and generates great varieties of tone colours.

Syncopation

A musical effect achieved by shifting the accents from strong to weak beats to give them special emphasis.

Timbre

The quality of a musical note or sound is referred to its timbre. It distinguishes one instrument or one voice from another.

Tonal

Music built upon a hierarchy of pitches and chords. If a piece is said to be in the key of C, it will usually begin and end with chords built on the note C. All other pitches and chords fall in strong or weak relation to that so-called tonic chord.

Tone and Semitone

A semitone is the smallest interval, in Western music, between two notes (the distance between adjacent notes on the piano). A tone comprises two semitones.

Triad

A triad is a three-note chord, usually consisting of notes arranged in intervals of thirds: the root, the third and the fifth.

Bibliography

Books

Alloway, Lawrence, *Nine Abstract Artists. Their Work and Theory,* London: Alec Tiranti Ltd., 1954 (republished Osborne Samuel)

Barber, Noël, *Conversations with Painters,* Collins, London, 1964

Bosseur, Jean-Yves, *Music,* New York: Rizzoli International Publications, 1991

Düchting, Hajo, *Paul Klee. Painting Music,* Munich/London/New York: Prestel Verlag, 2002

Frascina, Francis, Harrison, Charles, and Perry, Gill, *Primitivism, Cubism, Abstraction. The Early Twentieth Century,* New Haven and London: Yale University Press, 1993

Gage, John, *Colour and Culture. Practice and Meaning from Antiquity to Abstraction,* London: Thames and Hudson, 1993

Golding, John, *Paths to the Absolute. Mondrian, Malevich, Kandinsky, Pollock, Newman, Rothko and Still,* London: Thames and Hudson, 2000

Gooding, Mel, *Abstract Art,* Tate Publishing, London, 2001

Grunenberg, Christoph and Harris, Jonathan (Editors), *Summer of Love: Psychedelic Art, Social Crisis and Counter-Culture in the 1960s,* Liverpool University Press, Liverpool, 2005

Hall, Michael, *Leaving Home. A conducted tour of twentieth-century music with Simon Rattle,* Faber and Faber, 1996

Kandinsky, Wassily, *Über das Geistige in der Kunst (Concerning the Spiritual in Art),* translated and with an introduction by M. T. H. Sadler, New York: Dover Publications, 1977

Kandinsky, Wassily, *Punkt und Linie zu Fläche (Point and Line to Plane),* translated by Howard Dearstyne and Hilla Rebay, New York: Dover Publications, 1979

Kandinsky, Wassily, *Klänge (Sounds),* translated and with an introduction by Elizabeth R. Napier, New Haven and London: Yale University Press, 1981

Klee, Felix, *The Diaries of Paul Klee 1898–1918,* with an introduction by Felix Klee, Berkeley/Los Angeles/London: University of California Press, 1992

Klee, Paul, *Pädagogishes Skizzenbuch (Pedagogical Sketchbook),* introduction and translation by Sibyl Moholy-Nagy, London: Faber and Faber, 1953

Lankheit, Klaus (ed.), *Der Blaue Reiter Almanac (The Blue Rider Almanac),* with an introduction by Klaus Lankheit, translated by Henning Falkenstein, London: Tate Publishing, 2006

Maur, Karin von, *The Sound of Painting. Music in Modern Art,* London: Prestel, 1999

Phillips, Tom, *Music in Art,* London: Prestel, 1997

Phillips, Tom, *Tom Phillips: Works and Text,* London: Thames and Hudson, 1992

Ridley, Aaron, *The Philosophy of Music. Theme and Variations,* Edinburgh: Edinburgh University Press, 2004

Robins, Anna Gruetzner, *Modern Art in Britain 1910–14,* London: Merrell Publishers, 1997

Sekules, Veronica (ed.), *University of East Anglia Collection of Abstract and Constructivist Art, Architecture and Design,* Norwich: University of East Anglia, 1994

Shaw-Miller, Simon, *Visible Deeds of Music. Art and Music from Wagner to Cage,* New Haven and London: Yale University Press, 2002

Spencer, Robin (ed.), *Eduardo Paolozzi: Writings and Interviews,* Oxford: Oxford University Press, 2000

Tickner, Lisa, *Modern Life and Modern Subjects. British Art in the Early Twentieth Century,* New Haven and London: Yale University Press, 2000

Vergo, Peter, *That Divine Order. Music and the Visual Arts from Antiquity to the Eighteenth Century,* London: Phaidon Press Limited, 2005

Vergo, Peter et al, *Towards a New Art. Essays on the background to abstract art 1910–20,* Tate Gallery Publications Department, 1980

Whitford, Frank, *Bauhaus,* London: Thames and Hudson, 1984

Articles

Tucker, Michael, 'Hearing the Colours, Dancing the Heartspace', *Contemporary Art*, vol. 2, no. 1, Winter 1993-94

McKenzie, Dr. Janet, 'Mark Rowan-Hull. Seeing Music, Hearing Colour', *Studio International*, 2004, vol. 203, no. 1026

Exhibition Catalogues

Abstract Art in England 1913–1915, London: d'Offay, 1969

Vorticism and its Allies, London: Hayward Gallery, 1974

František Kupka 1871–1957. A Retrospective, New York: The Solomon R. Guggenheim Foundation, 1975

Soundings, Dore Ashton and Suzanne Delahanty, Neuberger Museum, NY, 1981

De Stijl: 1917–1931, Visions of Utopia, Walker Art Center, 1982

Vom Klang der Bilder. Die Musik in der Kunst des 20. Jahrhunderts (The Sound of Painting: Music in Art in the 20th Century), Karin von Maur, Staatsgalerie Stuttgart, 1985

The Poetic Trace. Aspects of British Abstraction since 1945, Mel Gooding, New York: Adelson Galleries, 1992

The Romantic Spirit in German Art 1790–1990, 1994 National Galleries of Scotland, Edinburgh, essays by Peter Vergo and John Gage, Thames and Hudson, London, 1994

Farben – Klänge. Kandinsky and Schönberg (Colours – Sounds: Kandinsky and Schönberg), Fondation Beyeler, 1998

Farbe zu Licht (Colour to Light), Fondation Beyeler, 2000

The Art of Noise. Exploring the Relationship between Art and Music, Manchester: Whitworth Art Gallery, 2001

Mondrian. The Transatlantic Paintings, exhibition catalogue, New Haven and London: Yale University Press, 2001

Ornament and Abstraction. The dialogue between non-Western modern and contemporary art, Fondation Beyeler, 2001

Ceri Richards. Themes and Variations. A select retrospective, Cardiff: National Museums and Galleries of Wales, 2002

Masters of Colour. Derain to Kandinsky. Masterpieces from The Merzbacher Collection, London: Royal Academy of Arts, 2002

Remix. Contemporary Art and Pop, London: Tate, 2002

Alan Davie. Jingling Space, Tate St Ives, 2003

Analogías Musicales. Kandinsky y sus contemporaneous (Musical Analogies: Kandinsky and his contemporaries), Madrid: Museo Thyssen-Bornemisza, 2003

Schoenberg, Kandinsky, and the Blue Rider, edited by Esther da Coseta Meyer and Fred Wasserman, New York: The Jewish Museum, New York in association with Scala Publishers, 2003

Sons et Lumières. Une histoire du son dans l'art du XXe siècle (Sound and Light: A history of sound in 20th century art), Paris: Centre Pompidou, 2004

Elements of Abstraction. Space, Line and Interval in Modern British Art, Southampton: Southampton City Art Gallery, 2005

Nine Abstract Artists Revisited, London: Osborne Samuel, 2005

Visual Music. Synaesthesia in Art and Music Since 1900, New York: Thames and Hudson, 2005

Kandinsky. The Path to Abstraction, London: Tate, 2006

Image on page 11,153 © Tate, London 2007; 12 © Musée d'Orsay, Paris, France/ Giraudon/ The Bridgeman Art Library; 13 © Osterreichische Galerie Belvedere, Vienna, Austria/ The Bridgeman Art Library; 17 © Musée National d'Art Moderne, Centre Pompidou, Paris, France/ Lauros / Giraudon/ The Bridgeman Art Library; 21 fig 1. © Arnold Schönberg Center, fig 2. © Photo CNAC/MNAM Dist. RMN / © Droits Réservés; 23 © Solomon R. Guggenheim Museum, New York, Gift, Solomon R. Guggenheim 1937 37.245, © ADAGP, Paris and DACS, London 2007; 24 © Städtische Galerie im Lenbachhaus, © ADAGP, Paris and DACS, London 2007, Munich, Germany/ Peter Willi/ The Bridgeman Art Library; 25 © Osterreichische Galerie Belvedere, Vienna, Austria/ The Bridgeman Art Library; 27 © Arnold Schönberg Center; 33 © Kunstmuseum, Basel, Switzerland/ The Bridgeman Art Library; 34 fig.2, © Fundación Joan Miró, © Succession Miró/ADAGP, Paris and DACS, London 2007, fig.3 © Succession Miró/ADAGP, Paris and DACS, London 2007; 36 fig.4 © Leeds Museums and Galleries (City Art Gallery) U.K./ The Bridgeman Art Library, © Estate of John David Roberts. By permission of the William Roberts Society, fig.5 © Kunsthalle, Bremen, Germany/ Peter Willi/ The Bridgeman Art Library, © DAC 2007; 38 © Haags Gemeentemuseum, The Hague, Netherlands/ The Bridgeman Art Library, © 2007 Mondrian/Holtzman Trust c/o HCR International Warrenton, VA; 42,61 © Jonathan Clark Fine Art on Behalf of the Wells Estate; 47,48,49 © M.K iurlionis National Museum of Art, Kaunas, Lithuania; 51,68,85,89,103,117,125, 129,133,155,159 © ADAGP, Paris and DACS, London 2007; 53,55,91,135,163,165 © DACS 2007; 57,58 © Bauhaus-Archiv, Berlin, © ADAGP, Paris and DACS, London 2007; 63, 65 photo © Ian A. Cameron at Cameron & Hollis, © Estate of Ceri Richards/ DACS 2007; 67 © The Artist; 73 © Tate, London 2007, © ADAGP, Paris and DACS, London 2007; 75,77,79,81 © Arnold Schönberg Center, © DACS 2007; 83 V&A Images, © ADAGP, Paris and DACS, London 2007; 87 © V&A Images, © ADAGP, Paris and DACS; 92 © Bauhaus-Archiv, Berlin, © ADAGP, Paris and DACS, London 2007; 101 © Photo CNAC/MNAM Dist. RMN / © Droits Réservés, © ADAGP, Paris and DACS, London 2007; 105 © Photo CNAC/MNAM Dist. RMN / © Jaques Faujour, © ADAGP, Paris and DACS, London 2007; 107 © L & M SERVICES B.V. The Hague 20070615; 109 © Bauhaus-Archiv, Berlin, © DACS 2007; 113 © bpk/ Nationalgalerie, Museum Berggruen, SMB/ Jens Ziehe © DACS 2007; 115 © Bauhaus-Archiv, Berlin, © ADAGP, Paris and DACS, London 2007; 119 © Photo CNAC/MNAM Dist. RMN / © Jean-Claude Planchet, © ADAGP, Paris and DACS, London 2007; 120,139,141 © Trustees of the Paolozzi Foundation, Licensed by DACS 2007; 127 © Tate, London 2007, © Estate of Duncan Grant / Licensed by DACS 2007; 131 © Bauhaus-Archiv, Berlin; 137 © The Joseph and Anni Albers Foundation/VG Bild-Kunst, Bonn and DACS, London 2007; 143,144,145 photos Courtesy of Flowers, London, © Trustees of the Paolozzi Foundation, Licensed by DACS 2007; 147 Image courtesy of Flowers, London © Jack Smith; 149,169 © Photo CNAC/MNAM Dist. RMN / © Droits Réservés, © ADAGP, Paris and DACS, London 2007; 157 image courtesy of Waterhouse and Dodd, London; 161 © Solomon R. Guggenheim Museum, New York/ © Myles Aronowitz; 167 © Tate, London 2007, © 2007 Mondrian/Holtzman Trust c/o HCR International Warrenton, VA; 171 © V&A Images, © Succession H Matisse/DACS 2007; 173, 175 © Clody E. Norton; 177,179 © Alan Davie; 181 © Succession Miró/ADAGP, Paris and DACS, London 2007; 183 © Harvey Daniels.